SEEING THROUGH THE EYE

This life's dim windows of the soul
Distorts the Heavens from pole to pole,
And leads you to believe a lie
When you see with, not through, the eye.

—William Blake

SEEING THROUGH THE EYE

MALCOLM MUGGERIDGE ON FAITH

EDITED BY CECIL KUHNE

INTRODUCTION BY
WILLIAM F. BUCKLEY JR.

IGNATIUS PRESS SAN FRANCISCO

Cover photograph:
Malcolm Muggeridge
Courtesy of the Malcolm Muggeridge Collection,
Wheaton College (*IL*).

Cover design by Roxanne Mei Lum

ISBN 978-1-58617-068-4
ISBN 1-58617-068-6
Library of Congress Control Number 2004107668
Printed in the United States of America ♾

CONTENTS

PART THREE
INTERVIEWS

PREFACE

In his candid autobiography, *Chronicles of Wasted Time*, Malcolm Muggeridge recounted the evening he tried to commit suicide by drowning. He had swum into the surf near Mozambique's Lourenço Marques, and looking back, noted that the lights of the town had grown dim. He started to flail, and then began to cry out for help.

> In some mysterious way it became clear to me that there was no darkness, only the possibility of losing sight of a light which shone eternally; that our clumsy appetites are no more than the blind reaching of a newly born child after the teat through which to suck the milk of life; that our sufferings, our affliction, are part of a drama—an essential, even an ecstatic, part—endlessly revolving round the two great propositions of good and evil, of light and darkness.

The next day Muggeridge reflected: "The bars of the window, as I looked more closely, took on the form of a Cross." He had reached a threshold that would lead to a spiritual quest for life's meaning, and before dying in 1990 would spend the last twenty years of his life telling others of his transforming relationship with Jesus Christ.

In a long and distinguished career as one of England's finest journalists, Muggeridge served as correspondent for the *Guardian* and *Daily Telegraph* and as editor of *Punch*, and in these roles he moved freely about the world, living in India, Egypt, the Soviet Union, and Washington, D.C. Known for his quick wit and sharp tongue, he became a popular, albeit controversial, commentator on the affairs of the day. Leaning back in his chair, with that inimitable glint in his eyes, Muggeridge could pierce the most elaborate façade—and do so with gentle humor. His criticism of the monarchy and all manner of power was notable, as he lambasted the likes of such cultural icons as H. G. Wells, George Orwell, Bertrand Russell, George Bernard Shaw, and D. H. Lawrence. Muggeridge was never one to shirk controversy.

Born in 1903, Muggeridge was raised in a home of Fabian Socialists, and his father, whom he adored, was a vocal proponent of utopianism and later elected to Parliament. The young Muggeridge attended Cambridge and graduated in 1924, but he found the experience less than satisfying: "Cambridge, to me, was a place of infinite tedium; of afternoon walks in a damp, misty countryside; of idle days, and foolish vanities, and spurious enthusiasms." His own Socialist leanings, which he adopted from his father, changed dramatically when he saw firsthand the workings of Communism in the Soviet Union, and he felt compelled to take a laboring oar against the tide of the press corps, pointing to the sham of the system they were extolling. "I felt furious about the whole experience, as though I had been personally cheated, and poured out my righteous indignation and hurt vanity in a series of articles as bitter and satirical as I knew how to make them." During the Second World War, Muggeridge joined the Army Intelligence Corps and served in Mozambique, Italy, and France, before resuming his illustrious career as columnist and social commentator.

Muggeridge was never clear in his writings about exactly when he became a Christian. In some of his writings, he suggests that he was a believer as early as his college days, and in others he seems to say that he did not become a true follower of Christ until he was in his sixties. The late 1960s, however, were pivotal years in this process, and it was then that he made public his belief in Christ. Saint Mugg, as he was affectionately called, was clear in his new-found faith: "It is the truth that has died, not God", and "Jesus was God or he was nothing." To Muggeridge, God was reality and the world, fantasy: "Built into life is a strong vein of irony for which we should only be grateful to our Creator. It helps us to find our way through the fantasy that encompasses us to the reality of our existence. God had mercifully made the fantasies—the pursuit of power, of sensual satisfaction, of money, of learning, of celebrity, of happiness—so preposterously unrewarding that we are forced to turn to him for help and for mercy." Only a self-confessed libertine like Muggeridge could write words of such force and power, as he did in his book *Jesus Rediscovered*:

> Many people have asked me how it was that I came ultimately to be convinced that Christ was the answer. It was because in this world of fantasy in which my own occupation has particularly involved me, I have found in Christ the only true alternative. The shadow in the cave is like the media world of shadows. In contradistinction, Christ shows what life really is, and what our true destiny is. We escape from the cave. We emerge from the darkness and instead of shadows

> we have all around us the glory of God's creation. Instead of darkness we have light; instead of despair, hope; instead of time and the clocks ticking inexorably on, eternity, which never began and never ends and yet is sublimely now.

The result of this revelation was expressed in his changed relationship with others: "All I can claim to have learnt from the years I have spent in this world is that the only happiness is love, which is attained by giving, not receiving; and that the world itself only becomes the dear and habitable dwelling place it is when we who inhabit it know we are migrants, due when the time comes to fly away to other more commodious skies."

Muggeridge later went on to produce a BBC television series and book (*Something Beautiful for God*) about Mother Teresa, which were credited with introducing her works of charity to the West. In turn, Mother Teresa was influential in Muggeridge's spiritual journey. Like many Christians, his path was a gradual one, with increasing maturity and insights as he spent more time in the Scriptures and God illuminated his heart. He later became an outspoken critic of abortion and euthanasia and eventually converted to Catholicism (in 1982) because of the Church's stand on those issues.

When in 1973 he resigned as rector of Edinburg University rather than approve the students' request for distribution of "pot and pills", Muggeridge noted that these young people—in whom society had lavished its wealth in the hope that they would someday lead progress and produce great work of art—were degrading themselves with "the resort of any old, slobbering debauchee anywhere in the world at any time—Dope and Bed." He said in his resignation address that the highest aspiration of man is to see God, and that purity of heart—not indulgence of the senses or enlightened thinking—is the key to knowing God and unlocking the mystery of life. Amazingly, not a single public statement was uttered in his behalf.

Muggeridge's favorite quote—which he used often—was one from William Blake:

> This life's dim windows of the soul
> Distorts the Heavens from pole to pole,
> And leads you to believe a lie
> When you see with, not through, the eye.

Muggeridge clearly saw *through* the eye. The former archbishop of Sydney, Doctor Marcus Loane, called him "the most significant layman since

C. S. Lewis, highly intelligent and an outstanding apologist for Christ". Reverend John Stott described him as a "true prophet of the twentieth century . . . a voice crying in the wilderness".

In his marvelous work *A Third Testament*, Muggeridge described the Christian legacies left by a host of philosophers: Saint Augustine, Blaise Pascal, William Blake, Søren Kierkegaard, Fyodor Dostoyevsky, Tolstoy, and Bonhoeffer. He reverently called them "God's spies"—that special role, he said, "which was none other than to relate their time to eternity".

It is wonderfully ironic how in his own life Malcolm Muggeridge too became one of God's spies.

Cecil Kuhne
Dallas, Texas

ACKNOWLEDGMENTS

Like so many people I have met over the years, I first became acquainted with Malcolm Muggeridge in the mid-1980s while watching a series of interviews conducted by William F. Buckley Jr. for his weekly program, *Firing Line*. These exchanges were replayed every year at Christmas time for the next decade or so, and they were a moving tribute to this man's spiritual odyssey toward Christianity. The images of those broadcasts still remain vivid—Malcolm's kind, furrowed face and that gentle, enthusiastic voice sounding out with such modesty how his conversion to Christ had rendered him full of gratitude, in spite of life's trials.

Moved by Malcolm's intellect and wisdom, I eagerly sought out his writings—*Chronicles of Wasted Time*, *Jesus Rediscovered*, *The End of Christendom*, and others. However, I soon became discouraged at how few of his writings remained in print.

Mr. Buckley encouraged me to move forward with the anthology you have before you, and eventually he put me in touch with Malcolm's niece, Sally Muggeridge, who has taken it on herself to perpetuate the legacy of her father, who had taken it on himself to perpetuate the legacy of his brother. As the president of the Malcolm Muggeridge Society, she has worked tirelessly to spread the influence of his writings for generations to come. My gratitude for their many kindnesses—and to Malcolm's son, Leonard, for granting permission to republish these works—is enduring. We all owe thanks to Wheaton College, and especially David Malone, for maintaining Malcolm's papers, and for acting as host to a memorable centennial celebration of his birth in the summer of 2003.

But most of all, I will never be able to repay the debt I owe to Malcolm for his wonderful words praising the One to whom we owe everything, our Lord Jesus Christ.

INTRODUCTION

BY WILLIAM F. BUCKLEY JR.

I don't remember what it was, exactly, that brought Malcolm Muggeridge to my program, *Firing Line*. The taping was done in London, in February 1968, the high holy year of the countercultural revolution. That was the year when Martin Luther King was assassinated, when Eugene McCarthy challenged President Johnson in New Hampshire, Lyndon Johnson declared he would not run for reelection, Robert Kennedy leaped into the presidential ring and was assassinated, colleges and universities were in tumult. And that was the year when, in articles published in British journals, Malcolm Muggeridge divulged that he had embraced the Christian faith.

The counter-countercultural declaration of Mr. Muggeridge's movement was especially eye-catching given the great legions traveling in the opposite direction. He had been prominent for many years. His larger public knew him through his work as a television host and critic. But all of literate England, and much of America, knew him as a learned and incisive journalist who (in 1933) had written *Winter in Moscow*. It was a searing exposé of Communism, written after his year in the Soviet Union for the *Manchester Guardian*, the leading liberal daily. He had seen at first hand the torture and starvation of the kulaks in the Ukraine. After his exposé he continued with his books, wrote copiously for British periodicals, and was an instant hit on radio for the BBC (as he would be later on television). During the war he did hazardous duty in British intelligence in Mozambique and soon after the war became the editor of *Punch* magazine, the oldest English-language humor magazine in the world (1841–1992).[1]

Originally published as "On Knowing Malcolm Muggeridge", in William F. Buckley Jr., *Nearer, My God* (New York: Doubleday, 1997).

[1] *Punch* was revived in the fall of 1996.

It was just after leaving *Punch* that he wrote a funny and condescending article about young Queen Elizabeth (she was "frumpy, frowzy, and banal"), published on the eve of her visit (1957) to the United States in the *Saturday Evening Post*, then a U.S. magazine of enormous circulation. The article, which took a droll view of royal pageantry, outraged the British establishment. Muggeridge was eased out of *Punch* and shunned by the BBC, but by the early 'sixties he had reconquered England with his humor, skepticism, and acuity of expression. Everyone laughed, except that day's victims. His intellect and historical savoir faire gave his criticisms a very long reach. In America he made regular appearances as book editor for *Esquire* magazine. No Englishman, Evelyn Waugh having died, was a more mordant, more attractive wit.

It goes without saying that, as regards religion, he was an extrovert atheist (though, his biographers reveal, he had had an early interest in religion); in politics, a socialist (though never, since his experience in Moscow, pro-Communist). For those who hadn't been in personal touch and didn't know in what direction his mind was turning it was a shock when, in April 1968, the three BBC television documentaries were broadcast. Muggeridge had directed them and provided the spoken commentary. The cameras, shooting in and about Jerusalem, took the viewer to sites about which Muggeridge spoke.

"After his decisive dialogue with Satan," Muggeridge's voice came over the screen as the camera panned in to the city, "Christ very humanly chose to begin his ministry in Nazareth, where he was known and had grown up. There in the synagogue with, I daresay, his family present in the congregation, he chose to read the splendid passage in which the prophet Isaiah proclaims,

> The Spirit of the Lord is upon me,
> because he hath anointed me to preach the gospel to the poor;
> he hath sent me to heal the brokenhearted,
> to preach deliverance to the captives,
> and recovering of sight to the blind,
> to set at liberty them that are bruised,
> to preach the acceptable year of the Lord.

Muggeridge then weighed in, which was his way, by unction and guile and excitement, grabbing his viewers by the hair and forcing them to consider his discomfiting words. "All would have been well if Christ had just left matters there. Nothing pleases the average congregation more—whether in synagogue, church, mosque, or other conventicle—than to be told about preaching deliverance to captives, healing the brokenhearted, etc., always provided nothing is expected of *them*. But Christ went on recklessly: *This day is this scripture fulfiled in your ears*. In other words, *he* was going to do it; the spirit of the Lord was upon *him*, Joseph's son, known to them all.

"It was intolerable. With one accord they rose up and turned him out of the synagogue and out of Nazareth. As far as we know, he never returned there."

Such was the temperament of Malcolm Muggeridge. His smile was ready, his blue eyes really did sparkle, his features exuded benevolence, he made his points in perfect diction, the historical and philosophical references were apt, his desire to communicate his insights earnest and engaging. When he came to *Firing Line*, commissioned to discuss "The Culture of the Left," I had not known about his turn to religion, which would be broadcast two months later on BBC. I did have the sense that something was exciting him. I would know soon what it was, and the world would know that this was not one of his passing fancies, because he lived in that excitement another twenty-seven years, about which one could reasonably say that they were a great modern pilgrimage.

In February of 1980 a wealthy Rumanian-Canadian approached me through an intermediary to ask if I would undertake an experimental documentary, exact size and shape undecided—that would be left in my hands. The single, and singular, asset of the Canadian, apart from his personal wealth, was exclusive access to the Sistine Chapel, on an appointed day one month away, for forty-eight hours. This privilege had never before been extended, and I never learned how it came to be that the Canadian magnate had got it; but the invitation to me was to fashion two half-hour programs to be filmed in the Sistine Chapel.

I consulted with Warren Steibel, the producer of *Firing Line*, and asked him to serve as director. After a few meetings the idea evolved to reflect in each of the programs on one biblical parable. My idea was to feature their imperishable relevance.

It was expected (the entrepreneur's intermediary made this plain) that I would attract a star or two to participate. With only two weeks before the Sistine deadline, I approached David Niven, a neighbor in Switzerland (where I spend February and March), and Princess Grace of Monaco, who regularly vacationed with her family nearby and who, with Niven, spent occasional evenings at our house, painting in oils. By telephone I got to Charlton Heston, who had played Michelangelo in one movie (*The Agony and the Ecstasy*), John the Baptist in another (*The Greatest Story Ever Told*), and Moses in a third (*The Ten Commandments*) and so was enticed by the prospect of doing something in Michelangelo's primary shrine, adorned by the great painting of the Creation.

We would read, in the first program, the parable of the Good Samaritan and, in the second, the parable of the Prodigal Son. After the reading, the host would ask our guests to give from their own experience contemporary examples of the lessons of the Good Samaritan and the Prodigal Son at work. I telephoned to Malcolm Muggeridge in England and asked if he would serve as my cohost. He agreed instantly.

In the following week we spoke over the telephone several times, discussing details of the program. The Canadian entrepreneur was much taken by the formula I had come up with and wanted some indication whether, if the program succeeded, I would be willing to pursue in other renowned church sites other parables, with other luminaries. Muggeridge counseled that we put off a consideration of the question until after we saw what we had come up with.

A few days before we would meet in Rome, he called me on the telephone. I remember his words almost exactly. "Bill, in my life I have met with practically every important person and almost without exception I have regretted it. But I think the present Pope [John Paul II] is an exception. I think he is an immense personal and historical figure. I would like to meet him while we are in Rome. Can you arrange that?"

It was agreed he would use his own resources, I mine; and, on arriving in Rome, Malcolm and I were notified by written message that we had an appointment for a private audience with the Pope the following day at one o'clock. Malcolm's invitation was addressed directly. Mine, to "Mr. Buckley e due personi." That translated into: me, David Niven, and my wife, Pat. (Chuck Heston and Grace Rainier, who had not been told about our maneuver, would be leaving Rome at noon, after the film shoot, before the scheduled audience.)

. . .

It was shortly before midnight when we began shooting. The chapel, the most famous and intimate in the world, had been turned over to us only after closing time for visitors late that afternoon. The engineers and electricians and lighting men had been several hours getting things in order. It was mid-February, and there was no heating.

The half hour began with Princess Grace, radiant, modest in dress and mien, reading the Bible verse:

> And a certain lawyer asked, "Who is my neighbor?" and Jesus, answering, said ...
>
> "A certain man went down from Jerusalem to Jericho and fell among thieves who stripped him of his raiment and wounded him and departed, leaving him half dead. And by chance there came down a certain priest that way, and when he saw him, he passed by on the other side. And likewise a Levite, when he was at the place, came and looked on him and passed by on the other side. But a certain Samaritan, as he journeyed, came where he was, and when he saw him he had compassion on him, and went to him and bound up his wounds, pouring in oil and wine, and set him on his own beast and brought him to an inn and took care of him. And on the morrow, when he departed, he took out two pence and gave them to the host and said unto him, Take care of him and whatever thou spendest more, when I come again, I will repay thee.
>
> "Which then of these three, thinkest thou, was the neighbor unto him that fell among the thieves?" And the lawyer said, "He that showed mercy on him." Then said Jesus unto him, "Go and do thou likewise."

After the parable was done the camera turned to me. I said, "Although we speak from the *sanctum sanctorum* of the Roman Catholic Church, only two of the participants in this program are Catholics [Grace and me]. My cohost is Malcolm Muggeridge, the British writer, who in recent years has devoted his energies to examining the life of the spirit. Mr. Muggeridge."

He spoke without notes. "In the beginning was the Word. That's how the Fourth Gospel opens, intimating that since the world began, God the Creator has been communicating with men, His creation. And what amazing diversity of communication there has been. Take, for instance, this Sistine Chapel, wherewith through the genius of Michelangelo, God has spoken to us. Or of course, the most sublime communication of all, [which] is in the first chapter of the Fourth Gospel. The Word dwelt among us and, full of grace, became flesh, whereby God, reaching down, became a man, Jesus Christ, in order that men might reach upward and relate themselves to God. So I find nothing strange or out of the way to be considering in this famous chapel the parables, their significance, their meaning, which played so tremendous a part in Jesus' ministry on earth."

I then asked Princess Grace, seated, to come up with a parallel, a more or less contemporary Good Samaritan. She spoke of Henri Dunant, who during the War of the Italian Risorgimento and its "bloody battle of Solferino" (1859—forty thousand casualties) thought to institutionalize medical services to help the wounded. "He founded what came to be known as the Red Cross."

WFB: "What happened to Dunant himself?"

GRACE: "After ten years he met with bankruptcy, and he retired to a small village and he was almost forgotten. It was by chance that a newspaperman found him and sort of rediscovered him when he was almost forgotten. And in—"

WFB: "Did the newspapers do their duty by him as Good Samaritans?"

GRACE: "They certainly did. And as a result, Henri Dunant received the first Nobel Peace Prize, in 1901."

Princess Grace thought the spontaneity of the act—caring for the wounded—was its distinguishing feature, though it seemed to me that the Good Samaritan must be expected to do the virtuous thing in every situation and that therefore, in the most commendable sense, his behavior was predictable.

Heston thought it significant that Christ had designated as a "priest," and then as a "Levite," the men who passed by without pausing to help the wounded traveler. Jesus must have astonished His listeners when He spoke of the Samaritan's intercession. "The Samaritans, to Jesus' audience, were an outcast people, subject to all kinds of discrimination, and yet he makes the Samaritan the good man. Christ was saying: No, we must consider all men our own and charity is for all. And I think this is one of the distinguishing features of His ministry, one of His central teachings. And surely in the story of the Good Samaritan, that's why He had the Samaritan be the one that rescued the beaten man and succored him."

David Niven spoke of the fear, in our litigious world, that many whose inclinations are philanthropic have of the lawyer-behind-the-bush. "[Even] doctors have to insure themselves before they give somebody a pill—they might get sued." He told then the engrossing story (I had never heard it) of a single episode in the chaotic flight from France after Dunkirk in 1940. One motley assembly, "Royal Air Force ground personnel who were trapped, Red Cross workers, women, ambulance drivers, and, finally, the embassy staff from Paris with their children—by the time they got to St. Nazaire at the mouth of the Loire, there were over three thousand of them and the British government sent an old liner called the *Lancastria* to come and take them away, with three destroyers to guard her. They were just pulling up the anchor when three dive bombers came. The destroyers did what they could, but one bomb hit, went down the funnel and blew a huge hole in the side, and she quickly took on a terrible list.

"In the hold there were several hundred soldiers. Now there was no way they could ever get out because of the list, and she was sinking. And along came my own favorite Good Samaritan, a Roman Catholic priest, a young man in Royal Air Force uniform. He got a rope and lowered himself into the hold to give encouragement and help to those hundreds of men in their last dreadful hour—"

WFB: "Knowing he couldn't get out?"

NIVEN: "Knowing he could never get out, nor could they. The ship sank and all in that hold died. The remainder were picked up by the destroyers and came back to England to the regiment I was in, and we had to look after them, and many of them told me that they were giving up even then, in the oil and struggle, and the one thing that kept them going was the sound of the soldiers in the hold singing hymns."

...

It was weighty-thought time. I began with what became, in the edited film, a voice-over: "Inevitably when a text is examined and reexamined, the spirit of the exegete is aroused and the fine print comes into scrutiny. Were there hidden lessons planted in the parable? What did Christ mean when he spoke of a 'neighbor'? Malcolm Muggeridge [he was dressed in his overcoat to guard against the midnight cold of the Sistine Chapel] has, I'm sure, something to say on the subject."

Facing the camera, Muggeridge said that he understood the parable as "showing people reality." Christ didn't "accept human categories." He was not intending categorical slurs on priests or Levites, or special praise for Samaritans. "What he was saying really was that the people who are professionally compassionate—which those people were—when it comes to the crunch, often aren't. And that those who are not professionally compassionate are. And therefore I feel he was answering a trick question. He knew perfectly well this lawyer had no particular interest in what Jesus had decided was his true neighbor. The neighbor was the man who was compassionate, that's what He was saying."

A dialogue ensued on "Who is your neighbor?" It became, all too soon, a semantic excursion, but reached agreement that, in Christ's sense of the word, the neighbor isn't simply the man who lives next door. Muggeridge summed up. "Jesus would say if you want to know who your neighbor is, your neighbor is the man who is neighborly *in his behavior*. I mean, to me this is absolutely clear. He wasn't going to simply say to the lawyer, 'Well, a neighbor is a man who happens to live next door to you or up the road; you must love *him* as yourself.' Your neighbor is a man to whom you owe compassion, love, help. Insofar as you give it, you are loving your neighbor. Insofar as you don't give it, you are not loving him."

...

In the subsequent program on the Prodigal Son, Muggeridge had said, "I see the parable more than anything else as literature."

WFB: "Moral literature?"

MUGGERIDGE: "No, just literature. Life. Pictures of life."

WFB: "But I am surprised to hear you dispute that they are *moral* literature."

MUGGERIDGE: "All literature is in a sense moral. I mean—"

WFB: "*The Story of O* isn't. Well ... in a sense it is."

MUGGERIDGE: "If in anything in literature, there is truth, then it's moral, whatever the scene might be being described. Jesus was taking us to the very roots of our existence with these stories. That's why they've interested artists and writers. If they were merely moralistic tales, then they wouldn't."

I asked Malcolm if he could come up with a parable whose meaning was unambiguous. Muggeridge replied that parables never ceased for him to be grounds for fruitful exploration. But he ventured on nonetheless. "Now here is a parable for you. It came to me one day. I was actually watching a caterpillar in the path of my garden, a furry caterpillar. And I thought to myself: Now, supposing the caterpillars have an annual meeting, the local society of caterpillars. They meet to discuss their affairs and how things are going. And my caterpillar, an older caterpillar, addressing them, says, 'You know, it's an extraordinary thing, but we are all going to be butterflies.' 'Okay,' the caterpillars say. 'You poor fool, you are just an old man who is frightened of dying, you're inventing something to comfort yourself.' [But] these are all the things that people say to me when I say I am looking forward to dying because I know that I am going to go into eternity. You see?"

Please explain, I asked.

"And so he—the caterpillar—abashed, draws back, but in a short time he is in his chrysalis, and sure enough, he's right. He extricates himself from the chrysalis, and he is no longer a creeper, which is what caterpillars are; he is flying away."

Muggeridge was inexhaustibly inventive. He volunteered a second parable. "Some very humane, rather simpleminded old lady sees the play *King Lear* performed and she is outraged that a poor old man should be so humiliated, made to suffer so. And in the eternal shade she meets Shakespeare and she says to him, 'What a monstrous thing to make that poor old man go through all that.' And Shakespeare says, 'Yes, I quite agree. It was very painful, and I could have arranged for him to take a sedative at the end of Act I. But then, ma'am, there would have been no play.' "

I ventured that King Lear might have preferred that there should have been no play than that he should have lived through Acts II and III.

"But then he would have been a cowardly man, and, of course, he did in fact have to go through that suffering in order to understand why there had to be a play; and, of course, in that marvelous speech of his—one of my favorite things in all Shakespeare—when he to Cordelia says, 'Come, let's away to prison'—you know—'and take upon us the mystery of things.' It's a beautiful phrase, isn't it? It expresses exactly what I mean. This affliction *has* to be, and that of course is why one is drawn irresistibly as a West European to the Christian faith and to Christ, because this is the central point: the Cross."

Muggeridge pressed on: "There's another parable I've often thought of. When St. Paul starts off on his journeys, he consults with an eminent public relations man: 'I've got this campaign and I want to promote this gospel.' And the man would say, 'Well, you've got to have some sort of symbol. You've got to have an image. You've got to have some sign of your faith.' And then Paul would say, 'Well, I have got one. I've got this cross.' The public relations man would have laughed his head off: 'You can't popularize a thing like *that* . . . It's absolutely mad!' "

And Muggeridge extemporized, with television cameras filming him, his haunting sentences. "But it wasn't mad. It worked for centuries and centuries, bringing out all the creativity in people, all the love and disinterestedness in people; this symbol of suffering, *that's* the heart of the thing. As an old man, Bill, looking back on one's life, it's one of the things that strike you most forcibly—that the only thing that's taught one anything is *suffering*. Not success, not happiness, not anything like that. The only thing that *really* teaches one what life's about—the joy of understanding, the joy of coming in contact with what life *really* signifies—is suffering, affliction."

It hurt to think how many who had run into this theme of Malcolm Muggeridge would dismiss it, this quaint joy that comes to some from suffering. But *Schadenfreude* is pleasure taken from the suffering of others, and Muggeridge I thought of as engaged in a kind of total submission, on the order of what it was that gave Francis of Assisi the ecstasy he radiated.

It was some years after Malcolm died that I came upon a few lines of his in which I thought he captured beatifically the submission for which in his later years, animated by his meditation on the Crucifixion, he yearned. What he wrote I could not myself repeat with any pretense to projecting my own imperfect devotion, but reading what he said, I have as true an idea as ever I had of the saintly calling.

He had been writing of the impact on him of reading William Blake.

> I can remember the first time my eyes rested on lines by Blake (actually, "Ah, Sun-flower! weary of time"), and the extraordinary feeling I had of some unique distillation of understanding and joy, a unique revelation of life's very innermost meaning and significance.
>
> I find it more difficult to recall and recount the feelings I had about the Cross even before it meant anything to me as such. It was, I know, an obsessive interest; something I avidly sought out, as inflamed senses do erotica. I might fasten bits of wood together myself, or doodle it. This symbol, which was considered to be derisory in my home, was yet also the focus of inconceivable hopes and desires—like a lost love's face, pulled out and gazed at with sick longing. As I remember this, a sense of my own failure lies leadenly upon me. I should have worn it over my heart; carried it, a precious standard never to be wrested out of my hands; even though I fell, still borne aloft. It should have been my cult, my uniform, my language, my life. I shall have no excuse; I can't say that I didn't know. I knew from the beginning, and turned away. The lucky thieves were crucified with their Saviour; You called me, and I didn't go—those empty years, those empty words, that empty passion!

But the director was signaling. Our time was up.[2]

And the next morning we had an appointment with the Pope!

. . . It was wonderful! We were summoned to his private quarters at 12:45 for our 1:00 appointment. Wednesday was the day when during the morning, before any scheduled private audience, he met with pilgrims to Rome. We could see on the television screen in the private chamber where we sat that though it was after twelve—the appointed hour for the end of the public conference—John Paul II was still talking, making, in a half dozen languages, statements addressed to the curiosities of the large assembly. Finally he gave them his blessing, and we were asked to stand abreast of each other; he would arrive soon now, and indeed presently he was there, the slight benign smile still on his face, though a fatigue was discernible (the next day he would be hospitalized with influenza). As in the auditorium, he wore his white cassock, on his head, the zucchetto. And, around his neck, the loose gold necklace with the pectoral cross. Several clerical aides were in attendance.

My wife, Pat, had been drawn slightly to one side by an attendant monsignor, the (correct) assumption being that she was not one of the official party. The Pope passed by her, bowing his head in greeting. He approached Malcolm Muggeridge and extended his hand.

The words in the ensuing exchanges are etched exactly in my memory.

The Pope now addressed Muggeridge, in his serviceable though highly accented English. "Yes. You are radio?"

What possible answer can one give to that question, so posed? Malcolm smiled and managed to say that, yes, he had done considerable work on radio. The Pope wished nothing further, smiled, and offered his hand

[2] No network bid for the Sistine Chapel programs. The coroners' principal finding (this was the judgment of Warren Steibel, Muggeridge, and me) was that too much was being asked of the viewer, who had exactly the same view of things in that epochal chamber that cardinals have when they are seated there with the august responsibility of electing a Pope. A camera's eye strolling over the arch of the Sistine Chapel is almost required to travel deliberately, lasciviously. But the viewer, his attention arrested by Michelangelo, was being asked simultaneously to struggle over what live human beings were having to say in a serious discussion about serious matters. And when the camera did level on the actors, the viewer found himself staring at Grace Kelly, thinking thoughts like, *For gawd's sake—she hasn't made a movie in twenty years!* And at Charlton Heston, reciting lines different from any that had ever sounded from his lips, in a hundred-odd movies; and David Niven, a similar problem. And then there were Muggeridge and Buckley to cope with.

to David Niven. To whom he said, "Yes. You were very close to my predecessor."

David's eyes widened, and he stammered out, "I had great admiration for him, Your Holiness." So much for David Niven, on whom he smiled, turning and extending his hand to me.

I had to act quickly, I thought, if there was any hope of rescuing our papal audience. Clearly the machinery in the Vatican had got tangled. One bureaucracy had authorized the private interview with the important gentlemen who had been given the Sistine Chapel for their work. One of his visitors, the bureaucracy might have informed the Holy Father, was perhaps the most eloquent English-speaking Christian alive. Another was a renowned and greatly loved actor and—together with Princess Grace of Monaco and another famous actor, both of whom had had to leave Rome—all were at work on an unprecedented documentary in the Sistine Chapel with the Catholic American journalist influential in conservative thought ... It flashed through my mind that a second bureaucracy had probably briefed the Pope about an entirely different set of people, one of whom was "radio," another perhaps a biographer of Pope Paul VI.

I thought I might give the Pope a lifesaving lead, so after shaking hands, before he could speak, I said to him, smiling, "It's going to be *very* hard, Your Holiness, for me to get used to my own private chapel back home having spent so many hours in *yours*!"

Far from serving to alert the Holy Father to what was going on, my words clearly startled him, and he stepped back a pace, which motion signaled his attendants—who instantly escorted him to the conventional site, politely nudging my wife into the company. A photographer materialized, shot his picture, the Pope blessed us, smiled again, and left the chamber.

There can never have been such revelry in the Vatican elevator that took us down to our waiting car. At lunch Malcolm practiced "being radio," and David demanded attention so that he could proceed with the life story of Pope Paul VI. When in future days Malcolm's voice would come in over the long-distance line, he would always hear from me, "Is this Radio on the line?"

But when I visited him at his little country cottage in Sussex, there were here and there a few pictures of his family, and one of him and Pope John Paul II.

PART ONE

WRITTEN WORDS

1. Jesus: The Man Who Lives

I remember the precise moment of illumination very well. It was in the Church of the Nativity in Bethlehem. I was sitting in the crypt waiting for the time when the public were excluded and we could begin to film. Earlier in the day we had been filming in nearby fields where, reputedly, shepherds were tending their flocks when they heard the tidings of great joy, that a Saviour had been born in Bethlehem whom they would find there in a manger wrapped in swaddling clothes. Sure enough, in the fields there was a shepherd with his flock—sheep and goats duly separated, just as required. When he caught sight of us and our equipment he picked up one of his sheep in his arms, precisely as in the coloured pictures I remembered so well from Scripture lessons in my childhood. Then, when he had established his posture, and our cameraman was focusing for a shot, he put down the sheep and came forward to haggle over his fee. It was after settling this unseemly transaction, and getting our footage of the shepherd and his flock, that we went into the Church of the Nativity, having the greatest difficulty in making our way because of the press of beggars and children offering picture postcards, rosaries and other souvenirs for sale.

Still smarting from their persistent importunity, I had found a seat in the crypt on a stone ledge in the shadow cast by the lighted candles which provided the only illumination. How ridiculous these so-called 'shrines' were!, I was thinking to myself. How squalid the commercialism which exploited them! Who but a credulous fool could possibly suppose that the place marked in the crypt with a silver cross was veritably the precise spot where Jesus had been born? The Holy Land, as it seemed to me, had been turned into a sort of Jesusland, on the lines of Disneyland.

Originally published as a portion of Part I, entitled "Jesus Comes into the World", in Malcolm Muggeridge, *Jesus: The Man Who Lives* (San Francisco: Harper and Row, 1975, 1976), pp. 14–33.

Everything in the crypt—the garish hangings which covered the stone walls, the tawdry crucifixes and pictures and hanging lamps—was conducive to such a mood. The essential point, after all, about Jesus's birth was its obscurity, which made a perfect contrast with an Aphrodite rising in all her beauty and splendour out of the sea, or an Apollo radiant and masterful even by comparison with his fellow deities. How foolish and inappropriate, then, even from the point of view of fabricating a shrine, to furbish up what purported to be Jesus's birthplace with stage effects, decking out his bare manger to look like a junk-shop crammed with discarded ecclesiastical bric-a-brac! Rather, the shrine should surely aim at accentuating the bareness, the lowliness, of the occasion it celebrated, so that the humblest, poorest visitor might know that the Son of God was born into the world in even humbler, poorer circumstances than his.

As these thoughts passed through my mind I began to notice the demeanour of the visitors coming into the crypt. Some crossed themselves; a few knelt down; most were obviously standard twentieth-century pursuers of happiness for whom the Church of the Nativity was just an item in a sightseeing tour—as it might be the Taj Mahal, or the Chamber of Horrors in Madame Tussaud's Waxworks Show in London, or Lenin's embalmed corpse in his mausoleum in the Red Square in Moscow. None the less, as I observed, each face as it came into view was in some degree transfigured by the experience of being in what purported to be the actual scene of Jesus's birth. This, they all seemed to be saying, was where it happened; here he came into the world! here we shall find him! The boredom, the idle curiosity, the vagrant thinking all disappeared. Once more in that place glory shone around, and angel voices proclaimed: *Unto you is born this day . . . a Saviour, which is Christ the Lord!*, thereby transforming it from a tourist attraction into an authentic shrine. 'Everything possible to be believed is an image of truth', Blake wrote. And: 'Truth can never be told so as to be understood and not be believed.' The story of Jesus as recounted in the Gospels is true to the degree that it can be, and is, believed; its truth must be looked for in the hearts of believers rather than in history, or in archaeological dust or anthropological bones. *Where two or three are gathered together in my name*, Jesus promised, *there I am in the midst of them.* The promise has been kept even in the unlikeliest of places—his own ostensible birthplace in the crypt of the Church of the Nativity in Bethlehem.

Looking for Jesus in history is as futile as trying to invent a yardstick that will measure infinity, or a clock that will tick through eternity. God moulds history to His purposes, revealing in it the Fearful Symmetry which is His language in conversing with men; but history is no more than the clay in which He works. Who would look for Michelangelo's *Pietà* in the quarry where the marble to make it was procured? Or for Shakespeare's King Lear in history? If this is true of mortal genius, how much more so when the artist is God Himself, concerned to send us a self-portrait in the lineaments, and using the language, of mortality in order to open up for us new vistas of hope and understanding. This was the Incarnation, described in the opening words of the Fourth Gospel, in a passage surely among the greatest ever to be written at any time or by any hand. From its triumphant opening: *In the beginning was the Word, and the Word was with God, and the Word was God*, to its beautiful and comforting conclusion: *And the Word was made flesh, and dwelt among us . . . full of grace and truth*, it conveys with perfect clarity why the Incarnation had to be, and what it meant for mankind, at the time and for ever after.

* * *

So the story of Jesus has to begin with the Incarnation; without it, there would be no story at all. Plenty of great teachers, mystics, martyrs and saints have made their appearance at different times in the world, and lived lives and spoken words full of grace and truth, for which we have every reason to be grateful. Of none of them, however, has the claim been made, and accepted, that they were Incarnate God. In the case of Jesus alone the belief has persisted that when he came into the world God deigned to take on the likeness of a man in order that thenceforth men might be encouraged to aspire after the likeness of God; reaching out from their mortality to His immortality, from their imperfection to His perfection. It is written in the Old Testament that no man may see God and live; at the same time, as Kierkegaard points out, God cannot make Man His equal without transforming him into something more than Man. The only solution was for God to become Man, which He did through the Incarnation in the person of Jesus. Thereby, He set a window in the tiny dark dungeon of the ego in which we all languish, letting in a light, providing a vista, and offering a way of release from the servitude of the flesh and the fury of the will into what St. Paul called *the glorious liberty of the children of God.*

This is what the Incarnation, realized in the birth of Jesus, and in the drama of his ministry, death and Resurrection, was to signify. With it, Eternity steps into Time, and Time loses itself in Eternity. Hence Jesus; in the eyes of God, a man, and in the eyes of men, God. It is sublimely simple; a transcendental soap-opera going on century after century and touching innumerable hearts; from some bleak, lonely soul seeking a hand to hold when all others have been withdrawn, to vast concourses of joyful believers singing their *glorias*, their *kyries*, their *misereres*. There have been endless variations in the script, in the music, in the dialogue, but one thing remains constant—the central figure, Jesus. After the great Jehovah before whose wrath even the Gentiles bow down, the Lamb of God; after the immutable Law handed down to Moses from on high, grace and truth embodied in a gospel of love; after the Creation, the Incarnation, when the momentous announcement: *Fiat Lux!* which begins our human story finds its fulfilment in another: *Ecce Homo!* Let there be Light!, and then: Behold the Man! With the Light came the universe, and all its creatures; illimitable space to be explored, and the tiniest atoms to be broken down into yet tinier ones. With the Incarnation came the Man, and the addition of a new spiritual dimension to the cosmic scene. The universe provides a stage; Jesus is the play.

The exigencies of the play require that his birth shall be both miraculous and ordinary. Wise Men attend it, and also shepherds; a new star announces it, and yet it takes place in the lowliest of circumstances—in a manger, with the beasts of the field that are housed there looking on expressionlessly as Jesus emerges from his mother's womb. Gifts of gold, frankincense and myrrh signify a royal birth, the coming of a prince of the House of David; the homely greetings of the shepherds welcome a friend of the poor, the lowly and the oppressed—a man for others. Similarly, Mary, in delivering Incarnate God into the dangerous world, has to be, at once, the most radiant and warm-blooded of mothers whose breasts gush with milk, and a virgin untouched by any sensual hand or carnal experience. The Holy Child has to come, fleshly, out of her flesh, and, at the same time, not through fleshly processes. As she proclaims in her *Magnificat*, God has regarded her lowliness, and made her blessed in the eyes of future generations, by bestowing upon her the inestimable privilege that in her womb the Incarnation happens.

Until comparatively recent times Christians found little difficulty in combining these two themes of perfect motherhood and perfect virginity. The Madonnas of the Middle Ages, endlessly painted, sculpted, celebrated in verse and prose and Plainsong, are glowingly alive without being involved in our human concupiscence. One comes across them in obscure churches as in great cathedrals and abbeys—faces of transcendental beauty that are also enchantingly homely, and even droll, in wood and stone and marble; still with candle flames flickering in front of them and flowers heaped before them, and a few figures kneeling, touched with wonder at a Mother of God, who was, at once, so sublimely motherly, and so humanly divine. Such faces, blending physical and spiritual beauty into a sort of celestial coquetry, are likewise to be seen among nuns—or were until they put aside their habits and rules to follow Demas and the fashions of this present world. In humanistic times like ours, a contemporary virgin—assuming there are any such—would regard a message from the Angel Gabriel that she might expect to give birth to a son to be called the Son of the Highest as ill-tidings of great sorrow and a slur on the local family-planning centre. It is, in point of fact, extremely improbable, under existing conditions, that Jesus would have been permitted to be born at all. Mary's pregnancy, in poor circumstances, and with the father unknown, would have been an obvious case for an abortion; and her talk of having conceived as a result of the intervention of the Holy Ghost would have pointed to the need for psychiatric treatment, and made the case for terminating her pregnancy even stronger. Thus our generation, needing a Saviour more, perhaps, than any that has ever existed, would be too humane to allow one to be born; too enlightened to permit the Light of the World to shine in a darkness that grows ever more oppressive.

To a twentieth-century mind the notion of a virgin birth is intrinsically and preposterously inconceivable. If a woman claims—such claims are made from time to time—to have become pregnant without sexual intercourse, no one believes her. Yet for centuries millions upon millions of people never doubted that Mary had begotten Jesus without the participation of a husband or lover. Nor was such a belief limited to the simple and unlettered; the most profound and most erudite minds, the greatest artists and craftsmen, found no difficulty in accepting the Virgin Birth as an incontestable fact—for instance, Pascal, who in the versatility of his gifts and the originality of his insights was regarded as the Aristotle of his time. From a contemporary point of view, this is the more surprising in that little effort would seem to have been made to achieve consistency or credibility in the account in the Gospels of Jesus's birth. Thus, the genealogical table purporting to establish Jesus's descent from King David in accordance with Messianic prophecy is traced through Joseph, with whom, if the Virgin Birth really happened, he had no blood relationship.

Are we, then, to suppose that our forebears who believed implicitly in the Virgin Birth were gullible fools, whereas we, who would no more believe in such notions than we would that the world is flat, have put aside childish things and become mature? Is our scepticism one more manifestation of our having—in Bonhoeffer's unhappy phrase—come of age? It would be difficult to support such a proposition in the light of the almost inconceivable credulity of today's brain-washed public, who so readily believe absurdities in advertisements and in statistical and sociological prognostications before which an African witch-doctor would recoil in derision. With Pascal it was the other way round; while accepting, with the same certainty as he did the coming of the seasons, the New Testament account of Jesus's birth, he had already seen through and scornfully rejected the pretensions of science. Now, three centuries later, his intuition has been amply fulfiled. The dogmatism of science has become a new orthodoxy, disseminated by the Media and a State educational system with a thoroughness and subtlety far exceeding anything of the kind achieved by the Inquisition; to the point that to believe today in a miraculous happening like the Virgin Birth is to appear a kind of imbecile, whereas to disbelieve in an unproven and unprovable scientific proposition like the Theory of Evolution, and still more to question some quasi-scientific shibboleth like the Population Explosion, is to stand condemned as an obscurantist, an enemy of progress and enlightenment.

Does this mean that we must consider Pascal as having been, in his scientific capacity, an admitted genius, but, in his capacity of apologist for the Christian religion, a credulous fool? Is his work on the vacuum, his invention of the computer, of dazzling originality, but his *Pensées* no more than the vain imaginings of a naturally sceptical mind seeking for transcendental certainties at any cost? On the contrary, it is through the *Pensées* that his fame has been kept alive; it is to the *Pensées* that innumerable seekers after truth, up to and including our own time, have turned for enlightenment and inspiration, and never in vain. The key to this seeming disparity between Pascal the scientist, scrupulously observing facts and weighing their relevance, and Pascal the Christian, bowing his head, bending his knees, humbling his proud mind, before the Virgin Mother of Jesus, lies in the one word 'faith': what the writer of the Epistle to the Hebrews called *the substance of things hoped for, the evidence of things not seen.* Faith that bridges the chasm between what our minds can know and what our souls aspire after; faith which so dwarfs whatever we may consider ourselves to have achieved, or been, that it makes all men—the humblest, the simplest, the most, in worldly terms, foolish—our equals, our brothers; faith which so irradiates our inner being and outward circumstances that the ostensible exactitudes of time and measure, of proof and disproof, lose their precision, existing only in relation to eternal absolutes which everything in the universe proclaims, and in which all life has its being—the stones and the creatures, the pig's grunt and the nightingale's song, the trees and the mountains, the wind and the clouds, height and depth, darkness and light, everything that ever has been, or ever will be, attempted, or done, till the end of time—all swelling the chorus of faith.

It was precisely to revivify and replenish the world's stock of faith that the Bethlehem birth took place. Seen with the eye of faith, the shepherds rejoice, the Wise Men prostrate themselves and offer their gifts, the very stars are rearranged—though I have always considered myself that it was probably the Morning Star in its familiar place that the Wise Men followed, shining so wondrously on that momentous occasion that it was taken to be a new intruder into the heavens. Seen with the eye of faith, everything falls perfectly into place, faith being the key which enables us to decipher God's otherwise inscrutable communications. The centrepiece is, of course, Mary, a Virgin Mother, with God sucking voraciously at her breast; bearing in her arms the new light that has come into the world to lighten, not just the Jews, but the Gentiles, all mankind, as well. So it has been celebrated year by year through the centuries of Christendom, in carols, in crèches, in plays and processions, in a combination of public worship and private acts of giving, until now, when faith seems to be expiring, and the light has grown correspondingly dim, it has become a mighty exercise in salesmanship, a gala occasion in the great contemporary cult of consumption, an act of worship directed towards our latest deity—the Gross National Product.

Apart from the one dubious reference in Josephus, in his own lifetime Jesus made no impact on history. This is something that I cannot but regard as a special dispensation on God's part, and, I like to think, yet another example of the ironical humour which informs so many of His purposes. To me, it seems highly appropriate that the most important figure in all history should thus escape the notice of memoirists, diarists, commentators, all the tribe of chroniclers who even then existed, and, four centuries later, were so scarified by St. Augustine in the days when he held what he called his 'Chair of Lies' in Milan. Historically, Jesus is, strictly speaking, a non-person. Anthropologically, too, he is without interest; we know, in this respect, more about Neanderthal Man than about the Son of Man. Likewise, sociologically Jesus is a non-starter. What did he earn? How did he vote? What examinations did he pass, and what countries did he visit? The Gospels do not tell us, and we have no other means of knowing, though this has not prevented invention from getting to work; even, of late, in the Kinsey field. A suffragan Anglican bishop has raised the question of whether Jesus may not have been a homosexual; a sometime theological instructor in Manchester has devised a theory, with all the ostensible appurtenances of scholarship, whereby the Gospels are no more than a phallic code; and in Scandinavia—inevitably there!—film-makers have turned their attention to Jesus's sex-life. Truly the myths of fact are the most absurd and misleading of all—this being, perhaps, designed by God to humble our pride when we discover that the myths of faith turn out to be, by comparison, our only truth. Even the most conscientious historians can study the past, as geologists do, only through its fossils; truth belongs essentially to a spiritual order where the categories of time and space, without which history cannot exist, are inapplicable. History is too fragile and indeterminate a structure to contain Jesus; like—using the imagery of one of his own parables—the old wineskins into which new wine cannot be put, or like the worn cloth which cannot be patched with new. How shabby, how patched and repatched, how threadbare and faded this fabric of history is, compared with the ever-renewed, gleaming and glistening garment of truth!

Through the eye of faith, then, Jesus is seen as, at once, God and Man, as Mary is seen as, at once, Virgin and Mother. His perfect humanity and perfect godhead combine, as do her perfect virginity and perfect motherhood, to produce, in the one case, the Son of God, in the other, the Mother of God. Suddenly, almost with a click, like a film coming into sync, everything has meaning, everything is real; and the meaning, the reality, shine out in every shape and sound and movement, in each and every manifestation of life, so that I want to cry out with the blind man to whom Jesus restored his sight: *One thing I know, that, whereas I was blind, now I see.* How, I ask myself, could I have missed it before? How not have understood that the grey-silver light across the water, the cry of the sea-gulls and the sweep of their wings, everything on which my eyes rest and my ears hear, is telling me about God.

> This life's dim Windows of the Soul
> Distorts the Heavens from Pole to Pole
> And leads you to believe a Lie
> When you see with, not thro', the Eye.

Thus Blake distinguishes between the fantasy that is seen with the eye and the truth that is seen through it. They are two clearly demarcated kingdoms; and passing from one to the other, from the kingdom of fantasy to the kingdom of reality, gives inexpressible delight. As when the sun comes out, and a dark landscape is suddenly glorified, all that was obscure becoming clear, all that was incomprehensible, comprehensible. Fantasy's joys and desires dissolve away, and in their place is one joy, one desire; one Oneness—God. In this kingdom of reality, Simone Weil tells us, nothing is so continually fresh and surprising, so full of sweet and perpetual ecstasy, as goodness; no desert so dreary, monotonous and boring as evil. There we may understand what St. Augustine meant when he insisted that 'though the higher things are better than the lower, the sum of all creation is better than the higher things alone', and how, in the light of this realization, all human progress, human morality, human law, based, as they are, on the opposite proposition—of the intrinsic superiority of the higher over the lower—is seen as written on water, scribbled on dust; like Jesus's scribble while he was waiting for the accusers of the woman taken in adultery to disperse. Alas, then the sun goes in again, and we are back in the kingdom of fantasy, where it is goodness that is flat and boring, and evil that is varied and attractive, profound, intriguing and full of charm. Where the higher is ardently sought on its own account, to be extracted like uranium, pure and unalloyed, from its earthy bed, which is the whole of creation. With how unutterable a longing does one yearn to leave the sunless land of fantasy and live for ever in the sunshine of reality!

Jesus himself makes the same distinction as Blake between what is seen with and through the eye when he directs his teaching specifically to those who have eyes to see and ears to hear. It is not enough, that is to say, just to look and listen; behind the looking and listening there has to be the perspective of faith. Only seeing through the eye, and across this perspective, does the true significance of Jesus and his teaching become clear. Those critics who seek to discover it by minutely and diligently investigating the details of his life, as Tolstoy points out, in reality discover nothing. Even if they were completely successful in their efforts, instead of for the most part trafficking in presumptions and fantasy, and so were able to tell us exactly the sort of person Jesus was, produce a convincing profile of him, they would still be as far as ever from unravelling the secret of his power over the hearts and minds of men, both while he was in the world, and subsequently. This secret is hidden, not in the circumstances of his life, in the people with whom he consorted and the history, superstitions, fashions and ideologies of the time, but in his teaching, at once so pure, so lofty and so simple. It was those luminous words of his, sealed with his death on the Cross, that led to his being recognized as God. After all, who but God would have dared to ask of men what he asked of them? Demanding everything and enduring everything, he set in train a great creative wave of love and sacrifice such as the world had never before seen or dreamed of.

It is commentators like Blake and Tolstoy, Simone Weil and Dostoyevsky, who pre-eminently bring Jesus to life, because they approach him through the imagination as artists rather than through the intellect as theologians. In him they observe the very process of art at work in the Word becoming flesh and dwelling among us full of grace and truth, and are no more concerned to discover him as an historical personage than they would be to go through the records of La Mancha for traces of Don Quixote's lineage, or through Burke's *Landed Gentry* for traces of Falstaff's. The process itself—making the Word flesh and vesting it with grace and truth—suffices. This is what every artist is endlessly seeking to do. Thus Jesus's story is a drama, not documentation, and the Word whose flesh he became is every true word ever written or spoken; every true note ever sounded, every true stone laid on another, every true shape moulded or true colour mixed. The whole creative achievement of Man is comprehended in it. Look for it in the light shining in El Greco's faces; listen for it in the notes of Plainsong; marvel at it in the spire of Salisbury Cathedral rising so exquisitely into the sky; read it in Blake's *Songs of Innocence* and *Songs of Experience*. Hold it in your hand in a grain of sand; in your mind in the universe, with all its planetary systems within systems, and ultimate vistas of everlasting space; in your soul in the contemplation of the creator of it all, the spirit which animates it all, the beginning and the end of what has no beginning and no end—God. Then, pinpoint it all, bring it all to a focus, concentrate it all in a Man, and that Man—Jesus.

However, wherever and in whatever circumstances Jesus was born, there was, we may be sure, a real baby, wrinkled and wizened and full of wind, as babies are, and a doting mother to offer her breast, and look down with pride and joy at the tiny head of the little creature ardently sucking at it. Though in our time motherhood has been greatly devalued, and the sick phrase 'unwanted child' been given currency, it still remains true, as any nurse or gynaecologist will confirm, that it is extremely rare for any child at the moment of birth to be other than wanted in its mother's eyes. Once when I was in Calcutta with Mother Teresa she picked up one of the so-called 'unwanted' babies which had come into the care of her Missionaries of Charity. It had been salvaged from a dustbin, and was so minute that one wondered it could exist at all. When I remarked on this, a look of exultation came into Mother Teresa's face. 'See,' she said, 'there's life in it!' So there was; and suddenly it was as though I were present at the Bethlehem birth, and the baby Mother Teresa was holding was another Lamb of God sent into the world to lighten our darkness. How could we know? How dared we prognosticate upon what made life worth while for this or that child? How many Lambs of God may not have been carried away in buckets of hospital waste?

Mary's joy and pride in the baby Jesus sucking at her breast will naturally have been magnified by the knowledge that had been conveyed to her of the great destiny awaiting this particular child; but her rejoicing would have been very great anyway. Every mother's son, particularly the first-born, is a Son of God; a miraculous being whose arrival in the world is a unique occasion, with great things lying ahead. If God chose to become incarnate as Jesus, then his birth, whatever marvels may have accompanied it, must have had the same characteristics as any other; just as, on the Cross, the suffering of the man into whom the Bethlehem child grew must have been of the same nature as that of the two delinquents crucified beside him. Otherwise, Jesus's humanity would have been a fraud; in which case, his divinity would have been fraudulent, too. The perfection of Jesus's divinity was expressed in the perfection of his humanity, and vice versa. He was God because he was so sublimely a man, and Man because, in all his sayings and doings, in the grace of his person and words, in the love and compassion that shone out of him, he walked so closely with God. As Man alone, Jesus could not have saved us; as God alone, he would not; Incarnate, he could and did.

Joseph and Mary had come to Bethlehem despite the lack of accommodation because, we are told, their presence was required there for a census that was being taken. Here, the finger of history momentarily intrudes. There was, it seems, some sort of census being taken round about this time by Caesar Augustus, then at the height of his fame. He had already been proclaimed a god, with appropriate rites for worshipping him; and his régime was considered to be so enlightened, stable and prosperous that it would go on for ever—a final solution to the problem of government and a guarantee of the continuing happiness and prosperity of all who were fortunate enough to be Roman citizens. Expiring civilisations are prone to such fantasies; for instance, ours, notable in the last half century, equally, for inane hope and inane despair. Of all the millions of souls numbered in Caesar Augustus's census, the one born in Bethlehem just in time to be included in it must have been, in wordly terms, about the most insignificant, and the least likely to figure, in the estimation of posterity, as having any comparable importance with that of the great Emperor. It was a confrontation of sorts between the man who passed for being the ruler of the world and the latest and lowliest of his subjects. Yet, of course, as it turned out, their rôles were to be reversed; for centuries to come Jesus would reign over men's minds and hearts, when Augustus's kingdom existed only in history books and ruins. Was it, I have often wondered, Augustus's head—it might have been, though by then Tiberius was reigning—on the coin that was produced apropos one of Jesus's most famous observations, about rendering unto Caesar the things that are Caesar's and unto God the things that are God's? If so, it would have been appropriate enough; Augustus being a Caesar who claimed to be a god, and Jesus being God in the likeness of a man.

After Jesus's birth, we are told, Joseph and Mary took him into Egypt. The occasion for the journey had prophetic support in the beautiful lines of Jeremiah: *A voice was heard in Ramah, lamentation, and bitter weeping; Rachel weeping for her children refused to be comforted, . . . because they were not.* This is taken as referring to a decree by King Herod that all children of two years old and under in the neighbourhood of Bethlehem should be put to death. Thereby he hoped to ensure the elimination of the child of the House of David destined to be King of the Jews, about whose prophesied birth the Wise Men had told him, and in whom he saw a possible rival. It was Herod who, in the first place, sent the Wise Men to spy out the land in Bethlehem, with strict instructions to report back to him on what they found there. Having found Jesus, being Wise Men, they decided that it would be more prudent to return to the Orient whence they came by another route that did not take in a return visit to Herod. They are portrayed as *Magi*, or magicians, skilled in reading the stars and in soothsaying, by the early illustrators of the New Testament in their exquisite Books of Hours and illuminated manuscripts and Missals. I prefer to think of them in contemporary guise as pundits or talking heads; a think-tank, or Brains Trust, an *Any Questions* team. Do the panel think ... ? In any case, having circumvented Herod's domain, the Wise Men disappear from view, leaving him to order the Massacre of the Innocents, another episode popular with early Christian illustrators. Sceptics who wonder if anything of the kind ever happened may reflect that Herod's efforts are quite put in the shade today, when for the highest humanitarian motives babies are slaughtered on an infinitely larger scale than ever he managed, even before they have left the womb—something Herod did not think of.

The episode of the Flight to Egypt, like numerous others in the Gospels, doubtless owes much to the fact that it may be taken as fulfiling a Jewish prophecy—*Out of Egypt did I call my son*. This notion of taking deliberate steps, actually devising events, in order that a prophecy might seem to have been fulfiled, was one of my earliest Biblical enigmas. If, I remember reflecting as a child, and perhaps asking some unfortunate teacher, this or that had to be done to fulfil a prophecy, how was it a prophecy at all? Surely, prophesying meant foreseeing something that was going to happen, not so arranging things that it happened. Subsequent experience of life, and brooding thereon, made me understand that two parallel processes are at work—prophesying, and surrendering to the logic of events whereby the prophecy comes to pass. Built into our mortal circumstances there is what Blake called a Fearful Symmetry—

Tyger, Tyger, burning bright
In the forests of the night,
What immortal hand or eye
Dare frame thy fearful symmetry?

—which, once understood, makes it possible to envisage the consequences of things. Thus, a sunflower seed has a built-in propensity to become a sunflower, spreading its yellow petals, and, as Blake so beautifully puts it, becoming weary of time as it counts the steps of the sun. Equally, to realize this propensity, unfold this Fearful Symmetry, the sunflower has to be planted and watered and nurtured. The Old Testament prophets, attuned to the Fearful Symmetry of God's purposes, are able to announce what lies ahead—the mercies and the glories and the wrath to come. As with the sunflower, however, in order that their prophecies may be fulfiled, the ground has to be prepared and watered; the young shoots, or embryonic happenings, have to be nurtured and helped to grow and develop into their full historical fulfilment. Likewise with more recent prophets like Dostoyevsky, who saw with extraordinary clarity as being implicit in the Russian scene, in the ramshackle texture and romantic credulity of the European liberal mind, the revolutionary upheaval that loomed ahead. In conveying this in his writings—notably in his novel *The Devils*—he facilitated its inevitable coming-to-pass. Again, Kierkegaard envisaged with uncanny precision just what the consequences of universal suffrage democracy, mass Media and the pursuit of happiness through material wellbeing and sensual indulgence were bound to be, and how the Christian Churches in these circumstances would be diverted into proclaiming an earthly kingdom, and so destroy themselves. Like the prophets of old, in so forcefully and correctly forecasting the future, he helped to bring it about; 'In order that the prophecy might be fulfiled' would have been a suitable epitaph to inscribe on his tomb, especially appropriate in present-day Copenhagen, his native city.

Similarly, it has become abundantly clear in the second half of the twentieth century that Western Man has decided to abolish himself. Having wearied of the struggle to be himself, he has created his own boredom out of his own affluence, his own impotence out of his own erotomania, his own vulnerability out of his own strength; himself blowing the trumpet that brings the walls of his own city tumbling down, and, in a process of auto-genocide, convincing himself that he is too numerous, and labouring accordingly with pill and scalpel and syringe to make himself fewer in order to be an easier prey for his enemies; until at last, having educated himself into imbecility, and polluted and drugged himself into stupefaction, he keels over, a weary, battered old brontosaurus, and becomes extinct. Many, like Spengler, have envisaged the future in such terms, and now what they prophesied is upon us.

2. The Crucifixion

One thing at least can be said with certainty about the Crucifixion of Christ; it was manifestly the most famous death in history. No other death has aroused one hundredth part of the interest, or been remembered with one hundredth part of the intensity and concern. Walking recently with an artist friend (actually, Graham Sutherland, who designed the great tapestry in the restored Coventry Cathedral) in hills overlooking the Mediterranean, I found he was always on the lookout for thorns, as though they were precious jewels—as indeed they are for him ever since he painted the crown on Christ's stricken head.

Practically every European artist, great and small, has planned or executed a representation of the Crucifixion, from the Italian primitives to Francis Bacon. Most writers likewise have made use of the scene and its imagery in their work, if only for the purposes of ridicule or blasphemy. *Nouvelle vague* film makers, and Hollywood impresarios in search of a sure-fire box-office success, equally turn to it for a theme.

The Cross, symbol of this macabre execution, has been carried pretty well everywhere, within and outside Christendom. No corner of the world is so remote and inaccessible that you may not find a cross there.

As for Europe, in countries like Italy and France it is impossible to go a hundred yards anywhere without being confronted with some version or other of the Crucifixion. Since that Golgotha happening, billions have been made, from exquisitely fashioned ones to the most tawdry, gimcrack, mass-produced ones; from huge, overpowering Calvaries to little, tiny, jewelled crucifixes to hang round the neck or over the heart, but always with the same essential characteristics: a man at the last extremity of a cruel death, with lolling head, and feet and hands viciously nailed to a wooden cross.

Originally published in the *Observer* (March 26, 1967). Reprinted from Malcolm Muggeridge, *Jesus Rediscovered* (Garden City, N.Y.: Doubleday, 1969), pp. 111–17.

In theory such a symbol should be depressing. It portrays the defeat of goodness by duplicity and power; a meek and broken victim of the kind of human brutality to which we, perhaps more than most generations of men, have had to accustom ourselves. In practice the symbol has inspired some of the gayest figures in history, like St. Francis of Assisi; has filled the cities of Renaissance Italy with a profusion of art that has been the admiration of Christian and non-Christian alike; and has stimulated audacities of thought and exploration that have carried the human race forward with immense strides toward understanding and mastering their material circumstances.

How unlikely anything of the kind would have seemed at the time! Who among the motley collection of spectators of so obscure an event could possibly have envisaged that there before their eyes another civilisation was being born, which would last for two thousand years, shining so long and so brightly? Not even the Apostles could have thought of that; what they looked for was an apocalyptic Second Coming and the end of the world, not the beginning of Christendom. Only St. Paul, converted *after* the Crucifixion from a persecutor of Christians to one of Christ's most ardent and brilliant followers, may have vaguely sensed something of the kind. I nourish a secret hope in my heart, as our civilisation decomposes into People's Hedonism, with, not one, but whole armies of crazed Neros sucking LSD sugar and babbling protest songs, that another obscure Crucifixion may have taken place that will in due course lighten the darkness now falling so thick and so fast. If so, we should not know: it would not get on television or into the newspapers.

A believing or orthodox Christian would, of course, account for the durability of the cross's appeal over the centuries by the divinity of the man crucified. God, he would say, was put to death by unredeemed men, and then rose from the dead; naturally, so unique and definitive an event has continued and ever will continue to hold the attention of mankind.

I have to confess that to me—as, I should suppose, to the great majority of present-day inheritors of the Christian tradition—such a line of thought is largely meaningless. With the utmost difficulty, and in the vaguest possible manner, I can grasp some sort of notion of a deity, and of his loving purpose, in which I, in common with all creation, am inextricably enmeshed. I can even, in moments of illumination, imagine myself to be in contact with such a deity, and surrender myself with inexpressible happiness to his will. To imagine this deity having a son in any particular sense, and this son to have been born of a virgin, and to have lived on earth for thirty years or so as a man; then to have died and to have risen from the dead, is, as far as I am concerned, beyond credibility.

I quite agree that we of the twentieth century are perfectly capable of believing other things intrinsically as improbable as Christ's incarnation. Toward any kind of scientific mumbo-jumbo we display a credulity that must be the envy of African witch doctors. While we shy away with contumely from the account of the Creation in the Book of Genesis, we are probably ready to assent to any rigmarole by a Professor Hoyle about how matter came to be, provided it is dished up in the requisite jargon and associated, however obliquely, with what we conceive to be "facts."

I suppose every age has its own particular fantasy; ours is science. A seventeenth-century man like Pascal, though himself a mathematician and scientist of genius, found it quite ridiculous that anyone should suppose that rational processes could lead to any ultimate conclusions about life, but easily accepted the authority of the Scriptures. With us it is the other way round.

What, then, does the Crucifixion signify in an age like ours? I see it in the first place as a sublime mockery of all earthly authority and power. The crown of thorns, the purple robe, the ironical title "King of the Jews," were intended to mock or parody Christ's pretensions to be the Messiah; in fact, they rather hold up to ridicule and contempt all crowns, all robes, all kings that ever were. It was a sick joke that backfired. No one, it seems to me, who has fully grasped the Crucifixion can ever again take seriously any expression or instrument of worldly power, however venerable, glittering, or seemingly formidable.

When Christ was tempted in the wilderness, he declined the Devil's offer to give him sway over the kingdoms of the earth (a refusal that must be intensely irritating to those who believe that it is possible through Christian good will to set up a Kingdom of Heaven on earth); the Crucifixion demonstrated why: because the Devil's offer was bogus. There are no kingdoms for him to bestow; only pseudo or notional ones presided over by mountebanks masquerading as emperors and kings and governments.

Look under the crown and you see the thorns beneath; pull aside the purple robe, and lo! nakedness; look into the grandiloquent titles and they are seen to be no more substantial than Christ's ribald one of King of the Jews scrawled above his cross. In Christ's day the Roman emperors claimed to be gods and induced their subjects to pay them divine honors. He, a man, exposed the hollowness of their claim by dying, thereby becoming God in the eyes of successive generations of men, who went on worshipping him long after the Roman Empire had ceased to exist.

In this sense, Christ's death on the cross may be seen as the exact converse of the next most famous death as far as our civilisation is concerned—that of Socrates. Socrates obediently drank hemlock and died to support and enhance the state: Christ died on the cross in derisive defiance of all states, whether Roman, Judaic, or any other.

From Socrates's death emanate all plans for the collective betterment of mankind, whether embodied in a nation, a regime, a leader, an ideology, a social system, or, for that matter, a Church; from the cross comes the notion of individual salvation, of individual souls journeying through life like Bunyan's Pilgrim, all equal in their capacity as children of God and in that Christ died for them equally, and all buoyed up by the expectation of deliverance through death from the demands and imperfections of their fleshly existence.

What, I often ask myself, was the Golgotha happening actually like? Clearly, in no wise as momentous in the eyes of those who witnessed it as the retrospective attention lavished upon it would seem to imply. Upon history at the time it made absolutely no impact. To understand this, one has to think of an administratively comparable incident in times past in one of the remoter parts of the then extant British Empire—for instance, the execution in Burma that Orwell attended when he was a young police officer there, and afterwards described so feelingly and perceptively.

I well remember the good-naturedly contemptuous attitude, in the days of the Raj, of the British soldiery in India to Hindu and Moslem religious fanaticism. The Roman soldiers in Palestine, I expect, took a similar attitude towards Jewish religious fanaticism. I doubt if Christ made any particular impression on them; in their eyes he was just another wog to be crucified. One imagines the conversation in the sergeants' mess that night, with some old hand pointing out to a slightly squeamish newcomer lately arrived from Rome that with the Jews you have to be firm and standoffish; give 'em an inch and they take an ell. I heard it all word for word in upcountry clubs in India forty years ago.

For some reason I always see in my mind's eye a fringe of Roman troops ringing the little crowd round the cross, and standing out against the Golgotha skyline in their breastplates and kilts—not very high-grade troops either, in that distant, unpopular station. They look on nonchalantly; their orders are not to interfere, but to make sure that if there's any trouble it doesn't spread. An NCO is in charge; the officers are away at the games, or maybe Their Excellencies, the Pilates, are giving a garden party to celebrate the Emperor's birthday.

As for the indigenous spectators (as they are described in the official report that Pilate gets the next day, and barely glances at), they consist of a few sharp-eyed rabbis making sure that everything goes according to plan; the usual sightseers attracted by executions, street accidents, or any other violence; some of the disciples, including Peter,[1] still, poor fellow, full of contrition about his denial of Christ the day before (who hasn't similarly heard the cock crow, alas?); Mary and one or two other women, and maybe a representative of the underground Jewish resistance movement just in case something cropped up, though not with much hope.

Christ's remark about rendering unto Caesar the things that are Caesar's effectively eliminated any momentary expectation that he might espouse the cause of liberating the Jews from their servitude to Rome. As it turned out, Palestine was to be liberated on numerous occasions in the course of a rather tragic history, but never by him.

It was the sort of incident—a man dying in that slow, public way—that must have generated its own immediate tension in the beholders, even though they were unaware of the nature and magnitude of the stupendous drama being enacted before them. In some vague way they expect something to happen, and so it does; the man expires, not with a gesture of defiance befitting a putative King of the Jews, but with a cry of despair. With that cry Christendom comes to pass. We are henceforth to worship defeat, not victory; failure, not success; surrender, not defiance; deprivation, not satiety; weakness, not strength. We are to lose our lives in order to keep them, to die in order to live.

It is true, of course, that professing Christians and ostensibly Christian societies and institutions have by no means been true to the cross and what it signified, especially today, when the nominally Christian part of the world is foremost in worship of expanding production—our Golden Calf—and in pursuit of happiness in the guise of sensual pleasure. Yet

[1] Although the Scriptures reveal that Peter and the apostles were "witnesses" to the fact that the Jewish authorities had killed Christ "by hanging him on a tree" (Acts 5:30), Peter was not physically present at the Crucifixion.—Ed.

there the cross still is, propounding its unmistakable denunciation of this world and of the things of this world.

There had to be a sequel; I quite see that. The man on the cross who had given up the ghost must rise from the dead as a living God; the Resurrection followed the Crucifixion as inevitably as day follows night. And, indeed, in a sense, it clearly happened. Otherwise, how should I, a twentieth-century nihilist, who asks nothing better than to live out his days without any concern for a God, living or dead, be worrying his head about this cross and a man who died on it two thousand years ago? Whether it happened as described in the Gospel narrative, and endlessly repeated by Christian apologists, is another question. In any case, what does it matter?

I even prefer to suppose that some body snatcher, accustomed to hanging about Golgotha to pick up anything that might be going, heard in his dim-witted way that the King of the Jews was up for execution. Good! he thinks, there are bound to be pickings there. So he waits till the job is done, finds out where the corpse has been laid, drags the stone away, and then, making sure no one is watching, decamps with the body.

What a disappointment for him! This King of the Jews has no crown, no jewels, no orb, no scepter, no ring; he is just a worthless, wasted, broken, naked body. The man contemptuously abandons the body to the vultures, who in their turn leave the bones to whiten in the sun—those precious, precious bones![2]

[2] Muggeridge was no doubt being a little facetious here. In his book *Jesus: The Man Who Lives*, he clearly stated: "That the Resurrection happened, and that in consequence of it Jesus's followers who had scattered drew together again, resolved to go about their Master's business, seems to me indubitably true. Likewise, Jesus's claim to be the Light of the World, and his related promise that through him we may be born into new men, liberated from servitude to the ego and our appetites into the glorious liberty of the children of God."

3. A Christian Credo

In trying to formulate what I believe, I have to begin with what I disbelieve. I disbelieve in progress, the pursuit of happiness, and all the concomitant notions and projects for creating a society in which human beings find ever greater contentment by being given in ever greater abundance the means to satisfy their material and bodily hopes and desires. In other words, I consider that the way of life in urbanized, rich countries as it exists today, and as it is likely to go on developing, is probably the most degraded and unillumined ever to come to pass on earth. The half century in which I have been consciously alive seems to me to have been quite exceptionally destructive, murderous, and brutal. More people have been killed and terrorized, more driven from their homes and native places, more of the past's heritage has been destroyed, more lies propagated and base persuasion engaged in, with less compensatory achievement in art, literature, and imaginative understanding, than in any comparable period of history.

Ever since I can remember, the image of earthly power, whether in the guise of schoolmaster, mayor, judge, prime minister, monarch, or any other, has seemed to me derisory. I was enchanted when I first read in the *Pensées* (Pascal being one of the small, sublime band of fellow humans to whom one may turn and say in the deepest humility: "I agree") about how magistrates and rulers had to be garbed in their ridiculous ceremonial robes, crowns, and diadems. Otherwise, who would not see through their threadbare pretensions? I am conscious of having been ruled by buffoons, taught by idiots, preached at by hypocrites, and preyed upon by charlatans in the guise of advertisers and other professional persuaders, as well as by demagogues and ideologues of many opinions, all false.

Originally published as "Credo", in Malcolm Muggeridge, *Jesus Rediscovered* (Garden City, N.Y.: Doubleday, 1969), pp. 119–25.

Nor, as far as I am concerned, is there any recompense in the so-called achievements of science. It is true that in my lifetime more progress has been made in unraveling the composition and mechanism of the material universe than previously in the whole of recorded time. This does not at all excite my mind, or even my curiosity. The atom has been split; the universe has been discovered, and will soon be explored. Neither achievement has any bearing on what alone interests me—why life exists, and what is the significance, if any, of my minute and so transitory part in it. All the world in a grain of sand; all the universe too. If I could understand a grain of sand, I should understand everything. Why, then, should going to the moon and Mars, or spending a holiday along the Milky Way, be expected to advance me further in my quest than going to Manchester and Liverpool, or spending a holiday in Brighton?

Education, the great mumbo-jumbo and fraud of the age, purports to equip us to live, and is prescribed as a universal remedy for everything, from juvenile delinquency to premature senility. For the most part, it only serves to enlarge stupidity, inflate conceit, enhance credulity, and put those subjected to it at the mercy of brainwashers with printing presses, radio, and television at their disposal. I have seen pictures of huge, ungainly, prehistoric monsters who developed such a weight of protective shell that they sank under its burden and became extinct. Our civilisation likewise is sinking under the burden of its own wealth, and the necessity to consume it; of its own happiness, and the necessity to provide and sustain the fantasies that embody it; of its own security, and the ever more fabulously destructive nuclear devices considered essential to it. Thus burdened, it, too, may well soon become extinct. As this fact sinks into the collective consciousness, the resort to drugs, dreams, fantasies, and other escapist devices, particularly sex, becomes ever more marked.

Living thus in the twilight of a spent civilisation, amidst its ludicrous and frightening shadows, what is there to believe? Curiously enough, these twilight circumstances provide a setting in which, as it seems to me, the purpose that lies behind them stands out with particular clarity. As human love only shines in all its splendor when the last tiny glimmer of desire has been extinguished, so we have to make the world a wilderness to find God in it. The meaning of the universe lies beyond history, as love lies beyond desire. That meaning shines forth in moments of illumination (which come and go so unaccountably; though, I am thankful to say, never quite ceasing—a sound as of music, far, far away, and drowned by other, more tumultuous noises, but still to be faintly and fitfully heard) with an inconceivable clarity and luminosity. It breaks like a crystalline dawn out of darkness, and the deeper the darkness the more crystalline the dawn.

Let me express it, as I have often thought of it, in terms of a stage. In the middle is the workaday world where we live our daily lives, earning a living, reading newspapers, exchanging money, recording votes, chattering and eating and desiring. I call this the Cafe Limbo. On the left of the stage is an area of darkness, within which shapes and movements can be faintly discerned and inconclusive noises heard; sounds and sweet airs that, as on Caliban's island, give delight and hurt not. I call this Life. The right of the stage is bright with arc lamps, like a television studio. This is where history is unfolded and news is made; this is where we live our public, collective lives, seat and unseat rulers, declare wars and negotiate peace, glow with patriotism and get carried away with revolutionary zeal, enact laws, declaim rhetoric, swear eternal passion, and sink into abysses of desolation. I call this the Legend.

Across this triple stage, between Life, the Café Limbo, and the Legend, a drama is endlessly presented. Two forces shape the play: the Imagination, which belongs to Life, and the Will, which belongs to the Legend. Out of the Imagination comes love, understanding, goodness, self-abnegation; every true synthesis ever grasped or to be grasped. Out of the Will comes lust, hatred, cupidity, adulation, power, oratory; every false antithesis ever propounded or to be propounded. Those who belong exclusively or predominantly to Life are saints, mystics, and artists. In extreme cases—Christ, for instance—they have to be killed. (This is superbly explained in the famous Grand Inquisitor passage in *The Brothers Karamazov*, Dostoyevsky being, like Pascal, of the small, sublime band.) Those who belong exclusively or predominantly to the Legend are power-maniacs, rulers, heroes, demagogues, and liberators. In extreme cases—Hitler, for instance—they bring about their own destruction. In Life there is suffering, deprivation, and sanity; in the Legend, happiness, abundance, and madness.

Most of us spend the greater part of our time in the Café Limbo, casting an occasional glance in the direction of Life, and more than an occasional one in the direction of the Legend. Laughter is our best recourse, with the bar to provide a fillip as and when required. The Café Limbo is licensed. When a character passes from the Legend into Life, he brings some of the light with him, shining like a glowworm, until gradually the light subsides and goes out, swallowed up in the darkness of Life.

This same pattern may be traced more particularly and tragically in a single countenance, as anyone will be aware who has had occasion to watch over a loved face hovering between sanity and madness. (And many have; for as we abolish the ills and pains of the flesh we multiply those of the mind. By the time men are finally delivered from disease and decay—all pasteurized, their genes counted and rearranged, fitted with new, replaceable, plastic organs, able to eat, copulate, and perform other physical functions innocuously and hygienically as and when desired—they will all be mad, and the world one huge psychiatric ward.) You study the loved, distracted face as a scholar might study some ancient manuscript, looking for a key to its incomprehensibility. What you see is a fight to the death between the Will and the Imagination. If the former wins, then the flickering light will be put out forever; if the latter, it will shine again, to burn with a steady radiance, and you can cry out from a full heart: "Oh, beloved, you have come back to me."

I am well aware that, psychiatrically speaking, this is nonsensical. Yet I believe it. I see these two forces struggling for mastery in each individual soul; in mine, in all men's; in each collectivity, throughout our earth and throughout the immeasurable universe. One is of darkness and one of light; one wants to drag us down into the dark trough to rut and gorge there, and the other to raise us up into the azure sky, beyond appetite, where love is all-embracing, all-encompassing, and the dark confusion of life sorts itself out, like an orderly, smiling countryside suddenly glimpsed from a high hill as the mists disperse in the sun's light and warmth. One is the Devil and the other God. I have known both, and I believe in both.

For us Western Europeans, the Christian religion has expressed this ancient and, as I consider, obvious dichotomy in terms of breath-taking simplicity and sublimity. It was not the first word on the subject, nor will it be the last; but it is still *our* word. I accept it. I believe, as is written in the New Testament; if we would save our lives we must lose them; we cannot live by bread alone; we must die in the flesh to be reborn in the spirit; the flesh lusts contrary to the spirit and the spirit contrary to the flesh; God cannot see a sparrow fall to the ground without concern, and has counted the hairs of each head, so that all that lives deserves our respect and reverence, and no one man can conceivably be more important, of greater significance, or in any way more deserving of consideration than any other.

God is our father, we are his children and so one family, brothers and sisters together.

It is true that these basic propositions of Christianity have got cluttered up with dogma of various kinds that I find often incomprehensible, irrelevant, and even repugnant.[1] All the same, I should be proud and happy to be able to call myself a Christian; to dare to measure myself against that sublimely high standard of human values and human behavior. In this I take comfort from another saying of Pascal, thrown out like a lifeline to all sceptical minds throughout the ages: whoever looks for God has found him.

At its most obscurantist and debased, the Christian position still seems to me preferable to any scientific-materialist one, however cogent and enlightened. The evangelist with his lurid tract calling upon me to repent, for the Day of Judgement is at hand, is a burning and shining light compared with the eugenist who claims the right to decide in his broiler-house mind which lives should be protracted and which must be put out, or with the colporteurs of sterility who so complacently and self-righteously display their assortment of contraceptives to the so-called "backward" peoples of the world as our civilisation's noblest achievement and most precious gift.

The absurdities of the Kingdom of Heaven, as conceived in the minds of simple believers, are obvious enough—pearly gates, angelic choirs, golden crowns, and shining raiment. But what are we to think of the sheer imbecility of the Kingdom of Heaven on earth, as envisaged and recommended by the most authoritative and powerful voices of our time? Wealth increasing forevermore, and its beneficiaries, rich in time-payment merchandise, stupefied with television and with sex, comprehensively educated, told by Professor Hoyle how the world began and by Bertrand Russell how it will end; venturing forth on the broad highways, three lanes a side, with lay-bys to rest in and birth pills to keep them *intacta*, if not *virgo*, blood spattering the Tarmac as an extra thrill; heaven lying about them in the supermarket, the rainbow ending in the nearest bingo hall, leisure burgeoning out in multitudinous shining aerials rising like dreaming spires into the sky; happiness in as many colors as there are pills—green and yellow and blue and red and shining white; many mansions, mansions of

[1] We do not know to which specific doctrines Muggeridge refers, but he wrote this thirteen years before he joined the Catholic Church in 1982.

light and chromium, climbing ever upwards. This kingdom, surely, can only be for posterity an unending source of wry derision—always assuming there is to be any posterity. The backdrop, after all, is the mushroom cloud; as the Gadarene herd frisk and frolic, they draw ever nearer to the edge of the precipice.

I recognize, of course, that this statement of belief is partly governed by the circumstance that I am old, and in at most a decade or so, will be dead. In earlier years I should doubtless have expressed things differently. Now the prospect of death overshadows all others. I am like a man on a sea voyage nearing his destination. When I embarked I worried about having a cabin with a porthole, whether I should be asked to sit at the captain's table, who were the more attractive and important passengers. All such considerations become pointless when I shall so soon be disembarking.

As I do not believe that earthly life can bring any lasting satisfaction, the prospect of death holds no terrors. Those saints who pronounced themselves in love with death displayed, I consider, the best of sense, not a Freudian death wish. The world that I shall soon be leaving seems more than ever beautiful; especially its remoter parts, grass and trees and sea and rivers and little streams and sloping hills, where the image of eternity is more clearly stamped than among streets and houses. Those I love I can love even more, since I have nothing to ask of them but their love; the passion to accumulate possessions, or to be noticed and important, is too evidently absurd to be any longer entertained.

A sense of how extraordinarily happy I have been, and of enormous gratitude to my creator, overwhelms me often. I believe with a passionate, unshakable conviction that in all circumstances and at all times life is a blessed gift; that the spirit that animates it is one of love, not hate or indifference, of light, not darkness, of creativity, not destruction, of order, not chaos; that, since all life—men, creatures, plants, as well as insensate matter—and all that is known about it, now and henceforth, have been benevolently, not malevolently, conceived, when the eyes see no more and the mind thinks no more, and this hand now writing is inert, whatever lies beyond will similarly be benevolently, not malevolently or indifferently, conceived. If it is nothing, then for nothingness I offer thanks; if another mode of existence, with this old, wornout husk of a body left behind, like a butterfly extricating itself from its chrysalis, and this floundering, muddled mind, now at best seeing through a glass darkly, given a longer range and a new precision, then for that likewise I offer thanks.

4. But Not of Christ

Built into life is a strong vein of irony for which we should only be grateful to our Creator. It helps us to find our way through the fantasy that encompasses us to the reality of our existence. God has mercifully made the fantasies—the pursuit of power, of sensual satisfaction, of money, of learning, of celebrity, of happiness—so preposterously unrewarding that we are forced to turn to him for help and for mercy. We seek wealth and find we've accumulated worthless pieces of paper. We seek security and find we've acquired the means to blow ourselves and our little earth to smithereens. We seek carnal indulgence only to find ourselves involved in the prevailing erotomania. Looking for freedom, we infallibly fall into the servitude of self-gratification or, collectively, of a Gulag Archipelago.

We look back on history and what do we see? Empires rising and falling, revolutions and counter revolutions, wealth accumulating and wealth disbursed, one nation dominant and then another. Shakespeare speaks of "the rise and fall of great ones that ebb and flow with the moon."[1] In one lifetime I have seen my fellow countrymen ruling over a quarter of the world, the great majority of them convinced, in the words of what is still a favourite song, that "God who's made the mighty would make them mightier yet." I've heard a crazed, cracked Austrian proclaim to the world the establishment of a German Reich that would last for a thousand years; an Italian clown announce that he would restart the calendar to begin with his own assumption of power; a murderous Georgian brigand in the Kremlin acclaimed by the intellectual elite of the Western world as wiser than Solomon, more enlightened than Asoka, more humane than Marcus Aurelius. I've seen America wealthier and in

Originally published in 1980 by Wm. B. Eerdmans Publishing, Grand Rapids, Mich. Reprinted from Malcolm Muggeridge, *The End of Christendom* (Eugene, Ore.: Wipf and Stock Publishers, 2003), pp. 49–56.

[1] *King Lear*, V.ii.18–19.

terms of weaponry more powerful than all the rest of the world put together, so that Americans, had they so wished, could have outdone an Alexander or a Julius Caesar in the range and scale of their conquests. All in one little lifetime. All gone with the wind. England now part of an island off the coast of Europe and threatened with dismemberment and bankruptcy. Hitler and Mussolini dead and remembered only in infamy. Stalin a forbidden name in the regime he helped to found and dominated for some three decades. America haunted by fears of running out of the precious fluid that keeps the motorways roaring and the smog settling, with troubled memories of a disastrous campaign in Vietnam and of the great victory of the Don Quixotes of the media when they charged the windmills of Watergate.

Can this really be what life is about, as the media insist? This interminable soap opera going on from century to century, from era to era, whose old discarded sets and props litter the earth? Surely not. Was it to provide a location for so repetitive and ribald a performance that the universe was created and man came into existence? I can't believe it. If this were all, then the cynics, the hedonists, and the suicides would be right. The most we can hope for from life is some passing amusement, some gratification of our senses, and death. But it's not all.

Thanks to the great mercy and marvel of the Incarnation, the cosmic scene is resolved into a human drama. God reaches down to relate himself to man, and man reaches up to relate himself to God. Time looks into eternity and eternity into time, making now always and always now. Everything is transformed by this sublime drama of the Incarnation, God's special parable for fallen man in a fallen world. The way opens before us that was charted in the birth, ministry, death, and resurrection of Jesus Christ, a way that successive generations of believers have striven to follow. They have derived therefrom the moral, spiritual, and intellectual creativity out of which has come everything truly great in our art, our literature, our music. From that source comes the splendour of the great cathedrals and the illumination of the saints and mystics, as well as countless lives of dedication, men and women serving their God and loving their Saviour in humility and faith.

If this Christian revelation is true, then it must be true for all times and in all circumstances. Whatever may happen, however seemingly inimical to it may be the world's going and those who preside over the world's affairs, the truth of the Incarnation remains intact and inviolate.

Christendom, like other civilisations before it, is subject to decay and must sometime decompose and disappear. The world's way of responding to intimations of decay is to engage equally in idiot hopes and idiot despair. On the one hand some new policy or discovery is confidently expected to put everything to rights: a new fuel, a new drug, détente, world government. On the other, some disaster is as confidently expected to prove our undoing. Capitalism will break down. Fuel will run out. Plutonium will lay us low. Atomic waste will kill us off. Overpopulation will suffocate us, or alternatively, a declining birth rate will put us more surely at the mercy of our enemies.

In Christian terms, such hopes and fears are equally beside the point. As Christians we know that here we have no continuing city, that crowns roll in the dust and every earthly kingdom must sometime flounder, whereas we acknowledge a king men did not crown and cannot dethrone, as we are citizens of a city of God they did not build and cannot destroy. Thus the apostle Paul wrote to the Christians in Rome, living in a society as depraved and dissolute as ours. Their games, like our television, specialized in spectacles of violence and eroticism. Paul exhorted them to be stedfast, unmovable, always abounding in God's work, to concern themselves with the things that are unseen, for the things which are seen are temporal but the things which are not seen are eternal.[2] It was in the breakdown of Rome that Christendom was born. Now in the breakdown of Christendom there are the same requirements and the same possibilities to eschew the fantasy of a disintegrating world and seek the reality of what is not seen and eternal, the reality of Christ.

I expect that you're all familiar with Plato's image of the shadows in a cave. The people in the cave saw shadows passing by and mistook these shadows, supposing that the shadows were people and that the names they gave them were real. I feel that this is an image of our existence. Our television is an outward and visible sign of this fantasy with which we preoccupy ourselves.

Many people here have asked me how it was that I came ultimately to be convinced that Christ was the answer. It was because in this world of fantasy in which my own occupation has particularly involved me, I have found in Christ the only true alternative. The shadow in the cave is like the media world of shadows. In contradistinction, Christ shows what life

[2] 1 Corinthians 15:58; 2 Corinthians 4:18.

really is, and what our true destiny is. We escape from the cave. We emerge from the darkness and instead of shadows we have all around us the glory of God's creation. Instead of darkness we have light; instead of despair, hope; instead of time and the clocks ticking inexorably on, eternity, which never began and never ends and yet is sublimely now. What then is this reality of Christ, contrasting with all the fantasies whereby men seek to evade it, fantasies of the ego, of the appetites, of power or success, of the mind and the will, the reality valid when first lived and expounded by our Lord himself two thousand years ago? It has buoyed up Western man through all the vicissitudes and uncertainty of Christendom's centuries, and is available today when it's more needed, perhaps, than ever before, as it will be available tomorrow and forever. It is simply this: by identifying ourselves with Christ, by absorbing ourselves in his teaching, by living out the drama of his life with him, including especially the passion, that powerhouse of love and creativity—by living with, by, and in him, we can be reborn to become new men and women in a new world.

It sounds crazy, as it did to Nicodemus, an early intellectual and a potential BBC panelist who asked how in the world it was possible for someone already born to go back into the womb and be born again. It happens. It has happened innumerable times. It goes on happening. The testimony to this effect is overwhelming. Suddenly to be caught up in the wonder of God's love flooding the universe, made aware of the stupendous creativity which animates all life, of our own participation in it, every colour brighter, every meaning clearer, every shape more shapely, every note more musical, every word written and spoken more explicit. Above all, every human face, all human companionship, all human encounters, recognizably a family affair. The animals too, flying, prowling, burrowing, all their diverse cries and grunts and bellowings, and the majestic hilltops, the gaunt rocks giving their blessed shade, and the rivers faithfully making their way to the sea, all irradiated with this same glory for the eyes of the reborn. What other fulfilment is there, I ask, that could possibly compare with this? What going to the moon or exploration of the universe, what victory or defeat, what revolution or counterrevolution, what putting down of the mighty from their seats and exaltation of the humble and meek, who then of course become mighty in their turn and fit to be put down? This is a fulfilment that transcends all human fulfiling and yet is accessible to all humans, based on the absolutes of love rather than the relativities of justice, on the universality of brotherhood rather than the particularity of equality, on the perfect service which is freedom rather than the perfect servitude which purports to be freedom.

Nor need we despair to be living in a time when we have lost an empire on which the sun never set. It's in the breakdown of power that we may discern its true nature, and when power seems strong and firm that we're most liable to be taken in and suppose it can be used to enhance human freedom and well-being. We become forgetful that Jesus is the prophet of the losers' not the victors' camp, the one who proclaims that the first will be last, that the weak are the strong and the fools are the wise.

Let us then as Christians rejoice that we see around us on every hand the decay of the institutions and instruments of power, see intimations of empires falling to pieces, money in total disarray, dictators and parliamentarians alike nonplussed by the confusion and conflicts which encompass them. For it is precisely when every earthly hope has been explored and found wanting, when every possibility of help from earthly sources has been sought and is not forthcoming, when every recourse this world offers, moral as well as material, has been explored to no effect, when in the shivering cold the last faggot has been thrown on the fire and in the gathering darkness every glimmer of light has finally flickered out, it's then that Christ's hand reaches out sure and firm. Then Christ's words bring their inexpressible comfort, then his light shines brightest, abolishing the darkness forever. So, finding in everything only deception and nothingness, the soul is constrained to have recourse to God himself and to rest content with him.

5. Is There a God?

Well, is there? I myself should be very happy to answer with an emphatic negative. Temperamentally, it would suit me well enough to settle for what this world offers, and to write off as wishful thinking, or just the self-importance of the human species, any notion of a divine purpose and a divinity to entertain and execute it. The earth's sounds and smells and colors are very sweet; human love brings golden hours; the mind at work earns delight. I have never wanted a God, or feared a God, or felt under any necessity to invent one. Unfortunately, I am driven to the conclusion that God wants me.

God comes padding after me like a Hound of Heaven. His shadow falls over all my little picnics in the sunshine, chilling the air; draining the viands of their flavor, talk of its sparkle, desire of its zest. God takes a hand as history's compere, turning it into a soap opera, with ham actors, threadbare lines, tawdry props, and faded costumes. God arranges the lighting—Spark of Sparks—so that all the ravages of time, like parched skin, decaying teeth, and rotting flesh, show through the make-up, however lavishly it may be plastered on. Under God's eye, tiny, hoarded glories—a little fame, some money . . . *Oh Mr. M! how wonderful you are!*—fall into dust. In the innermost recesses of vanity one is discovered as in the last sanctuaries of appetite, on the highest hill of complacency as in the lowest burrow of despair. One shivers as the divine beast of prey gets ready for the final spring, as the shadow lengthens, reducing to infinite triviality all mortal hopes and desires.

There is no escape. Even so, one twists and turns. Perhaps Nietzsche was right when he said that God had died. Progressive theologians with German names seem to think so. *Time* magazine turned over one of its

Originally published in the *New Statesman* (May 6, 1966). Reprinted from Malcolm Muggeridge, *Jesus Rediscovered* (Garden City, N.Y.: Doubleday, 1969), pp. 99–103.

precious covers to the notion. If God were dead, and eternity had stopped, what a blessed relief to one and all! Then we could set about making a happy world in our own way—happy in the woods like Mellors and his Lady Chatterley; happiness successfully pursued, along with life and liberty, in accordance with the Philadelphia specification; happy the Wilson way, with only one book to take to the post office—one book, one happiness; happy in the prospect of that great Red Apocalypse when the state has withered away, and the proletariat reigns forevermore. If only God were D. H. Lawrence, or Franklin D. Roosevelt, or Harold Wilson, or Karl Marx!

Alas, dead or alive, he is still God, and eternity ticks on even though all the clocks have stopped. I agree with Kierkegaard that "what man naturally loves is finitude" and that involvement through God in infinitude "kills in him, in the most painful way, everything in which he really finds his life ... shows him his own wretchedness, keeps him in sleepless unrest, whereas finitude lulls him into enjoyment." Man, in other words, needs protection against God as tenants do against exploiting landlords or minors against hard liquor.

Where is such protection to be found? One of the most effective defense systems against God's incursions has hitherto been organized religion. The various churches have provided a refuge for fugitives from God—his voice drowned in the chanting, his smell lost in the incense, his purposes obscured and confused in creeds, dogmas, dissertations, and other priestly pronunciamentos. In vast cathedrals, as in little conventicles, or just wrapped in Quaker silence, one could get away from God. Plain song held him at bay, as did revivalist eloquence, hearty hymns, and intoned prayers. Confronted with that chanting, moaning, gurgling voice—"Dearly beloved brethren, I pray and beseech you ..." or with that earnest, open, Peace Corps face, shining like the morning sun with all the glories flesh is heir to, God could be relied on to make off.[1]

Unfortunately, this defensive system has now proved to be a Maginot line, easily bypassed by hordes of happiness-pursuers, some in clerical collars and even miters, joyously bearing a cornucopia of affluence, and scattering along their way birth pills, purple hearts, and other goodies—a

[1] Muggeridge was wary of the way that man's ego—no matter how well-intentioned—inevitably seemed to raise its ugly head, as contrasted with the beautiful simplicity of God's plan for salvation.

mighty throng whose trampling feet clear a path as wide as a motorway, along which God can come storming in.

Another defense against God has been utopianism, and the revolutionary fervor that goes therewith. A passion to change the world and make it nearer to the heart's desire automatically excludes God, who represents the principle of changelessness, and confronts each heart's desire with its own nullity. It was confidently believed that a kingdom of heaven on earth could be established, with GOD, KEEP OUT notices prominently displayed. In practice, the various versions of this kingdom have one and all proved a failure, utopian hopes washed away in the blood of Stalin's purges, reduced to the dimensions of Mr. Harold Wilson, liberated out of existence.

Few any longer believe in the coming to pass of a perfect, or even a Great, society. There never was a less revolutionary climate than now prevails, when almost any status quo, however ramshackle, can stand—Tito's, Franco's, Ulbricht's. Why, tourism today is a more dynamic force than revolution, swaying, as it does, crowns and thrones; Thomas Cook and the American Express, not the *Internationale*, unite the human race. In Africa, it is true, regimes still totter and fall, but even there the wind of change blows as it listeth. Even when the great day comes, and the white oligarchs are dispossessed and replaced by Black ones, it will be history, not progress, that has spoken.

With the church no longer a sanctuary, and utopianism extinguished, the fugitive from God has nowhere to turn. Even if, as a last resort, he falls back on stupefying his senses with alcohol or drugs or sex, the relief is but short-lived. Either he will sink without trace forever into that slough, or, emerging, have to face the inescapable confrontation. It is a fearful thing to fall into the hands of the living God—thus Kierkegaard (and also Cromwell) groaned in desperation.

What living God? A being with whom one has a relationship, on the one hand, inconceivably more personal than the most intimate human one, to the point that, as we are told, God has actually counted the hairs of each head; on the other, so remote that in order to establish a valid relationship at all, it is necessary to die, to murder one's own flesh with the utmost ferocity, and batter down one's ego as one might a deadly snake, a cobra that has lifted its hooded head with darting, forked tongue, to sting. (I say "a being," which suggests a person, a spirit, a genie coming out of a bottle, and so is utterly inappropriate. There are no adequate words for any of the great absolutes, like life and death, good and evil;

only for trivialities like politics and economics and science. One falls back on the meaningless monosyllable God, as Hindu *sadhus* in their spiritual exercises endlessly repeat the equally meaningless monosyllable *Om*.)

What can be said with certainty is that, once the confrontation has been experienced—the rocky summit climbed, the interminable desert crossed—an unimaginably delectable vista presents itself, so vast, so luminous, so enchanting, that the small ecstasies of human love, and the small satisfactions of human achievement, by comparison pale into insignificance. Out of tactical despair comes an overwhelming strategic happiness, enfolded in which one is made aware that every aspect of the universe, from a tiny grain of sand to the light-years that measure its immeasurable dimensions, from the minutest single living cell to the most complex human organism, are ultimately related, all deserving of reverence and respect; all shining, like glowworms, with an intrinsic light, and, at the same time, caught in an all-encompassing radiance, like dust in a sunbeam.

This sense of oneness, with the consequent release from the burden of self, I take to be God—something that indubitably exists, that not only has not died, but cannot die. Such has been the testimony of those in the past whom I most revere—like Christ, St. Paul, St. Augustine, and St. Francis; Pascal, Bunyan, Blake, Tolstoy, and Dostoyevsky. To their testimony, with the greatest possible diffidence I add my own, so hesitant, fitful, and inarticulate.

6. Happiness

The sister-in-law of a friend of Samuel Johnson was imprudent enough once to claim in his presence that she was happy. He pounced on her hard, remarking in a loud, emphatic voice that if she was indeed the contented being she professed herself to be, then her life gave the lie to every research of humanity; for she was happy without health, without beauty, without money, and without understanding. It was rough treatment, for which Johnson has been much criticized, though it should be remembered that he spoke as an eighteenth-century man, before our present preoccupation with happiness as an enduring condition of life became prevalent. Actually, I think I see his point.

There *is* something quite ridiculous, and even indecent, in an individual claiming to be happy; still more, a people or a nation making such a claim. The pursuit of happiness, included along with life and liberty in the American Declaration of Independence as an inalienable right, is without any question the most fatuous that could possibly be undertaken. This lamentable phrase—the pursuit of happiness—is responsible for a good part of the ills and miseries of the modern world. To pursue happiness, individually or collectively, as a conscious aim, is the surest way to miss it altogether, as is only too tragically evident in countries like Sweden and America, where happiness has been most ardently pursued and where the material circumstances usually considered conducive to happiness have been most effectively constructed. The Gadarene swine were doubtless in pursuit of happiness when they hurled themselves to destruction over the cliff. Today, the greater part of mankind, led by the technologically most advanced, are similarly bent, and, if they persist, will assuredly meet a similar fate. The pursuit of happiness, in any case, soon

Originally a BBC broadcast (October 5, 1965). Reprinted from Malcolm Muggeridge, *Jesus Rediscovered* (Garden City, N.Y.: Doubleday, 1969), pp. 179–80.

resolves itself into the pursuit of pleasure, something quite different—a mirage of happiness, a false vision of shade and refreshment seen across parched sand.

Where, then, does happiness lie? In forgetfulness, not indulgence, of the self. In escape from sensual appetites, not in their satisfaction. We live in a dark, self-enclosed prison, which is all we see or know if our glance is fixed ever downward. To lift it upward, becoming aware of the wide, luminous universe outside—this alone is happiness. At its highest level such happiness is the ecstasy that mystics have inadequately described. At more humdrum levels it is human love; the delights and beauties of our dear earth, its colors and shapes and sounds; the enchantment of understanding and laughing, and all other exercise of such faculties as we possess; the marvel of the meaning of everything, fitfully glimpsed, inadequately expounded, but ever present.

Such is happiness—not compressible into a pill; not translatable into a sensation; lost to whoever would grasp it to himself alone, not to be gorged out of a trough, or torn out of another's body, or paid into a bank, or driven along a motorway, or fired in gun salutes, or discovered in the stratosphere. Existing, intangible, in every true response to life, and absent in every false one. Propounded through the centuries in every noteworthy word and thought and deed. Expressed in art and literature and music; in vast cathedrals and tiny melodies; in everything that is harmonious, and in the unending heroism of imperfect men reaching after perfection.

When Pastor Bonhoeffer was taken off by his Nazi guards to be executed, as I have read, his face was shining with happiness, to the point that even those poor clowns noted it. In that place of darkest evil, he was the happiest man—he the executed. I find this an image of supreme happiness.

7. Rapture

The most characteristic and uplifting of the manifestations of conversion is rapture—an inexpressible joy which suffuses our whole being, making our fears dissolve into nothing, and our expectations all move heavenwards. No earthly image can convey this adequately; music at its best—say, Mozart's *Exultate*—gets nearer to it than words. It is like coming to after an anaesthetic, with lost faces and voices and shapes again becoming recognizable. Or like getting film back into sync, so that the speaking and the pictures sort themselves out and become clear instead of confused. The so-called successes and achievements on which we pride ourselves, and which bring us such inordinate satisfaction, are, indeed, a kind of anaesthetic; emerging from them—Pascal calls them all diversions of one sort and another—we resume contact with reality.

Pascal's own conversion illustrates this. He had been thinking of Peter; of his thrice-repeated denial that he was in any way connected with Jesus, and then the cock crowing and his bitter tears. I have myself found that, reading of this, it is hard to keep back my own tears, so conscious am I of similar betrayals. Pascal, too, wept as he recalled his own disloyalty; and a dreadful desolation came upon him, which then suddenly melted away as he remembered that he, too, could be forgiven. In his methodical way, as though he were documenting one of his scientific experiments, he notes it all down, with the triumphant conclusion: "Certainty, certainty, joy, peace. God of Jesus Christ. *Deum meum et Deum vostram*. Oblivion of the world and of everything except God." He kept this record always about his person; when he died it was found sewn into his coat.

Then, at the other extreme, the dark night. The light has gone out, no glimmer anywhere, only darkness; no hope of any kind, except for death,

Reprinted from Malcolm Muggeridge, *Confessions of a Twentieth-Century Pilgrim* (New York: HarperCollins, 1988), pp. 21–23.

not to be, not to exist at all. Even flattery—the fan-letter *in excelsia*—falls like a lustreless kiss on a dead cheek. Heaven or hell a matter of indifference; let there be nothingness, *Fiat nihil!* Throughout nights of sleeplessness and misery, only one longing—for obliteration; likewise when the words will not come, the mind will not think, the pen will not write. And yet, as I am well aware, all this is so much theatre; and the billions upon billions of fellow humans who have lived, are living and will live on our little earth, have only one recourse—to put aside every other consideration, the backwards and the forwards, hope and despair, ardour and listlessness, and get down on their knees to pray with the utmost humility, and utterly meaning it: "Thy will be done", confident that our Creator's purpose for His creation is to do with love rather than power, with peace and not strife, with Eternity rather than Time, and with our souls rather than our bodies or our minds.

Thus in the turmoil of life without, and black despair within, it is always possible to turn aside and wait on God. Just as at the centre of a hurricane there is stillness, and above the clouds a clear sky, so it is possible to make a little clearing in the jungle of our human will for a rendezvous with God. He will always turn up, though in what guise and in what circumstances cannot be foreseen—perhaps trailing clouds of glory, perhaps as a beggar; in the purity of the desert or in the squalor of London's Soho or New York's Times Square. Once, in Times Square, I was glancing disconsolately, but also avidly, at the rows and rows of paperbacks, each with some lewd or sadistic picture for its cover, and noticed that by some strange accident my book on Mother Teresa, *Something Beautiful for God*, had got on to these sad shelves. Wondering how it could have happened, Herbert's beautiful lines came into my mind:

And here in dust and dirt, O here
The lilies of His love appear.

For every situation and eventuality there is a parable if you look carefully enough.

8. The Road to Emmaus

In Jerusalem Christ's mood was different—sterner and sadder; at times almost bitter. Every evangelist must believe in his heart that if only he tries hard enough to deliver his message people will pay heed. Surely, what seems so clear to him will be clear to others! The hungry sheep look up, and he longs to feed them. Then he realizes that even when they do follow, it is usually for the wrong reasons. They will as readily follow any other shepherd that comes along, true or false. Christ did not know, when he lived on earth, but could easily have guessed, that before he had been long dead men would be killing other men in his name, and setting golden crowns on the heads of popes and kings to his greater glory.[1]

What, I have occasionally asked myself, would the man whose fortunes we have been following have made of the Vatican or Lambeth Palace or the House of Lords? Christ was the Good Shepherd; he was listened to, certainly, but Tiberias, Capernaum, Caesarea, Jerusalem itself, went their ways regardless. In earthly terms, his mission was a failure; now he had to fulfil it in God's way—which led to the Cross.

I see Christ on the Mount of Olives, looking across at Jerusalem, deeply stirred, as any Jew must be, because of its tremendous place in Jewish life and history. The city was very different then, of course, with the huge, magnificent Temple dwarfing everything else, and the towers of Herod's palace rising into the sky. Different, and yet the same; then, as now, a place of violence, of furious passions and bigotries. Roman soldiers patrolled the uneasy streets as Israeli ones do today; strictly orthodox rabbis, or Pharisees, scornfully eyed their laxer fellow Jews, stonily averting their

Originally this was the commentary of three television programs on BBC 2 (April 10–12, 1968). Reprinted from Malcolm Muggeridge, *Jesus Rediscovered* (Garden City, N.Y.: Doubleday, 1969), pp. 34–43.

[1] Muggeridge may not have put a very fine gloss on the theological point here. Readers are referred to the *Catechism of the Catholic Church*, no. 472.

gaze from the gentiles in their midst, precisely as I've seen them doing on their way to the Wailing Wall, some of whose stones being all that remains of their once splendid Temple, where they ceremonially bemoan its passing, as well as all the transitoriness and unsatisfactoriness of human life. Strange, majestic, bearded men, to me rather appealing, who resolutely refuse to accommodate themselves to the twentieth century, which their more pliable countrymen have brought to their ancient city.

What could Christ do about Jerusalem—except die there? In his eyes, the city was doomed; its fine buildings, its crowded streets, its synagogues, the Temple itself, all marked for destruction. So, like the Hebrew prophets of old, Christ foresaw the wrath to come which duly came—army after army sweeping in, the latest a Jewish one; the Temple, razed to the ground to provide a site for other temples dedicated to other gods than Jehovah, now a mosque; Jerusalem destroyed, to rise again and be destroyed again.

It was as though here was the world's soul, where all its bitterest conflicts and most searching dilemmas must be worked out, whence would come also its truest understanding and sweetest hopes. Looking over at Jerusalem from the Mount of Olives and thinking of all this—of the suffering and privations involved, of the narrow path God had set to salvation—Christ wept.

It was in such a mood that Christ drove the money-changers out of the Temple. We all know the feeling—the blind rage that human beings should sully every place and everything with their hateful little cupidities. I confess that I have felt it in the Holy Land at the relentless exploitation of shrines and relics and credulities for gain. If I'd had the nerve I might well have hurled a stock of crowns of thorns at the head of their vendor! The next day, we may be sure, the money-changers were back in their places plying their trade as zealously as ever. They are at it still—in banks and stock exchanges, in casinos and bingo halls, wherever the money game is played—everywhere.

Christ liked to walk out from Jerusalem in the evening to nearby Bethany rather than stay in the city, where he was always in danger, and where—as I like to think—he felt choked and oppressed by the dust and restlessness of the streets. In Bethany there were two sisters, Mary and Martha, and their brother Lazarus, whom, when he had been thought to be dead, Christ had called forth from the tomb itself. One gets from the Gospels a delightful picture of this household where Christ was always welcome. The sisters were quite different in temperament—Mary thoughtful and imaginative, Martha practical and energetic. On one occasion, when Mary was seated at Christ's feet and listening to him with rapture, Martha, *cumbered about much serving*, humanly grew irritated. I see her in her working clothes, sleeves turned up, face flushed from the fire where she was preparing with loving care a supper she knew her guest particularly liked.

Lord, she expostulated, *dost thou not care that my sister hath left me to serve alone? bid her therefore that she help me.*

Christ's answer was perfect: *Martha, Martha, thou art careful and troubled about many things: But one thing is needful: and Mary hath chosen that good part, which shall not be taken away from her.* It was Mary who subsequently poured a whole pound of very costly spikenard ointment over Christ's feet, and wiped them with her hair, earning a rebuke from, of course, Judas, who spoke on behalf of all charitable prigs at all times when he complained that the money spent on the ointment should have been given to the poor. In Christ's reply one may detect again that note of astringent irony I like so much—*Let her alone: against the day of my burying hath she kept this. For the poor always ye have with you; but me ye have not always.* It is all perfectly described, and bears upon it every mark of truth.

Christ and his disciples celebrated the Passover together in the traditional way. Now he knew that his hour was drawing near, and insisted on washing the others' feet, showing them once more that every act of true humility is a sort of grace whereby the soul grows as the will, or ego, diminishes. Whosoever would be great in this world, he was always telling them, is small; and whoever, through his sense of God's greatness, realizes his own smallness, becomes spiritually great.

As things turned out, it was to be their last Passover; it was also —though, of course, they didn't know it—the first Communion service. For the first time those mysterious words were spoken:

> *Take, eat; this is my body. . . . this is my blood of the new testament, which is shed for many for the remission of sins.*

Words to be endlessly repeated, in every language, to the accompaniment of every variety of ritual, or in stark simplicity. At this original, austere, Last Supper, Christ showed how, through the Blessed Sacrament—the bread he broke and the wine he sipped with his disciples—he would remain always within our reach.

Thus the Christian religion was born here in Jerusalem two thousand years ago. It has brought to the world, as Christ said it would, not peace but a sword. Jerusalem itself remains a place of strife and fratricidal conflict, and Christianity's ostensible devotees remain divided, and flounder tragically and often absurdly in their rivalries and uncertainties. *In the world*, Christ said to his disciples, *ye shall have tribulation*. A generation like ours, which has seen the two most destructive and cruel wars of history, and all that followed from them, will not be inclined to question the inevitability of tribulation.

Christ, however, did not stop there: *but be of good cheer*, he went on; *I have overcome the world*. So he had—not as earthly conquerors do, by force of arms or fraudulent promises; rather, by seeing through the world and the evanescence of its hopes and desires, and the utopian dreams that embody them. He showed us how to escape from the little, dark cell our egos make, so that we may see and hear and understand, whereas, before, we had been blind and deaf and dumb.

It was at the Last Supper that Christ indicated his awareness that one of his disciples would betray him. He even pointed to Judas as being that disciple; Judas knew that Christ knew, and yet he could no more draw back than Macbeth could from murdering Duncan, or Vronsky from seducing Anna Karenina. Mystics and great artists know—what is often hidden from other men—that our free will is shaped by our passions into an inescapable destiny. Prometheus is both bound and free.[2]

At the Last Supper, too, Christ told Peter that that very night, before the cock crew, he would deny him thrice. Never! said Peter indignantly; never, never, never! Alas, poor Peter! He was, of course, subsequently forgiven, to become, as many Christians have believed, the rock on which Christ's Church would be built, *and the gates of hell shall not prevail against it*.

Christ now went with three of his disciples to the garden of Gethsemane, below the Mount of Olives. His soul, he said, was *exceeding sorrowful, even unto death*, and he wanted to be alone and to pray. So he left the disciples to sit and wait for him, and withdrew by himself. The earth's shapes and sounds and colours and living creatures, we should remember, were not less dear to Christ because of his divine destiny than they are to us; rather more so, if anything. To leave them behind, to die, so early in

[2] Muggeridge was well aware of the difficult theological enigma posed between a person's free will and God's will for that individual. In his biography *Chronicles of Wasted Time*, he wrote: "Free will, in my experience, is tactical rather than strategic; in all the larger shaping of a life, there is a plan already, into which one has no choice but to fit, or contract out of living altogether."

his earthly life, was still a deprivation, even though his death was to put an end forever to dying in the old pagan sense of finality.

We cry when we leave our homes to venture out into a world we long to explore. So Christ was sorrowful that the time had come when he must leave loving friends and disciples, the road to Bethany in the deepening dusk, the Sea of Galilee and the fishing boats coming in with their catches—all the familiar scenes and dear companionship he had known on earth. *O, my Father,* he prayed, *if it be possible, let this cup pass from me: nevertheless not as I will, but as Thou wilt,* reflecting, as he must have done, how easy it would be for him to slip away by himself, back to Galilee, and a happy private life there like other men, with a wife, children, and all the other mitigations of the loneliness and mystery of our human fate. How easy, and how impossible!

He found the disciples asleep, and rebuked them rather irritably: *What, could ye not watch with me one hour?* Then he again went off by himself to continue with his prayers, returning to find them once more asleep. This time he let them be. What did it matter now? Soon the garden of Gethsemane resounded with the noise of a mob armed with swords and staves (a few days before, it had been palm leaves) who were looking for him. Judas, to earn his thirty pieces of silver, proceeded to identify him with a kiss and a *Hail, Master!*—and Christ was apprehended. Someone drew a sword in his defense, but Christ quickly told whoever it was to put up his sword, *for all they that take the sword shall perish with the sword.* Thereupon, we are told, *all the disciples forsook him and fled.* He was alone.

Now began for Christ the farce of the judicial proceedings against him, intended to give his execution a show of legality. There is, of course, no such thing as earthly justice, and cannot ever be; only the will of the strong over the weak, dressed up with more or less propriety according to the antiquity of the procedure. Judges have to wear wigs and robes—as Pascal pointed out—to hide the inadequacy of the justice they dispense, which would otherwise be all too apparent. Christ maintained a contemptuous silence while witnesses of sorts were being cross-examined at the house of Caiaphas, the High Priest, where he had been taken. It was only when Caiaphas asked him point-blank if he was the Christ, the Son of God, that he deigned to reply, and then only to say: *Thou hast said.*

It was enough. Blasphemy! Caiaphas shouted. There was no need to hear any more witnesses, he went on, and asked those standing by what they thought. *He is guilty of death,* they obediently answered, and proceeded to mock and insult Christ, and knock him about, in a style that has become all too familiar in the various utopias of our time.

That same morning Judas tried to return his thirty pieces of silver to the priests and elders who had given him them, but they would not receive the money back. So he threw the coins on the temple floor and went and hanged himself; a man, it seemed, on whom all the darkness in the universe had settled. Was he, too, forgiven at last—a beneficiary from the death he helped to bring about? Surely Christ died even for Judas.

The high priest and the elders were not entitled to impose the death sentence; so they took Christ, bound, to Pontius Pilate, who was.

What was the cause of their relentless hostility to Christ? Neither his messianic claims, nor his occasional Jewish unorthodoxies, it seems to me, account for the bitter resentment he aroused in them. There were others at that time in Judea, each of whom claimed to be the Messiah, and for the most part Christ conducted himself like a strict and pious Jew.

No, as I see it, Christ's real crime was simply that he spoke the truth, which is intolerable to all forms of authority—but especially ecclesiastical. [*Y*]*e shall know the truth, and the truth shall make you free*, Christ said. In the eyes of Caiaphas and his associates, as later in the eyes of Dostoyevsky's Grand Inquisitor in *The Brothers Karamazov*, Christ had to die because the truth he spoke and the freedom he offered undermined the authority other men claimed and exercised.[3]

When Pilate—to me the embodiment of every colonial governor that ever was, so that I see him in a gray frock coat and topper—asked Christ whether he was King of the Jews, he replied: *To this end was I born, and for this cause came I into the world, that I should bear witness unto the truth.* Pilate, no fool, was impressed. *What is truth?* he muttered, and went out to Caiaphas's men to tell them that he found no fault in Christ, and to suggest that he should be released on the occasion of the Passover. No! they shouted. No! Give us Barabbas!—a Jewish partisan who was also due to be crucified. Pilate shrugged and gave way; it didn't matter much to him either way. How surprised he would have been to know that this obscure affair would keep his memory alive centuries after the Roman Empire he served had ceased to exist!

[3] Muggeridge's use of the word "authority" may be somewhat semantical. He would no doubt say that anyone claiming "authority" other than through Jesus Christ could not be trusted. A church or individual claiming to be *under* the authority of Christ would be an entirely different matter.

Now the Roman soldiers, bored with the whole affair, indulged in a sick joke. They stripped Christ and put a scarlet robe on him; then crowned him with a crown of thorns, affecting to pay him homage: *Hail, King of the Jews!* As so often happens with sick jokes, theirs rebounded on their own heads. Had they but known it, in making fun of this King of the Jews, they were mocking, not Christ, but their own caesar, and every caesar, king, or ruler that ever had been or was to be. They were making power itself derisory forever. Thenceforth, for all who had eyes to see, thorns sprouted underneath every golden crown, and underneath every scarlet or purple robe there was stricken flesh.

There followed the Crucifixion. Christ humped his cross along the *Via Dolorosa* (if that was indeed the way he took to Golgotha) until he was too weak to continue, when another took it for him. Three crosses were set up, with Christ's in the middle and a thief on either side, and the long agony began. The crowd of spectators, I imagine, consisted, as such crowds usually do, of the curious, the morbid, and some casual passers-by. In this particular case, there were doubtless a few of Caiaphas's men to keep the jeering going, and some Roman soldiers. A group of women, we are told, stood on the outskirts—his mother, Mary Magdalene, and others from Bethany and Galilee. At one point he was given vinegar to drink; just before he died he was heard to cry out in a loud voice: *My God, my God, why hast Thou forsaken me?*

Thus ostensibly it all ended in defeat and despair. Well, that's all over, Caiaphas and his friends must have thought. How wrong they were! It was only beginning. Not defeat, but a fabulous new hope, had been born; not despair, but an unexampled joy, had come into the world. Christ died on the Cross as a man who had tried to show his fellow men what life was about; he rose from the dead to be available forever as an intermediary between man and God.

How rose from the dead? After his death on the Cross, we are told, he was seen by the disciples and others on numerous occasions; the stone in front of the tomb where he had been laid was found to have been removed, and the tomb to be empty. These are matters of legitimate historical investigation; what is not open to question is that today, two thousand years later, Christ is alive. The words he spoke are living words, as relevant now as when they were first spoken.

Shortly after Christ's death on the Cross, two men were walking along the road to Emmaus, a village some seven or eight miles distant from

Jerusalem. One of them may have been Cleopas, who was connected by marriage with Christ's family. As they walked along, they naturally talked about the Crucifixion and its aftermath; so absorbed in their talk that they scarcely noticed when a third man drew alongside and walked with them. He broke in to ask them what they were talking about so earnestly, while looking so sad.

Obviously, Cleopas said, he must be a stranger if he hadn't heard of the recent happenings in Jerusalem. Then they told him how Christ had been crucified (although they—Cleopas and his companion—had *trusted that it had been he which should have redeemed Israel*), and how certain women of their company had gone to the tomb where he had been laid, and found it empty, seeing at the same time a vision of angels, who said that he was alive.

Thereupon the stranger went through the scriptures with them, showing that everything that had happened had been foretold. By this time they had reached the house in Emmaus they were making for, and the stranger would have gone on alone, but the others pressed him to stay with them, *for it is toward evening, and the day is far spent.* He accepted their invitation. When they sat down to eat, and he broke bread and blessed it, they recognized him at last. He was no stranger, but their Saviour. Then he disappeared. Cleopas and his companion could not even wait to finish their meal, but hurried back full of joy and hope to Jerusalem, along the road they had so lately traveled, to tell the others of their marvelous experience. On every walk, Christ came to tell us, whether to Emmaus or Wimbledon or Timbuktu, there is the same stranger waiting to accompany us along our way, if we want him.

The rest of the story of Christ belongs to history. Terrible things have been done in his name; the doctrine of unworldliness that he preached has been twisted to serve worldly purposes; the Cross on which he died, besides inspiring some of the noblest lives which have ever been lived, and some of the noblest thoughts and creations of man, has also served as a cloak for some of the basest; his gospel of love has been enforced with the rack and the whip, and driven home with the sword.

Let others better qualified than I work out, if they can, the gain and the loss in human terms. Here, where he was born, lived, and died, we may remember how miraculously, nonetheless, his light continues to shine in the dark jungle of the human will, as I—a true child of these troubled times, with a sceptical mind and a sensual disposition, most diffidently, unworthily, but with the utmost certainty—testify.

9. Paul, Envoy Extraordinary

I am a poor sightseer, and soon weary of archaeological remains. Already in my memory Ephesus and Caesarea and Corinth and Philippi and Troas are indistinguishable heaps of fallen masonry and rubble. This, incidentally, led to one of our sharper exchanges—at Pisidian Antioch, where I ventured to remark that I find travelling about Asia Minor and the Middle East, where every step taken is in the dust of some forgotten civilisation, for this very reason particularly pleasurable. My point was that in such circumstances all the pretentions of historians are automatically laid low; the historical past they try so hard to reconstruct is visibly obliterated, whereas Paul's words, handed down to us in what many regard as quasi-mythical records, ring out louder and clearer than ever. You would not have it so, of course; the historian, you insisted, also labours in the vineyard of truth, helping to signpost the way that a Paul sees in a blaze of light on the Damascus road, and thenceforth proclaims. It was a difference which, in one form and another, cropped up on numerous occasions, and one that I have pondered over endlessly. The truth that transcends the fact; the myth more real than reality; the Word that exists in the beginning before there are tongues to speak it and minds to remember and record it, and that goes on existing when the tongues and the minds and all their records have likewise passed away. An historical Jesus contained in the dimensions of time, and a transcendental Jesus bridging the gulf between eternity and now; making eternity now and now eternity.

Paul himself, in any case, as we both agreed, was very much a figure of history. An incorrigibly mortal man in the Falstaffian sense. He soon joined us on our travels; someone very solid, substantial, energetic, covering prodigious distances, presumably for the most part on foot, staying

Originally published as "A Letter to a Friend", in Malcolm Muggeridge, *Paul, Envoy Extraordinary* (New York: Harper and Row, 1972), pp. 22–30.

sometimes for longer or shorter periods with one or other of his congregations, but mostly on the move. Along those long, long roads, some of which, like the Via Egnatia, have survived to this day including the very paving-stones he trod on. Without a home, or even a room, to call his own; his books and manuscripts, his very clothes, scattered here and there. Plying his trade of tent-maker (whatever precisely that may have been), thereby jealously guarding his independence, in accordance with his own dictum that unless a man works he shall not eat.

His real work, of course, was telling everyone who would listen to him about the birth, ministry, death and resurrection of Jesus Christ, the so long expected Messiah. We followed him from synagogue to synagogue, at each of which he had been well received as a recognizable rabbi, and then been chased out when he moved inexorably on from expounding the scriptures to proclaiming the coming of Christ's kingdom, and the realization it brought of the glorious liberty of the children of God. One of the synagogues, at Beroea—I'm sure you remember it as vividly as I do—was so ancient, and on the identical site of the one Paul actually held forth in, coming there from Thessalonica, that we almost expected him to loom into view. A small, bald, bandy-legged, big-nosed man (I was happy that you were inclined to accept that second-century description), who sometimes had the face of an angel. I could easily guess what some, at any rate, of the occasions for this transformation must have been; surely his amanuensis will have recalled how brightly his face shone when, in the midst of dictating polemics, admonitions, instructions of one sort and another, he suddenly broke off into one of those truly sublime utterances of his—

> *Though I speak with the tongues of men and of angels . . . Who shall separate us from the love of Christ? . . . But the fruit of the Spirit is love, joy, peace, longsuffering . . .*

—which belong not only to the highest flights of mysticism, but also to the greatest literature of all time.

Reading Paul's letters over and over with you, I fell completely in love with them, coming to see belatedly that, from any point of view, they are among the most remarkable documents to come down to us from antiquity. How, hurriedly dictated, as they must have been, at odd moments, they yet convey with astonishing vividness and verisimilitude the whole character and circumstances of the early churches and the first Christians. They came to seem in my eyes a kind of sublime journalism; transcendental reporting of the very highest order—the kind that Blake engaged in when he stepped out of the world of time to survey with a painter's careful exact eye the eternity that lay around it. What comfort for me, too, in that directive to the Christians at Colossae to *let your speech be always with grace, seasoned with salt, that ye may know how ye ought to answer every man!* Who that has ever tried, however inadequately, to reach up with words to the mystery of things will not echo Paul's prayer for a door of utterance, *to speak the mystery of Christ . . . that I may make it manifest as I ought to speak?* The words were, to me, the more wonderful because they were so patently not studied, but poured out just as they came, presenting, I daresay, some difficulty to whoever had the task of transcribing them. That the letters were thus composed seems to me to be abundantly clear in the very choice of words and structure of the sentences. Take, for instance, the categories in the famous passage about what may separate us from the love of Christ—*tribulation, or distress, or persecution, or famine, or nakedness, or peril, or sword*; then the succeeding list of the ones that assuredly will not be able so to separate us—*neither death, nor life, nor angels, nor principalities, nor powers, nor things present, nor things to come, nor height, nor depth, nor any other creature.* Is it not obvious that these, so arbitrarily yet marvellously chosen, come, as it were, warm and inspired, straight from his mouth rather than being first chosen and arranged in his mind?

Inside Paul the mystic, providing that other face—shrewd and calculating, if not crafty—there was the Pharisee, preoccupied with Old Testament prophesies and all the multitudinous intricacies of the Law, as he had studied it under Gamaliel and expounded it as a young man with great brilliance to the admiration of his elders. The same mind which had led him to persecute the Christians so relentlessly functioned after his Damascus road experience no less energetically and masterfully on their behalf. It is the contrast between these two sides of his nature that made him, while he was alive, and subsequently, so complex and controversial a figure. We found it most interesting, and at times diverting, to assemble some of the divers opinions which have been expressed about him. Our assembly could have been far more extensive; there is scarcely a single questing soul in the last two thousand years who has not at one time or another expressed an emphatic opinion about Paul.

The opinions, as will be seen from our selection, vary enormously; he is a man about whom no final judgement ever has, or, it is safe to predict, ever will, be reached. One of those unique men who defy all categorization and all tabloid assessments. I remember discussing this with you on the roof of St. Peter's in Rome, as we looked down at the vast concourse of people making their way across the piazza and up the steps into the church which has so long been the centre of the Christendom Paul, as Christ's emissary, may be said to have founded. What would he make of the scene, we asked ourselves, without finding a clear answer, and went on to wonder whether it was this very enigmatic quality in him which accounted for the paucity of statues and pictures of him compared with other apostles which we had noticed in Rome. Did the very artists draw back from committing themselves to a representation of such a man?

Certainly, we never lacked for a theme; I really believe we could have gone on talking about him almost indefinitely, as we might have spent far more time than the two months at our disposal following him on his restless journeys from city to city, up and down the highways and the seaways of the great Roman Empire as it existed in his time. One conversation that sticks out in my mind with particular clarity was at Paphos, in the ancient basilica adjoining the ruins of the residence of the Roman proconsul, in Paul's day, Sergius Paulus. There we discussed the burning topic, more than ever crucial today, of what a Christian owes to Caesar and what to God; standing side by side in those tall narrow stalls like upturned coffins that you find in Greek churches, while the bearded priest brought in green boughs in preparation for Easter.

There was a time when I should have regarded it as almost blasphemous to fall in with Paul's insistence that all earthly authority, even the Emperor Nero's under whose dispensation, as a Roman citizen, he perforce lived, must be regarded as coming from God, and that whoever resists such authority automatically puts himself at enmity with God. Now, conscious of belonging to a society visibly falling apart, morally and in every other way, I can see more clearly what he meant. What a difficult balance to strike between the exigencies of order and of freedom! You, who care as little for authority as anyone I have ever known, can still see clearly why Paul felt bound to commend even the shaky corrupt rule of a Nero as providing some sort of scaffolding for the ramshackle edifice of public order in an already decomposing Roman Empire. Subsequently, I had the same discussion with Enoch Powell, the two of us this time occupying the twin pulpits in the beautifully restored Wren church of St. Mary-le-Bow. He—assuredly no hater of authority—saw the dilemma from Caesar's side, and wondered how anything could be salvaged from his exigencies to give to God. My own impulse is so strongly the other way that every Caesar and commissar who ever was or is to be seems stuffed with straw.

Paul, in any case, in forming his estimate of what was due to Caesar had the great advantage of believing that the millenium was near, and the curtain about to fall for ever on our human scene. Such a prospect, as you justly remarked, quoting Dr. Johnson on a man about to be hanged, wonderfully concentrates the mind. There would be little point in throwing Nero to his own lions, even supposing such an enterprise to be otherwise desirable, if in the near future the heavens were going to unfold like a scroll and the Son of Man appear in all his glory riding on a cloud. Furthermore, most of Paul's flock were slaves with no stake in the Roman State anyway, so that the notion of overthrowing, or bettering, it would have had little appeal, especially in the light of the lasting liberation through Christ that Paul proclaimed. A congregation of slaves convinced that the world must soon end would seem to constitute the ideal progenitors of the Christian religion. Today we have plenty of slaves; all that remains is to persuade the Archbishop of Canterbury, the Cardinal Archbishop of Westminster, the Moderator of the General Assembly in the Church of Scotland and one or two others that the millenium is near. This should not be too difficult.

The readiness in Paul to accept any secular authority on any terms doubtless accounts in part for his unpopularity today, when all change is considered to be for the better, and each new acceptance of servitude is hailed as liberation. Actually, it is the very gospel he did so much to propagate which has offered, and continues to offer, the only basis there is for being free at all in our mortal condition; as is exemplified in his enchanting Letter to Philemon, which I first read with you beside Lake Eğridir, and now almost know by heart. The runaway slave is sent back to his master as an act of restitution, but with this admonition: *That thou shouldest receive him for ever; not now as a servant, a brother beloved, specially to me, but how much more unto thee, both in the flesh and in the Lord.* As he dictated these words, far more than any Spartacus uprising, Paul made the institution of slavery inconceivable in Christian terms, even though twenty centuries later, in our own time, when chattel slavery had been abolished, new variants, racial, economic and ideological, were to make their appearance and claim their millions of victims.

Another aspect of his present unpopularity is undoubtedly his attitude to marriage and sexual indulgence, which we discussed at Cenchraea, one of the ports of Corinth, dabbling our feet in the sparkling water of the Mediterranean there. It was a problem which must have posed itself with particular urgency—how were Christians to be induced to live chastely or virtuously in a society as permissive and decadent in its time as ours is. Paul called upon them, in their new-found freedom, to eschew the vices and debaucheries which were going on around them, reminding them in the magnificent eighth chapter of his Letter to the Romans that to be *carnally minded is death, but to be spiritually minded is life and peace.* No doctrine could be less acceptable today, not only to the many who have turned away from Christianity, but also to many ostensible Christians, including ministers and priests and bishops. Among the divergent opinions about Paul, we quote the late Bishop Pike's that he was 'wrong about sex'. The remark was made to me as we walked amicably together out of a BBC Television studio. It echoed in my mind when I read of his tragic death in the desert near Jericho.

The maintenance of Christian standards in so inimical a moral climate which Paul required of Christians was not possible through mere observance of the Law; he had tried this himself, and almost been destroyed in the process. It could only come through grace; the rebirth which had befallen him on the Damascus road, followed by his emergence as a new man. Of all the things I learnt with you in our Pauline travels and discussions, I value most this clear distinction between the Law with its necessary definitions, and the new dispensation of love which Christ instituted in the world, and confirmed with his death and resurrection. The Law sufficed to sustain the synagogues as citadels of virtue in a decadent and declining civilisation, but Christ's dispensation of love provided the light of hope and joy and creativity out of which a new one would be born. If now this new one is in its turn waning, the light is still there; as when Paul first took it from Jerusalem to the Hellenistic world, in the process transforming what might have been merely a Judaic cult into a universal religion.

I must say the moment when, at the behest of the mysterious man from Macedonia, he decided he must go to Europe, was for me the most dramatic of all. We stood, you will remember, on a hill at Troas looking out at the sea he crossed, and then on another hill at Kavalla, in his day Neapolis, watching the boats come in, as it might have been his. What a truly momentous occasion that was, and, like all the most important events, passing largely unnoticed, human beings in all ages having a wonderful faculty for becoming preoccupied with what matters least and averting their eyes from what matters most. So he pressed on, we hot on his heels, until we reached Athens, where, on Mars' hill, we fell into a somewhat acrimonius dispute about whether the philosophers who gathered there to listen to Paul were more like dons or journalists, I, not surprisingly, inclining to the former view, and you to the latter. Whether dons or journalists, we could agree that they were very like their twentieth-century equivalents, with their passion for always *telling or hearing something new*. There was so much in Paul's world to remind us of ours; like the demo at Ephesus when the mob shouted monotonously for two hours on end: *Great is Diana of the Ephesians*, or, for that matter, the games, with their presentation of spectacles of violence and eroticism for the edification of multitudes of listless viewers.

It is a curious thing, but in retrospect it seems as though I took my leave of Paul, not in Rome where he was martyred, but at Miletus where he said goodbye to the elders of the church in Ephesus, and then went on to Jerusalem to grapple with the always rather cantankerous church there, and to hand over the money he had so assiduously collected for them from his mostly Gentile congregations. The events in Rome are only vaguely in my mind, but this parting at Miletus is as vivid to me as though I had been one of the elders myself. Do you remember that we both agreed that we sensed Paul's presence more strongly than anywhere else in that desolate stretch of marshland, once Miletus's busy harbour, where the sea had receded—rather like Romney Marsh. Perhaps it was the virtual absence of ruins and of tourists, perhaps the very desolation and remoteness of the place, but as you read his speech to the elders about how they would see his face no more, and how he commended them to God and the word of his grace, I felt like joining them in weeping sore and falling on his neck. So I shall always think of him there, on that moving occasion, so resolute, so eloquent, so faithful a servant of Christ; desperately needed then in the world of round about 50 A.D., and as I think, and I know you do, too, no less desperately needed today....

10. A Door of Utterance

Doing something beautiful for God is, for Mother Teresa, what life is about. Everything, in that it is for God, becomes beautiful, whatever it may be; as does every human soul participating in this purpose, whoever he or she may be. In manifesting this, in themselves and in their lives and work, Mother Teresa and the Missionaries of Charity provide a living witness to the power and truth of what Jesus came to proclaim. His light shines in them. When I think of them in Calcutta, as I often do, it is not the bare house in a dark slum that is conjured up in my mind, but a light shining and a joy abounding. I see them diligently and cheerfully constructing something beautiful for God out of the human misery and affliction that lies around them. One of their leper settlements is near a slaughter-house whose stench in the ordinary way might easily make me retch. There, with Mother Teresa, I scarcely noticed it; another fragrance had swallowed it up.

For those of us who find difficulty in grasping with our minds Christ's great propositions of love which make such dedication possible, someone like Mother Teresa is a godsend. She is this love in person; through her, we can reach it, and hold it, and incorporate it in ourselves. Everyone feels this. I was watching recently the faces of people as they listened to her—just ordinary people who had crowded into a school hall to hear her. Every face, young and old, simple and sophisticated, was rapt, hanging on her words; not because of the words themselves—they were ordinary enough—but because of her. Some quality that came across over and above the words held their attention. A luminosity seemed to fill the school hall, illumining the rapt faces, penetrating into every mind and heart.

Reprinted from Malcolm Muggeridge, *Something Beautiful for God* (San Francisco: Harper & Row, 1971), pp. 126–39.

When she had finished and the meeting was over, they all wanted to touch her hand; to be physically near her for a moment; to partake of her, as it were. She looked so small and frail and tired standing there, giving herself. Yet this, I reflected, is how we may find salvation. Giving, not receiving; the anti-ad, the dispensing rather than the consuming society; dying in order to live. One old man, not content just to take her hand, bent his grey head down to kiss it. So they do to queens and eminences and great seigneurs. In this particular case, it was a gesture of perfect thankfulness to God—in which I shared—for helping our poor stumbling minds and fearful hearts by showing us his everlasting truth in the guise of one homely face going about his work of love.

The Christian religion finds expression thus, in the love of those who love Christ, more comprehensibly and accessibly than in metaphysical or ethical statements. It is an experience rather than a conclusion, a way of life rather than an ideology; grasped through the imagination rather than understood through the mind, belonging to the realm of spiritual rather than intellectual perception; reaching quite beyond the dimension of words and ideas. As St. Augustine found on that wonderful occasion at Ostia with his mother shortly before she died, when they were carried together to somewhere near the very presence of God, and then, returning, found words as clumsy instruments as a surgeon might find a hacksaw, or an artist a house-painter's brush—'And while we spoke of the eternal Wisdom, longing for it and straining for it with all the strength of our hearts, for one fleeting instant we reached out and touched it. Then, with a sigh, leaving our spiritual harvest bound to it, we returned to the sound of our own speech, in which each word has a beginning and an ending—far, far different from your Word, our Lord, who abides in Himself for ever, yet never grows old and gives new life to all things.'

As it is so beautifully put in the opening chapter of the Fourth Gospel: *And the Word was made flesh, and dwelt among us, full of grace and truth.* The Christian story is simply an endless presentation of this process of the Word becoming flesh and dwelling gracefully and truthfully among us. Whether in the ultimate silence of the mystic, such as befell St. Augustine and his mother—a silence that comprehends all that ever has been, will be and can be said and understood and sensed, from before the beginning of time to beyond its ending. Or in a Mother Teresa and her Missionaries of Charity going about the world and shining their light in its darkest places. Or in the splendour of artistic creation; in the great cathedrals climbing into the sky to God's greater glory; in the glowing words, the sentient stone and paint, the swelling sounds of music. Or in the solitary soul questing for truth, in the tiniest mechanisms of our mortal existence, as in the universe's illimitable reaches. Or in the beatific soap opera of worship, with its monotonously repeated pleas, confessions and expectations, its *glorias* and its *misereres*, its plainsong and hallelujah choruses; eyes piously downcast, and knees piously kneeling on the world's cold stone. In each and every manifestation of our mortal seeking the immortal, or our temporal seeking the eternal, or our imperfect seeking the perfect. Of men reaching up to God, and God in love and compassion bending down to men.

Each day Mother Teresa meets Jesus; first at the Mass, whence she derives sustenance and strength; then in each needing, suffering soul she sees and tends. They are one and the same Jesus; at the altar and in the streets. Neither exists without the other. We who are imprisoned in history; castaways on the barren shores of time, past, present and to come—we seek another Jesus. A Jesus of history, which is actually a contradiction in terms; like an eternity clock or an infinity tape-measure. Jesus can only exist now; and, in existing now, makes now always. Thus, for Mother Teresa the two commandments—to love God and to love our neighbour—are jointly fulfiled; indeed, inseparable. In her life and work she exemplifies the relation between the two; how, if we do not love God we cannot love our neighbour, and if we do not love our neighbour we cannot love God.

It may strike a contemporary mind as extraordinary that someone like Mother Teresa, in contact all the time with human suffering at its most acute and most desolate, should herself convey such an impression of total serenity, and be so confident of God's love and care for the creatures of his creation. Maybe it is partly this very circumstance which draws to her in an almost magical way those who see and hear her. Suffering crystallizes, as nothing else does, the dilemmas and nightmares of life without God. It is an inflamed nerve which, touched, gives rise to howls of rage and anguish, especially today. Surely, when we can go to the moon, and ride through space faster than light; when our very genes are counted, and our organs replaceable; when we can arrange to eat without growing fat, to copulate without procreating, to flash a gleaming smile without being happy—surely suffering should be banished from our lives. That *we* should have to go on suffering, and watch others suffering, is an outrage;

and a deity who, having the power to stop it, still allowed it to continue, would be a monster, not a loving God. So Simone de Beauvoir, watching her mother die in agony of cancer, saw it as 'an unjustifiable violation'; as something 'as violent and unforeseen as an engine stopping in the middle of the sky'. The image is significant. When machines jam and go wrong, we hate them utterly, and look round for a manufacturer or mechanic to curse. In the eyes of those who see men as machines, God is that manufacturer, and the mechanic his priest.

Mother Teresa, of course, sees it quite differently. Suffering and death, to her, are not the breakdown of a machine, but part of the everlasting drama of our relationship with our creator. Far from being an unjustifiable violation, an outrage, they exemplify and enhance our human condition. If ever it were to be possible—as some arrogant contemporary minds are crazy enough to believe—to eliminate suffering, and ultimately death, from our mortal lives, they would not thereby be enhanced, but rather demeaned, to the point that they would become too insignificant, too banal, to be worth living at all. Rather as though, out of humanitarian pity for poor old King Lear, at the end of Act I he were to be given a sedative strong enough to let him sleep through the other four acts. Thereby he would be spared, true, but there would be no play. So for us, too, if the eugenist's dream were ever to be realized—the sick and the old and the mad, all who were infirm and less than physically complete and smooth-working, painlessly eliminated, leaving only the beauty queens and the athletes, the Mensa IQs, and the prizewinners to be our human family—if this ever came to pass (a possibility shudderingly envisaged at some refrigerated Scandinavian bacchanalia, or along the ice-bound corridors of cash), God really would be dead. The only way God ever could die would be if we retreated so far into our egos and our flesh, put between us and him so wide a chasm, that our separation became inexorable. Then, and only then, God would be dead, and the curtain would fall for ever on us and our tiny earth.

It so happened that just when I was thinking about all this *à propos* Mother Teresa, I participated in a television programme about suffering, as a result of which I received hundreds of letters, nearly all of them recounting some experience of suffering, or of watching over suffering. Just because television, unlike any other means of communication which has ever existed, reaches more or less everyone, at all social and mental levels, the correspondence it gives rise to covers a similarly wide swath.

The letter-writers range between near-illiterates and dons, clergymen, civil servants and the like. In this particular case, the deep concern felt by one and all broke through the differing styles and idioms. As between a professor's neat missive quoting Blake and the stumbling scribble of some crippled pensioner there seemed, for once, little difference; the majesty of the matter at issue dwarfed variations in the manner and competence of presentation. I was conscious, turning over these letters, more poignantly than ever before, of how all of us are at one, if not in our hopes and desires, then in the scars and bruises we bear, or have watched with anguish being inflicted on some beloved flesh—still more agonizedly on some beloved mind, bringing down the darkness upon it. We can still gather together round the Cross even though we shut our ears to the words of the *Man* who died on it.

It was altogether a harrowing correspondence, though with many beautiful and uplifting accounts of suffering overcome and affliction turned to good purposes—as sometimes dark clouds which gather turn to glory when the sun sets. Thus, a lady describes how, through a mental breakdown suffered some years ago, she became 'a much better person than I used to be. My fellow patients help me when I am "down", and I help them when they need it.' In their common affliction they drew together in mutual helpfulness and love, forming attachments which continued and grew stronger when they emerged from the shadows of their sickness. This, too, is something beautiful for God, shining through the desolation of the drugged faces and listless bodies which haunt one after a visit to a psychiatric ward.

Another lady thanks me for the programme 'which I watched through the mirror of my iron lung'. What fabulous, God-given courage! I who find the confines of my own easeful circumstances an intolerable constriction—how, I ask myself, should I fare in an iron lung? 'It seems to me a wonderful thing,' she goes on, 'that God has taken this evil suffering and overlaid it with so much positive good, the compassion and learning of which you spoke. As for the individual, I think this is one way in which we are made "more than conquerors". Not only do we have strength available to bear the suffering, but we can also make this evil an instrument for good to other people.' Yet another correspondent—a sufferer from muscular dystrophy—describes how, when the doctors told him he must get worse, and he was put on a régime that required swallowing some twenty tablets daily, he took his 'sickness to the Great

Physician, and he healed me completely. Since then I've never taken a tablet, and my health is perfect.' 'Suffering,' he concludes, 'I know why I suffered. It was to teach me compassion, and more, it was to keep me humble in the knowledge of his wondrous grace.'

I could go on and on with such quotations, not, heaven knows, with any desire to spread complacency about others' misfortunes; rather, taking pride in belonging to the same human family as these heroic souls—exemplars of the enchanting lines of Blake I often say over to myself when afflicted by a sense of the seeming injustice with which the gifts and pains of life are distributed:

Joy and woe are woven fine,
A clothing for the soul divine;
Under every grief and pine
Runs a joy with silken twine.
It is right it should be so;
Man was made for joy and woe;
And when this we rightly know,
Through the world we safely go.

On the other side, there were some—but by no means as many—letters complaining, with varying degrees of bitterness, of the seemingly pointless suffering which they, or those dear to them, had been forced to endure. Let me give one example. A mother writes of how she had a lovely son who was born a blue baby. Two major heart operations, one when he was five and the other when he was thirteen, overcame some of his disability. He grew into a cheerful youth, won a maths exhibition at Oxford, and altogether 'blossomed and matured'. A last operation, finally to close up the hole in his heart, remained. He had it, returned home; then, a few weeks later, had to return to hospital, where it was discovered that the hole had opened again. One more desperate operation failed, and he died.

'He was just twenty-two,' his mother writes. 'His last words to me in reply to my, "Then I'll see you tomorrow, Ralph," were: "I don't think you will. I'm sorry, Goodbye." Such a firm goodbye, said with closed eyes and ashen face. I went away to take away from him the burden of my concern and sorrow; he sent me away to save me pain.'

'Where is God,' she goes on, 'and why does he allow such cruel things to happen? I have been an agnostic with Christian leanings—so was my son. I felt there was a benign influence in the world, and was happy.... Other people have even worse tragedies—though my loss is made more cruel through the tremendous faith and hope I had that my son would one day be well. Had he died when he was a small sick boy I could have cuddled and comforted him, and accepted that he was better off out of this world. But why should he have to go when he had struggled and battled to reach a fine young manhood? He did not want to die.... Perhaps I am only thinking of myself, and my son is indeed better off where he is—but how can I *know* this? I can only feel the great desolation that he has gone from this world, leaving a grievous gap in the lives of his parents and his brother. *Where is your God?*'

Where is my God? Dear Mrs ——, he is everywhere; even in the hole in your son's heart, or nowhere. I look out of my window, as I write these words, at a wintry countryside. The bees and the badgers are asleep; the birds perch hungrily on the bare twigs; nature seems dead for ever. Yet not so. Faith tells me that soon the badgers and the bees will awake, the trees load themselves with leaves, the birds sing joyously as they once more build their nests, the dead earth renew itself and wear all the greenery of yet another harvest.

This is a faith easily held. We know—or think we do—that spring will always return. Now I turn my glance from the window into my own heart, seeing there the litter and the dust of wasted years. Old envies not quite spent, old appetites that still could be reanimated, old hopes and desires that flounder on even though whatever outcome they might expect to have has long ago proved illusory. This, too—the interior of my heart—seems a dead landscape. Yet faith tells me that it, likewise, can have a spring in the rebirth promised to us all in the new dispensation which Christ brought to the world. The old envies budding with holy love; the old lusts burning with spiritual appetite; the old hopes and desires finding a new destination in the bright radiance of God's universal love.

Over and above any spring we may know, outside our windows or in our hearts, there is the illimitable sweep of God's concern for his creation and his creatures; comprehending both suffering and beatitude, and transcending both. No one who has been spared—certainly not I—dare say to the afflicted that they are blessed in their affliction, or offer comfort in universal terms for particular griefs. Yet one can dimly see and humbly say that suffering is an integral and essential part of our human drama. That it falls upon one and all in differing degrees and forms whose comparison lies beyond our competence. That it belongs to God's purpose for us here on earth, so that, in the end, all the experience of living has to teach us is to say: Thy will be done. To say it standing before a cross; itself signifying the suffering of God in the person of a Man, and the redemption of a Man in the person of God. The greatest sorrow and the greatest joy co-existing on Golgotha.

11. The Prospect of Death

The one sure thing about mortal existence is that it will end; the moment we are born, we begin to die. This basic fact of death is today highly unpalatable, to the point that extraordinary efforts are made, linguistically and in every other way, to keep death out of sight and mind.

Even those who for one reason or another advocate killing off unborn children and the debilitated old seek to clothe their murderous intentions in elusive terms; such as Retrospective Fertility Control for abortion, and Mercy Killing for euthanasia. A month spent in Florida in the company of fellow geriatrics gave me some idea of the lengths to which the old are induced to go in order to distract their thoughts from their impending demise. In, let us call it, Sunshine Haven, everything was done to make us feel that we were not really aged, but still full of youthful zest and expectations; if not teenagers, then keen-agers, perfectly capable of disporting ourselves on the dance floor, the beach, or even in bed. Withered bodies arrayed in dazzling summer wear, hollow eyes glaring out of garish caps, skulls plastered with cosmetics, lean shanks tanned a rich brown, bony buttocks encased in scarlet trousers—it all served to make a Florida beach on a distinct view a macabre version of Keats's Grecian Urn:

> What men or gods are these? What maidens loath?
> What mad pursuit? What struggle to escape?
> What pipes and timbrels? What wild ecstasy?

Nearer at hand, the impression was more in the vein of Evelyn Waugh's *The Loved One*. At Forest Lawn, the original of Waugh's Whispering Glades, the cadavers are scented and anointed and dressed for their obsequies in their exotic best, down to underclothes; in Sunset Haven, pre-cadavers

Reprinted from Malcolm Muggeridge, *Confessions of a Twentieth-Century Pilgrim* (San Francisco: Harper & Row, 1988), pp. 142–50.

likewise array themselves for social occasions like young debutantes and their squires out on a spree, and behave accordingly, though sometimes with creaking joints and inward groans. Of all the amenities available in Sunset Haven—bingo, swimming pool, books, billiards and golf—the one never spoken of or advertised in any way is the crematorium, discreetly hidden away among trees and bushes, and unmentioned in the illustrated brochures. Yet evidently business is brisk through the winter months, despite the sunshine and the geriatric *joie de vivre* so much in evidence. Death becomes the dirty little secret that sex once was. Eros comes out of hiding, and old Father Time tries to secrete his scythe.

Another method of, as it were, keeping death under the carpet is to stow away the debilitated old in state institutions, where they live in a kind of limbo between life and death, heavily sedated and inert. Private institutions for the affluent old are naturally better equipped and staffed, but can be very desolating, too. Those under Christian auspices, especially when they are run by nuns, usually have long waiting lists, not so much because the prospective inmates are particularly pious, as because they want to be sure that some zealot for mercy killing will not finish them off arbitrarily by administering excessive sedation; or, if they happen to need to be in an iron lung or attached to a kidney machine, by pulling the plug, as it is put in today's rather disgusting medical jargon.

In any case, disposing of people who live inconveniently long, and of defectives of one sort and another, has, from the point of view of governments, the great advantage of saving money and personnel without raising a public hullabaloo—something governments are always on the look out for. It is, of course, inevitable that in a materialist society like ours death should seem terrible, and even inadmissible. If Man is the very apex of creation, with nothing greater than himself in the universe; if his earthly life exhausts the whole content of his existence, then, clearly, his definitive end, his death, is too outrageous to be contemplated, and so is better ignored.

Simone de Beauvoir, in her book *A Very Easy Death*, describes her mother's death from cancer as being "as violent and unforeseen as an engine stopping in the middle of the sky". The image is significant; death is seen, not as the finale of a drama; nor as the end of an act, to be followed by a change of scene and the rest of the play; not even as an animal expiring, but as the breakdown of a machine which suddenly and maddeningly stops working. "There is no such thing as a natural death",

Madame de Beauvoir concludes. "All men must die, but for every man his death is an accident, and, even if he knows it and consents to it, an unjustifiable violation." In the light of such an attitude, death becomes a monstrous injustice, an act of brutal oppression, like, say the Vietnam War, or *apartheid* in South Africa. One imagines a demo led by Madame de Beauvoir, and all the demonstrators chanting in unison: "Death out! Death out! Death out!"

The slogan is not quite as preposterous as might at first glance be supposed; the crazy notion that some sort of drug might be developed which would make its takers immortal, a death pill to match the birth pill, has been seriously entertained. And how wonderfully ironical that *soma*, the drug in Aldous Huxley's *Brave New World* that was to make everyone happy for evermore, should have been the name originally chosen for thalidomide! Nor is it fanciful to detect in the mania for transplants of hearts, kidneys and other organs, perhaps even genitals, a hope that it may become possible to keep human beings going indefinitely, like vintage cars, by replacing their spare parts as they wear out.

Again, experimentation in the field of genetics would seem to hold out the prospect of being able in due course to produce forms of life not subject to death. Jonathan Swift, in *Gulliver's Travels*, showed a clearer sense of our true human condition when he made the immortal Stuldbrugs, encountered by Gulliver on his third voyage to the flying island of Laputa, not, as Gulliver had supposed they would be, wise, serene and knowledgeable, but rather the most miserable of creatures, excruciatingly boring to themselves and to others. Whenever they see a funeral Gulliver learns, they lament and repine that others are gone to a harbour of rest, at which they themselves never can hope to arrive.

Indeed, sanely regarded, death may be seen as an important factor in making life tolerable; I like very much the answer given by an octogenarian when asked how he accounted for his longevity—"Oh, just bad luck!" No doubt for this reason among others, death has often in the past been celebrated rather than abhorred; for instance, very exquisitely, by the Metaphysical Poets, among whom John Donne may be regarded as the very lauriate of death. So alluring did he find the prospect of dying that when he was Dean of St. Paul's he had himself painted in his shroud so as to be reminded of the deliverance from life that lay ahead. Sleep, he points out, even just for a night, wonderfully refreshes us; how much more, then, will sleeping on into eternity be refreshing! And then:

One short sleep past, we wake eternally,
And Death shall be no more, Death thou shalt die.

In our own time, Dietrich Bonhoeffer manifested a similar attitude to death when, with his face shining in joyful expectation, he said to the two Nazi guards who had come to take him to be executed: "For you it is an end, for me a beginning." Likewise Blake when, on his deathbed, he told his wife Catherine that to him dying was no more than moving from one room to another. As his end approached he sang some particularly beautiful songs, which, he told Catherine, were not of his composition, but came directly from heaven.

Alas, I cannot claim total certainty of this order, and fall back on Pascal's famous wager, which requires us to bet on eternal survival or eternal extinction. Confronted with such a choice, as Pascal points out in his *Pensées*, the obvious course must be to back the former possibility, since then, "if you win, you win everything; if you lose, you lose nothing". So, I back eternal survival, knowing full well that if eternal extinction should be my lot, I shall never know that I have lost my bet, and taking no account of exotic notions like Reincarnation, or of the so-called "evidence" provided by people who have been in a coma and imagined they were dead. The fact is that to know what being dead is like, you have to die, just as to know what being born is like you have to be born.

I can say with truth that I have never, even in times of greatest preoccupation with carnal, worldly and egotistic pursuits, seriously doubted that our existence here is related in some mysterious way to a more comprehensive and lasting existence elsewhere; that somehow or other we belong to a larger scene than our earthly life provides, and to a wider reach of time than our earthly allotment of three score years and ten. Thus, death has seemed more alluring than terrible, even perhaps especially, as a belligerent of sorts in the 1939–45 war; for instance, wandering about in the London Blitz, and finding a kind of exaltation in the spectacle of a bonfire being made of old haunts like Fleet Street, Paternoster Row, the Inner Temple, as though, not only might I expect to die myself, but the world I knew, the way of life to which I belonged, was likewise fated to be extinguished. Now, death seems more alluring than ever, when, in the nature of things, it must come soon, and transmits intimations of its imminence by the aches and pains and breathlessness which accompany old age.

It has never been possible for me to persuade myself that the universe could have been created, and we, *homo sapiens*, so-called, have, generation after generation, somehow made our appearance to sojourn briefly on our tiny earth, solely in order to mount the interminable soap opera, with the same characters and situations endlessly recurring, that we call history. It would be like building a great stadium for a display of tiddly-winks, or a vast opera house for a mouth-organ recital.

There must, in other words, be another reason for our existence and that of the universe than just getting through the days of our life as best we may; some other destiny than merely using up such physical, intellectual and spiritual creativity as has been vouchsafed us. This, anyway, has been the strongly held conviction of the greatest artists, saints, philosophers and, until quite recent times, scientists, through the Christian centuries, who have all assumed that the New Testament promise of eternal life is valid, and that the great drama of the Incarnation which embodies it, is indeed the master drama of our existence. To suppose that these distinguished believers were all credulous fools whose folly and credulity in holding such beliefs has now been finally exposed, would seem to me to be untenable; and anyway I'd rather be wrong with Dante and Shakespeare and Milton, with Augustine of Hippo and Francis of Assisi, with Dr. Johnson, Blake and Dostoyevsky, than right with Voltaire, Rousseau, Darwin, the Huxleys, Herbert Spencer, H. G. Wells and Bernard Shaw.

It must be admitted that as the years pass—and how quickly they pass, their passing speeding up with the passage of time!—our world and living in it come to seem decidedly overrated. As Saint Theresa of Avila put it, no more than a night in a second-class hotel. Even so, it is extraordinary how even in old age, when ambition is an absurdity, lechery a bad joke, cupidity an irrelevance—how even then I find myself, as the General Confession in the Book of Common Prayer puts it so beautifully, following too much the devices and desires of my own heart. Talking to the young I have noticed with wry amusement how they assume that round the late sixties a kind of cut-off operates whereby the world, the flesh and the Devil automatically lose their appeal. If only it were so!

The best I can hope for in my dotage is to emulate the state of mind of the Sage in Dr. Johnson's *Rasselas*, reflecting that of his creator:

> My retrospect of life recalls to my view many opportunities of good neglected, much time squandered upon trifles and more lost in idleness and vacancy. I

> leave many great designs unattempted, and many great attempts unfinished. My mind is burdened with no heavy crime, and therefore I compose myself to tranquillity; endeavour to abstract my thoughts from hopes and cares which, though reason knows them to be vain, still keep their old possession of the heart; expect with serene humility, that hour which nature cannot long delay; and hope to possess in a better state, that happiness which here I could not find, and that virtue which here I have not attained.

None the less, the mystery remains; and ever must. Some eight decades ago I came into the world, full of cries and wind and hiccups; now I prepare to leave it, also full of cries and wind and hiccups. Whence I came I cannot know, least of all in the light of contemporary myths like Darwinian evolution, Freudian psychology, situational ethics, Marxist prophecy, and so on—surely the most absurd ever. Whither I go, if anywhere, I can only surmise helped thereto by the testimony of true visionaries like the author of *The Cloud of Unknowing*, Blake, Dostoyevsky, and, of course, above all Jesus Christ. By inspired works of art like Chartres Cathedral and the *Missa Solemnis*, by the dedicated lives of saints and mystics; above all, by the Incarnation and all its consequences, in history, in what we still call Western Civilisation, now toppling into its final collapse, in providing infallible signposts in the quest for God.

The hardest thing of all to explain is that death's nearness in some mysterious way makes what is being left behind—I mean our earth itself, its shapes and smells and colours and creatures, all that one has known and loved and lived with—the more entrancing; as the end of a bright June day somehow encapsulates all the beauty of the daylight hours now drawing to a close; or as the last notes of a Beethoven symphony manage to convey the splendour of the whole piece. Checking out of St. Theresa of Avila's second-class hotel, as the revolving doors take one into the street outside, one casts a backward look at the old place, overcome with affection for it, almost to the point of tears.

So, like a prisoner awaiting his release, like a schoolboy when the end of term is near, like a migrant bird ready to fly south, like a patient in hospital anxiously scanning the doctor's face to see whether a discharge may be expected, I long to be gone. Extricating myself from the flesh I have too long inhabited, hearing the key turn in the lock of Time so that the great doors of Eternity swing open, disengaging my tired mind from its interminable conundrums and my tired ego from its wearisome insistencies. Such is the prospect of death.

I am eighty-four years old, an octogenarian who has done much that he ought not to have done and left undone much that he ought to have done, and lived fourteen years longer than the three score years and ten which, the Bible tells, will be but labour and sorrow, they pass away so soon.

For me, intimations of immortality, deafness, failing eyesight, loss of memory, the afflictions of old age, release me from preoccupation with worldly fantasy and free me to meditate on spiritual reality, to recall Archbishop Fulton Sheen's remark that Christendom is over but not Christ.

And so I live, just for each day, knowing my life will soon be over, and that I, like Michelangelo at the end of his life "... have loved my friends and family. I have loved God and all His creation. I have loved life and now I love death as its natural termination ..." [1], knowing that although Christendom may be over—Christ lives!

[1] From "*The Agony and the Ecstasy*" by Irving Stone.

PART TWO

SPEECHES AND SERMONS

1. A World of Fantasy

I have tried to show that, as I see it, the media have created, and belong to, a world of fantasy, the more dangerous because it purports to be, and is largely taken as being, the real world. Christ, on the other hand, proclaimed a new dimension of reality, so that Christendom, based on this reality, could emerge from the fantasy of a decomposing Roman civilisation.

Now we, the legatees of Christendom, are in our turn succumbing to fantasy, of which the media are an outward and visible manifestation. Thus the effect of the media at all levels is to draw people away from reality, which means away from Christ, and into fantasy, whether it be at the lowest possible level, in appeals to our cupidity, our vanity, our carnality in overtly pornographic publications and spectacles, or, in more sophisticated terms, by displaying in words or in pictures, in one context or another, the degeneracy and depravity, the divorcement from any concept of good and evil, the leaning towards perversion and violence and the sheer chaos of a society that has lost its bearings, and so is materially, morally and spiritually, adrift.

There is a passage in Pascal's *Pensées*, a book I greatly admire, that I often quote, and that seems to me highly relevant:

> It is in vain, O men, that you seek within yourselves the cure for your miseries. All your insight only leads you to the knowledge that it is *not* in yourselves that you will discover the true and the good. The philosophers promised them to you, and have not been able to keep their promise. They do not know what your true good is, or what your true state is. How should they have provided you with a cure for ills which they have not even understood? Your principal maladies are pride, which cuts you off from God, and sensuality, which binds

A sermon originally entitled "Looking through the Eye", delivered at the 1976 London Lectures in contemporary Christianity. Reprinted from Malcolm Muggeridge, "Seeing through the Eye", in *Christ and the Media* (Vancouver, B.C.: Regent College Publishing, 1977), pp. 60–77.

> you to the earth, and they have done nothing but foster at least one of these maladies. If they have given you God for your object, it has been to pander to your pride—they have made you think you were like him, and resembled him by your nature; and those who have grasped the vanity of such a pretention have cast you down into the other abyss by making you believe that your nature is like that of the beasts of the field, and have led you to seek your good in lust, which is the lot of animals.

Substitute for 'philosophers', 'the media', and the passage is perfectly applicable today. What it says is that without God we are left with a choice of succumbing to megalomania or erotomania, and heaven knows, there is plenty going on in the world, and in the hearts and minds of contemporary men, to justify that proposition. In this retreat from reality fostered by the media, their purportedly serious offerings, especially in the field of television, are often more morally misleading and harmful than mere disgusting pornography of the kind which traffickers in this particular squalid commodity market and sell, whether in books, periodicals, films or ostensible entertainment. Such material is at least easily recognisable for what it is, except perhaps in the eyes of some deluded intellectuals, and the aspiring ones who trail along in their wake, including, alas, trendy clergymen and even bishops.

The ostensibly serious offerings of the media, on the other hand, represent a different menace precisely because they are liable to pass for being objective and authentic, whereas actually they, too, belong to the realm of fantasy. Here, the advent and exploration of visual material with the coming of the camera, has played a crucial rôle. This applies especially to news and so-called documentaries, both of which are regarded as factual, but which, in practice, are processed along with everything else in the media's fantasy-machine. Thus news becomes, not so much what has happened, as what can be seen as happening, or seems to have happened. As for documentaries, anyone who has worked on them, as I have extensively, knows that the element of simulation in them has always been considerable, and has only increased as making and directing them has become more sophisticated and technically developed. Christopher Ralling, a gifted BBC producer, in an article in the *Listener*, has expressed his concern about how documentary-makers tend more and more to venture into a no-man's-land between drama and documentary.

Four lines by Blake, like so much of what he wrote, now seem prophetic, almost as though he foresaw the coming of the camera (surely not by chance originally called 'camera obscura'!), and all it would do to us in the way of inducing us to accept fantasy as reality:

> This life's dim windows of the soul
> Distorts the Heavens from pole to pole,
> And leads you to believe a lie
> When you see with, not through, the eye.

Has there ever been a more perfect instrument for seeing with rather than through the eye, than the camera? And as it has developed from bleary daguerreotypes to the latest video product, what a multitude of lies it has induced belief in, ranging between the crazy claims of advertising and the sophisticated practice of Orwell's Newspeak and Doublethink, not to mention mounting Big Brother's—or Sister's—appearances! To see through the eye is to grasp the significance of what is seen, to see it in relation to the totality of God's creation—'All the world in a grain of sand', again to quote Blake. Just looked at, seen with the eye, which is all the camera can do, a grain of sand is but one among innumerable other identical grains, making up a sea shore or a desert. So the camera is mindless, an instrument for merely looking. As such, it is more and more taking over the media. In newspapers, magazines and colour supplements, on location, in the studio and the cutting room, increasingly the camera tends to have the last word, and, in all seriousness, it may not be very long before television production, like so much else, is almost wholly automated, with no need for any human participation, other than to maintain the machines and programme the computers.

On the prowl for news, what the camera wants is an exciting or dramatic scene which will hold viewers, thus bringing into play its own particular expertise. Pictures are all. If there is footage available of, say, an air disaster, that takes precedence as news over some other disaster—say, an earthquake—of which there is no available footage. A murder in Belfast is less newsworthy than one in Fulham because of its familiarity; famines only occur when they have been filmed, the others—and there are many, alas—are likely to continue unnoticed. News cameramen want to lead the TV news bulletins as reporters want to lead the front page of the newspapers they serve, and are always on the look-out for some scene which will photograph strikingly. The temptation to set one up is correspondingly very great. When the Berlin Wall was completed, two *vopos*—East German policemen—decided to jump off it into West Berlin. I was told by a cameraman present on the occasion that they had to jump three times before their performance was considered to be visually satisfactory.

Then there are those pictures from the Vietnam War of GI's setting fire to huts or shooting a Vietcong prisoner out of hand. The chances of such a scene presenting itself just when a camera is ready to roll, with the correct positioning, lighting and so on, is about a billion to one against. None the less, they were the camera's truth, and so valid, and incidentally in the end decisive in bringing about an ignominious American defeat. One of the most famous shots in the 1939–45 War, used many times subsequently for documentary purposes, is of Hitler doing a weird little dance of triumph on hearing the news that France had fallen to the Wehrmacht. Now this, too, turns out to have been a fake, procured by the simple device of removing a few frames from film of Hitler walking. The Führer's tread was unremarkable, but in the camera's version he will dance on through history for ever.

The most horrifying example I know of the camera's power and authority, which will surely be in the history books as an example of the degradation our servitude to it can involve, occurred in Nigeria at the time of the Biafran War. A prisoner was to be executed by a firing squad, and the cameras turned up in force to photograph and film the scene. Just as the command to fire was about to be given, one of the cameramen shouted 'Cut!'; his battery had gone dead, and needed to be replaced. Until this was done, the execution stood suspended. Then, with his battery working again, he shouted 'Action!', and bang, bang, the prisoner fell to the ground, his death duly recorded, to be shown in millions of sitting rooms throughout the so-called civilised world. Some future historian may speculate as to where lay the greatest barbarism, on the part of the viewers, the executioners, or the cameras. I think myself that he would plump for the cameras.

As for the words that accompany the pictures, they have, of course, to be edited down and made to fit, and so are as malleable as the footage, if not more so. There are many authenticated cases of word-faking, like picture-faking. In the case, for instance, of the award-winning television programme *The Selling of the Pentagon*, some of the interviews have been shown to be edited in a way that gives a completely false impression of what was actually said. It goes without saying that none of the awards were withdrawn when the faking was exposed. Nor did the esteem in which the programme was held, diminish. The fraudulence of it apparently did not particularly interest viewers; in their eyes, it just did not matter. Another example of the same sort of fraudulence is Marcel Ophuls's *The Sorrow and the Pity* (*Le Chagrin et la Pitié*), a study of French Resistance in the 1939–45 War, which was shown on BBC 2 and much praised. It happens to be a subject I know quite a lot about because I was a liaison officer with the Gaullist Intelligence set-up, and spent the last year of the war in Paris with them. I can only say, in the light of this experience, that Ophuls's film is distorted and slanted to an almost incredible degree. This, however, as with *The Selling of the Pentagon*, did not prevent it from having an enthusiastic reception. The faking possibilities especially in the cutting room are well-nigh illimitable, and people now clamouring for the televising of Parliament should realise this, and the great power it will put in the hands of whoever edits the footage. He will have to work quickly to get an early screening, which means with little effective supervision, and it will be all too easy for him to make the performance of any MP seem admirable, absurd or contemptible just according to how he puts the footage together.

When I first went to Washington as a newspaper correspondent in 1946, there was a regular White House Press Conference; accredited journalists would gather round the President's desk in the famous Oval Room and ask him questions, which he would answer off-the-cuff. We were not allowed to quote his answers, or to attribute them, but, of course, the procedure was enormously helpful. Then, under President Eisenhower the Press Conference was put on the air, and, with the coming of the Kennedys, lavishly televised. This meant inevitably that the cameramen needed to know in advance who was going to ask questions, because otherwise they couldn't be sure of getting their picture correctly. From this, it is a very small step to start organising the right sort of question. Again, whereas in informal exchanges a President would speak with some frankness, the moment the cameras came they took over, and the whole operation became completely artificial, and ultimately useless, to the point that serious journalists like James Reston never nowadays bother to attend the Press Conference at all. This is assuredly what will happen in Parliament if MP's fall into the trap, and allow their proceedings to be televised. The camera will prove much more effective than Guy Fawkes in destroying Parliament as a deliberative assembly and organ of government.

Faking of the words and pictures to fit the theme has been particularly prevalent in compilation programmes which purport to reconstruct out of stock footage some historical scene or happening. There was the case, for instance, of a programme which celebrated the fiftieth anniversary of the Russian Revolution and used clips taken from Eisenstein's film of the storming of the Winter Palace in Petrograd. This representation of the scene bore little or no relation to what actually occurred, but there it is, on the record. Visually speaking, that is what happened; the footage proves it. The accumulated documentation of our time will be so vast, and for one reason and another, so slanted, that posterity will know nothing about us for sure. The first Dark Ages are lost in the mists of antiquity, with virtually no records; the coming Dark Ages will be equally lost in the blaze of studio lighting, with a superabundance of records, almost all falsified.

In recording contemporary events the camera likewise holds sway. I remember once returning to my hotel in New York and noticing on the way that a crowd had assembled outside what was obviously an embassy or consulate of some sort—I found out afterwards that it belonged to one of the Arab countries. There were the usual students assembled—bra-less girls, bearded men, holding placards with slogans on them; also a police van in attendance, and a number of cops standing by with their truncheons—everything set for a demo. 'What's going on?' I asked, and was told, as though it should have been obvious, that the cameras hadn't yet turned up. I lingered on until they came, and watched them set up and start rolling. Then, 'Action!' whereupon, placards were lifted, slogans shouted, fists clenched; a few demonstrators were arrested and pitched into the police van, and a few cops kicked, until, 'Cut!' Soon the cameras, the cops, and the demonstrators had all departed, leaving the street silent and deserted. Later, in the evening, in my hotel room, I watched the demo on the screen in one of the news programmes. It looked very impressive.

So I suggest that the cameras are our ego's eyes, our age's focus, the repository and emanation of all our fraudulence. Take them to any place of conflict and strife, and hey presto!—in a matter of minutes, trouble stirs for them to register. In his book, called *Do It*, Jerry Rubin, one of the principals in the Chicago conspiracy trial some years ago, has some sage words to say on the subject:

> Television creates myths bigger than reality. Whereas a demo drags on for hours and hours, TV packs all the action into two minutes—a commercial for the revolution. On the television screen news is not so much reported as created. An event happens when it goes on TV and becomes myth ... Television is a non-verbal instrument, so turn off the sound, since no one ever remembers any words that they hear, the mind being a technicolour movie of images, not words. There's no such thing as bad coverage for a demo. It makes no difference what's said: the pictures are the stories.

These observations irresistibly recall to me a remark made in Dostoyevsky's uncannily prophetic novel *The Devils*, by the character Peter Verkovensky, who bears a more than passing resemblance to Jerry Rubin and his like. 'A generation or two of debauchery,' Peter Verkovensky exults, 'followed by a little drop of nice fresh blood, just to accustom people, and then the turmoil will begin.' Well, it duly began in Russia, just as Dostoyevsky foretold, and seems now to be well under way elsewhere. It would seem to me that the camera may well take its place along with nuclear weaponry and the birth pill as one of the three major apocalyptic portents of our time; the first signifying power in terms of destruction, the second sex in terms of sterility, and the last, actuality in terms of fantasy.

Does this mean that the camera and all its works are wholly evil and incapable of fulfiling God's purposes? Of course not. Everything and everyone ministers to this fulfilment. Even Judas had an essential rôle in the sublime drama of the Passion. God ensures that, whatever we may do in the way of deceiving ourselves, ultimately reality will out. To every fantasy he provides an antidote, just as wherever stinging nettles are, there are also dock leaves to take away the sting. So the camera has to lie, if only to convince us that truth cannot be seen with, but only through, the eye, as Blake said. In the same sort of way, we love money; then along comes inflation to reveal money's absurdity; we are obsessed with eroticism, then along comes porn, the *reductio ad absurdum*, or, better perhaps, *ad disgustum*, of sex; we believe in the coming of a kingdom of heaven on earth, and we get the Gulag Archipelago; we crave for facts, and we get computers; we are avid for news, and *Newzak* assails us—news without end, amen.

It is not only to perform his wonders, but also to reveal his ironies that God moves in a mysterious way. It could not possibly be the case that something men have invented, like the media, could never be serviceable to God. If he put into his creatures gifts which enabled them to send words gyrating round the earth and through the stratosphere, then somehow and some time this must serve his purposes. For me personally the media have come to give off a whiff of sulphur, and yet at the end of the day I have to admit that they can enrich as well as debase a life. For instance, once when I was standing waiting for a train in an underground station, a little man—actually, he turned out to be of Greek extraction—came up to me and asked permission to shake my hand. I gladly, and rather absent-mindedly, extended a hand, assuming that he had mistaken me for A.J.P. Taylor, or maybe Mike Yarwood. As we shook hands, he remarked that some words of mine in a radio programme had prevented him from committing suicide. The humbling thing was that I couldn't remember the particular programme he had in mind; doubtless some panel or other, to me buffoonery, and yet a human life had hung on it.

A more ribald example of how incalculable are the consequences of what one does on television was provided by the sequel to a discussion I once had with Archbishop Anthony Bloom on the meaning of pain and affliction. When our session before the cameras was over, for once I felt reasonably satisfied with the exchanges that had taken place between us. The Archbishop is a man of great spirituality, and it seemed to me that we had made a serious, enlightened, and possibly enlightening contribution to a subject that troubles many today. Well, the following morning, when I took a cab at Charing Cross Station, the driver said to me in a jovial, appreciative tone of voice, as though commenting on some particularly neat piece of play in a game of football: 'I saw you last night on the telly with that bloke with a beard; you certainly knocked hell out of him'—an observation which shows once again that in Blakean terms, people look at a television screen with, not through, the eye, and so see on it what they expect, or have been induced to expect, to see.

Then, I have to say that I owe to the media, specifically television, what has proved to be one of the greatest blessings of my life—meeting Mother Teresa. This occurred by chance. I was asked to interview her for BBC television, and on the way to London for the purpose, in the train, looked over some material about her which had been provided. The moment I saw her I realised that, in the words of the prophet Amos, 'the Lord had taken her'. Subsequent acquaintance only confirmed this. She has told me more about our Lord, and helped me to understand more about the Christian faith, far, far more, than anything I have ever read, or thought, or heard on the subject. In the television programme that we made about her, *Something Beautiful for God*, the fact that she does truly live in Christ, and he in her, shines triumphantly through the camera's fraudulence. With God, all things are possible, as Jesus told the disciples when, after he had spoken about rich men and the eye of the needle, they went on to draw the conclusion that there would be no millionaires in heaven. Yes, with God, all things are possible, even bringing the reality of Christ on to the television screen.

We had only five days' filming in Calcutta to make the forty-minute programme on Mother Teresa. The normal allowance for a film of that length would have been two to three months. At every point we had to take all sorts of chances, one of them being to film in the very poor light of her home for the dying, where derelicts from the streets of Calcutta are brought, mostly to die, sometimes to live. To everyone's amazement, including the cameraman, Ken MacMillan's, and mine, this particular footage came out very well, showing the home for the dying, formerly a temple to the Hindu God Khali, bathed in a soft and very beautiful light. There has been some dispute about this. My own feeling was, and remains, that love carried to the point that Mother Teresa has carried it, has its own luminosity, and that the medieval painters who showed saints with halos, were not so wide of the mark as a twentieth-century mind might suppose. In any case, the programme has been shown many times, in many different places, always with great impact.

The moral would seem to be that what is required to make a successful Christian television programme is merely to find a true Christian, and put him or her on the screen. This, rather than any televisual skills or devices, would seem to be the key. Though my own part in making the programme was quite small—just doing the commentary, which meant letting Mother Teresa speak, and then producing a book about her, which meant holding a pen for her to write—it is a source of great satisfaction and joy to me, and something for which I am truly grateful to the media, that when I meet her Missionaries of Charity, which I quite often do, it usually turns out that a good number of them were drawn into the order by the film or the book.

One of the great attractions of Christianity to me is its sheer absurdity. I love all those crazy sayings in the New Testament—which, incidentally, turn out to be literally true—about how fools and illiterates and children understand what Jesus was talking about better than the wise, the learned and the venerable; about how the poor, not the rich, are blessed, the meek, not the arrogant, inherit the earth, and the pure in heart, not the strong in mind, see God. This is very much in Mother Teresa's vein. Most of what she and her Missionaries of Charity do is, in worldly terms, patently absurd. For instance, salvaging derelicts from the streets, just for them to have the comfort of seeing, even for a few hours or minutes, a loving face, and receiving loving care, rather than closing their eyes on a world implacably hostile, or at best indifferent, whether they lived or died. In purely human terms, such a procedure is clearly ridiculous—so much effort put out for so small a purpose. When the needs of the living are so great, surely, it might be thought, the best thing to do for the dying is just to let them die with perhaps a hypodermic jab to induce forgetfulness and put them to sleep. Mother Teresa sees it differently. When I asked her once what was the difference, in her eyes, between the welfare services and what her Missionaries of Charity do, she said that welfare workers do for an idea, a social purpose, what she and the Missionaries of Charity do for a Person. What we will do for a person is quite different from what we will do as a duty to the society we live in, or in fulfilment of a social idea or ideal. Mothers have starved for their children, wives have trudged for miles and faced appalling dangers when their husbands are in concentration camps to take them food parcels, clean clothes. There is no limit to what love will do, to the point of laying down a life for someone else. Mother Teresa insists that in every single suffering human being she sees the suffering Christ. So a grizzled head, a stricken face laid low in the gutter, is He to whom all care and all love are due. This is more in the nature of a passion than an enlightened purpose. It cannot be taught, but only caught, like a virus, picked up where the saints cherish the poor. Mother Teresa is a notable carrier of infection.

There is something else which I owe to television that has brought me great comfort and joy. Through having a face that, because of television, is liable to be recognised, and being nowadays known as someone who takes a Christian position, people quite often come up to me and, by one means or another, indicate that they, too, are Christians. Thus, when I'm leaving a restaurant, perhaps, a waiter comes padding after me, and silently shakes my hand. Or, in of all crazy places, a make-up room, the girl who is attending to my ancient visage whispers in my ear, 'I love the Lord'. Or turning a corner, I come face to face with a West Indian who, with an enormous grin of recognition, shouts out, 'Dear brother in Christ!' Or an air hostess, stooping to arrange my seat, manages to whisper that she, too, has recently become a Christian. I could go on giving examples for ever.

The experience is altogether delightful, but there is more in it than that. Notice, that it never for a moment occurs to me to want to know whether these diverse people who greet me so charmingly are educated or uneducated, bourgeois or proletarian, Roman Catholics or Anglicans or Jehovah's Witnesses, or brown or white or yellow, what their IQ is, how much they earn, or what sort of accent they have. All the different categories we have devised just don't apply. There is but one category:

our common fellowship in Christ. This, it seems to me, is a true image of Christian brotherhood. Work-a-day encounters, glorified by participation in a common lot, as children of the same God, redeemed by the same Saviour, destined for the same salvation. Marx saw the apogee of human existence in a victorious proletariat living happily ever after in a society in which government has withered away. Bunyan saw us as souls, for whom, when our pilgrimage is over, the trumpets will sound on the other side. I am for Bunyan.

All through these lectures I have been contrasting the fantasy of the media with the reality of Christ. About the former, the fantasy of the media, I have had much to say—some might contend too much! Let me, then, in conclusion speak about the reality of Christ, and how we may not just recognise it, but live with and by it, making it part of ourselves. Anthony Smith, an old media hand and friend who has been wise enough to take the golden road from Shepherd's Bush to Oxford University, preferring dreaming spires to dreaming aerials, in his excellent book, *The Shadow in the Cave*, uses Plato's famous image of the prisoners in the cage to illustrate the rôle of the media. It is apt indeed.

The prisoners, Socrates explains to Glaucon, are living in a cave which has a wide mouth open towards the light. They are kept in the same place, looking forward only away from the mouth of the cave and unable to turn their heads, for their legs and necks have been fixed in chains from birth. Higher up behind them a fire is burning, and between it and the prisoners there is a road with a low wall built at its side, like the screen over which puppet players put up their puppets. Men walk past under cover of this wall carrying all sorts of things, copies of men and animals, in stone or wood or other material; some of them may be talking and others not.

'It's a strange sort of image,' Glaucon remarks, 'and these are strange prisoners.'

'They're like ourselves,' Socrates replies. 'They see nothing of themselves but their own shadows, or one another's, which the fire throws on the walls of the cave. And so too with the things carried past. If they were able to talk to one another wouldn't they think that the names they used were those of the shadows that went by? And if their prison sent back an echo whenever one of those who went by said a word, what could they do but take it for the voice of the shadow? ... *The only real thing for them would be the shadows of the puppets.*'

Thus the media world of shadows. In contra-distinction, Christ shows us reality, what life really is, what it is really about, and our true destiny in belonging to it. We escape from the cave, we emerge from the darkness, and instead of shadows we have all around us the glory of God's creation; instead of darkness, light, instead of despair, hope, instead of time and the clocks ticking inexorably on, eternity, which never began and never ends, and yet is sublimely NOW.

What, then, is this reality of Christ, contrasting with all the fantasies whereby men seek to evade it—fantasies of the ego, of the appetites, of power or success, of the mind and the will; valid when first lived and expounded by our Lord himself two thousand years ago, buoying up Western man through all the vicissitudes and uncertainties of Christendom's centuries, and available today, when it is more needed, perhaps, than ever before, as it will be available tomorrow and for ever? It arises simply out of the circumstances that by identifying ourselves with Christ, by absorbing ourselves in his teaching, by living out the drama of his life with him, including especially the Passion—that powerhouse of love and creativity; by living with, by and in him we can be reborn to become new men and women in a new world.

It sounds crazy, as it did to Nicodemus, an early intellectual and potential BBC panelist, who asked how in the world it was possible for someone already born to go back into the womb and be born again. Yet it happens; it has happened innumerable times; it goes on happening. The testimony to this effect is overwhelming. Suddenly caught up in the wonder of God's love flooding the universe, made aware of the stupendous creativity which animates all life, of our own participation in it—every colour brighter, every meaning clearer, every shape more shapely, every note more musical, every word written and spoken more explicit: above all, every human face, all human companionship, all human encounters recognisably a family affair. The animals too, flying, prowling, burrowing, all their diverse cries and grunts and bellowings, and the majestic hilltops, the gaunt rocks giving their blessed shade, and the rivers faithfully making their ways to the sea—all irradiated with this same new glory in the eyes of the reborn.

What other fulfilment is there that could possibly compare with this? What going to the moon, or exploration of the universe, what victory or defeat, what revolution or counterrevolution, what putting down of the mighty from their seats and exalting of the humble and meek, who then, of course, become mighty in their turn and fit to be put down? A fulfilment that transcends all human fulfiling and yet is accessible to all humans; based on the absolutes of love rather than the relativities of justice, on the universality of brotherhood rather than the particularity of equality, on the perfect service which is freedom rather than on the perfect servitude which purports to be freedom.

Now a last personal word. It so happens that for the past months, here and elsewhere, I have been wholly preoccupied with thinking and talking about this reality of Christ in contradistinction to the fantasy so evident on every hand in our twentieth-century world. It might seem a little thing, but for me it has been a rather tremendous experience, culminating in being here in this church and speaking these words to you. From what I have said, you know I am convinced that hard and testing days lie ahead; the more so because the prophecy about false shepherds within the fold will be amply fulfiled, indeed, is being fulfiled already. In the nature of things, my own part in these apocalyptic prospects is strictly limited, and I cannot pretend that I wish it were otherwise. How beautiful always is the end of a journey! How exquisite the twilight when a day is ending! How glorious are the closing bars of the *Missa Solemnis*, triumphantly echoing, as they do, all that has gone before! Even so, I felt induced to renew my purpose to serve and live in the reality of Christ, and scribbled down, as it were, my operational orders for such time as remains to me in this world. I venture now to repeat them in case they might be helpful to any who hear or read what I have had to say in these lectures. Here they are:

1. Seek endlessly for God and for his hand in all creation, in the tiniest atom or electron as in the wide expanse of the universe, in our own innermost being as in all fellow-creatures. So, looking, we find him, finding him, we love him, and realise that in every great word ever spoken or written we hear his voice, as in every mean or sordid word we lose it, shutting ourselves off from the glory of his utterance.

2. Live abstemiously. Living otherwise—what Pascal calls 'licking the earth'—imprisons us in a tiny dark dungeon of the ego, and involves us in the pitiless servitude of the senses. So, imprisoned and enslaved, we are cut off from God and from the light of his love.

3. Love and consider all men and women as brothers and sisters, caring for them exactly as we should for Jesus himself if we had the inexpressible honour of ministering to him.

4. Read the Bible and related literature, especially mystical works like the Metaphysical Poets and *The Cloud of Unknowing*. These are the literature of

the Kingdom proclaimed in the New Testament; words which became flesh and have dwelt among us, full of grace and truth. Who would live in a new country and not bother to study its literature? I would add here an extra little codicil particularly my own: Love laughter, which sounds loudly as heaven's gates swing open, and dies away as they shut.

Finally:

5. Know Jesus Christ and follow his Way, like Bunyan's Pilgrim, whithersoever it may lead; through pleasant pastures, over formidable hills, into sloughs and along the Valley of the Shadow of Death itself, but always with the light of the Celestial City, not just in prospect, but *in* one's very eye. Thereby we may learn to live and learn to die.

Thus fortified, we can laugh at the media as Rabelais, in the person of Panurge, laughed at the antics of carnal men; as Cervantes, in the person of Don Quixote, laughed at the antics of crusading men; as Shakespeare, in the person of Sir John Falstaff, laughed at the antics of mortal men.

Nor need we despair to be living at a time when we have lost an Empire on which the sun never set, and acquired a Commonwealth on which it never rises. It is in the breakdown of power that we may discern its true nature, and when power seems strong and firm that we are most liable to be taken in and suppose it can really be used to enhance human freedom and wellbeing, forgetful that Jesus is the prophet of the loser's, not the victor's, camp, and proclaimed that the first will be last, that the weak are the strong, and the fools, the wise. Let us, then, as Christians rejoice that we see around us on every hand the decay of the institutions and instruments of power; intimations of empires falling to pieces, money in total disarray, dictators and parliamentarians alike nonplussed by the confusion and conflicts which encompass them. For it is precisely when every earthly hope has been explored and found wanting, when every possibility of help from earthly sources has been sought and is not forthcoming, when every recourse this world offers, moral as well as material, has been explored to no effect, when in the shivering cold the last faggot has been thrown on the fire and in the gathering darkness every glimmer of light has finally flickered out—it is then that Christ's hand reaches out, sure and firm, that Christ's words bring their inexpressible comfort, that his light shines brightest, abolishing the darkness for ever. So, *finding in everything only deception and nothingness, the soul is constrained to have recourse to God himself and to rest content with him.*

2. Another King

Nowadays when I occasionally find myself in a pulpit—one of those bad habits one gets into in late middle age—and never, by the way, in a more famous pulpit than this one—I always have the same feeling as I look round, as I do now at your faces: a deep, passionate longing to be able to say something memorable, to shed some light.

I am the light of the world, the founder of the Christian religion said. What a stupendous phrase! And how particularly marvelous today, when one is conscious of so much darkness in the world! *Let your light shine before men*, he exhorted us. You know, sometimes on foolish television or radio panels, or being interviewed, someone asks me what I most want, what I should most like to do in the little that remains of my life, and I always nowadays truthfully answer—and it *is* truthful—"I should like my light to shine, even if only very fitfully, like a match struck in a dark, cavernous night and then flickering out."

How I should love to be able to speak to you with even a thousandth part of the certainty and the luminosity of St. Paul, for instance, in Thessalonica, when he and his companions were, in the most literal sense, turning the world upside down by insisting, contrary to Caesar's decrees, *that there* [was] *another king, one Jesus*. Golden words, a bright and shining light indeed. Now something had happened to him, as it had to Christ's disciples, transforming them from rather inarticulate, cowardly men who ran away for cover when their leader was arrested, into the most lion-hearted, eloquent, quick-witted, yes, and even gay evangelists the world has ever known. Irresistible in their oratory, indomitable in their defiance, captivating in their charm; overwhelming in the love which shone in their faces, in their words, and in their deeds. Well, what had happened

Originally a sermon delivered at the University of Edinburgh Service, in the High Kirk of St. Giles (January 14, 1968). Reprinted from Malcolm Muggeridge, *Jesus Rediscovered* (Garden City, N.Y.: Doubleday, 1969), pp. 69–76.

to them? We can call it what we like as far as I'm concerned: "the Holy Ghost descending," "Damascus road conversion," "speaking with tongues," anything you like. I don't mind. The point is that, as they said themselves, they were reborn. They were new men with a new allegiance, not to any form of earthly authority but to this other king, this Jesus. Ever since their time, with all the ups and downs, confusions and villainies of institutional Christianity, this notion has persisted, of being reborn, of dying in order to live, and I want to consider whether such a notion, as I understand it the very heart of the Christian religion, has any point or validity today.

In the boredom and despair of an expiring Roman civilisation, with all the inevitable accompaniments of permissive morality, addiction to vicarious violence, erotic and narcotic fantasies, it offered a new light of hope, a new joy in living, to one and all, including, perhaps especially including, the slaves. In our uncannily similar circumstances, has it anything to offer today? That's my question. Of course I can't answer it as St. Paul and the disciples did. They were the beginning; we are the end. I, too, belong to the twentieth century, with a twentieth-century sceptical mind and sensual disposition, with the strange mixture of crazy credulity in certain directions, as, for instance, in science and advertising (if you happen to cast an eye through the advertisements in your colour supplements, you will see displayed there a credulity which would be the envy of every witch doctor in Africa) and equally crazy scepticism, so that illiterate schoolboys and half-baked university students turn aside with contemptuous disbelief before propositions which the greatest minds and the noblest dispositions of our civilisation—Pascal, say, and Tolstoy—accepted as self-evident. That is our twentieth-century plight. Let me, then, in true twentieth-century style, begin with a negative proposition—what I consider to be the ineluctable unviability and absurdity of our present way of life.

How can anyone, apart from an occasional "with it" cleric, provost of King's, or Hungarian economist, seriously believe that by projecting present trends into the future we arrive at enduring human felicity—producing more and more and consuming more and more year by year under the impetus of an ever more frenzied persuasion by mass-communications media, and at the same time watching the rest of mankind get hungrier and hungrier, in ever greater want; growing ever stronger, with the means at our disposal to blow ourselves and our earth itself to smithereens many times over, and at the same time becoming ever more neurotic about the imminence of global nuclear war; moving ever faster and further afield, exploring the universe itself, and pursuing happiness, American style; "grinding out our appetites," as Shakespeare so elegantly put it, ever more desperately, with physical and even moral impunity, and spiritual desolation. It is a state of affairs at once so bizarre and so tragic that I alternate between laughing hilariously at it and looking forward eagerly to my departure from the scene, quite soon now—in at most a decade or so. This year, at sixty-five years old, I move into the N.T.B.R. (Not To Be Resuscitated) bracket, when some high-minded, highly skilled doctor will look me over and decide in his infinite wisdom and humanity whether I am worth keeping alive. As I have said, I alternate between a sense of the utter absurdity of it all and a desire to get out of so nonsensical a world.

May I, moving from general things to more particular ones, consider for instance the situation in this ancient university, with which through the accident of election I find myself briefly associated. The students here in this university, as in other universities, are the ultimate beneficiaries under our welfare system. They are supposed to be the spearhead of progress, flattered and paid for by their admiring seniors, an *élite* who will happily and audaciously carry the torch of progress into the glorious future opening before them. Now, speaking for myself, there is practically nothing that they could do in a mood of rebelliousness or refusal to accept the ways and values of our run-down, spiritually impoverished way of life for which I shouldn't feel some degree of sympathy or, at any rate, understanding. Yet how infinitely sad; how, in a macabre sort of way, funny, that the form their insubordination takes should be a demand for pot and pills, for the most tenth-rate sort of escapism and self-indulgence ever known! It is one of those situations a social historian with a sense of humor will find very much to his taste. All is prepared for a marvelous release of youthful creativity; we await the great works of art, the high-spirited venturing into new fields of perception and understanding—and what do we get? The resort of any old, slobbering debauchee anywhere in the world at any time—dope and bed.

The feeling aroused in me by this, I have to confess, is not so much disapproval as contempt, and this, as you may imagine, makes it difficult, in fact impossible, for me as Rector to fulfil my functions. Here, if I may, I should like to insert a brief word of personal explanation. I, as Rector, and Allan Frazer as my Assessor, find ourselves, as you know, responsible for passing on to the university authorities the views and requests of the student body as conveyed to us by their elected officers, and as set forth in their magazine *Student*, for whose conduct they are responsible. Their request concerning the birth pill is as it happens highly distasteful to us, as we have not hesitated to let it be known. The view of the elected officers of the Student Representative Committee, as expressed by some of them and not repudiated publicly by any of them, is that the Rector and his Assessor are bound not only to pass on but to recommend whatever the SRC may decide. This is a role which, in my opinion, no self-respecting Rector or Assessor could possibly countenance, and I have therefore asked the Principal to accept my resignation, as has my Assessor.

So, dear Edinburgh students, this is likely to be the last time I address you, and this is what I want to say—and I don't really care whether it means anything to you or not, whether you think there is anything in it or not. I want you to believe that this row I have had with your elected officers has nothing to do with any puritanical attitudes on my part. I have no belief in abstinence for abstinence's own sake, no wish under any circumstances to check any fulfilment of your life and being. But I have to say to you this: that whatever life is or is not about, it is not to be expressed in terms of drug stupefaction and casual sexual relations. However else we may venture into the unknown it is not, I assure you, on the plastic wings of *Playboy* magazine or psychedelic fancies.

I have recently, as you might have heard, been concerned in making some films for BBC Television on the New Testament, and it involved, along with much else, standing on what purports to be, and, unlike most shrines, may well be, the hill of Beatitudes, where the most momentous of all sermons was preached some two thousand years ago. It was rather marvelous standing there looking down on the Sea of Galilee and trying to reconstruct the scene—the obscure teacher and the small, nondescript, mostly illiterate crowd gathered round him. For the Christian religion began, let us never forget, not among brilliant, academic minds, not among the wealthy, or the powerful, or the brilliant, or the exciting, or the beautiful, or the fascinating; not among television personalities or leader-writers on the *Guardian*; it began among these very simple, illiterate people, and one was tremendously conscious of them gathered there.

And then those words, those incomparable words, which were to echo and re-echo through the world for centuries to come; even now not quite lost. How it is the meek, not the arrogant, who inherit the earth.

How we should love our enemies, and do good to them that hate us. How it is the poor, not the rich, who are blessed, and so on. Words which have gone on haunting us all, even though we ignore them; the most sublime words ever spoken.

One of the Beatitudes that had for some reason never before impressed me particularly, this time stuck in my mind and has stayed there ever since. It is: *Blessed are the pure in heart: for they shall see God.* May I commend this Beatitude to you as having some bearing on our present controversies and discontents. To see God is the highest aspiration of man, and has preoccupied the rarest human spirits at all times. Seeing God means understanding, seeing into the mystery of things. It is, or should be, the essential quest of universities like this one, and of their students and their staff. Note that the realization of this quest is achieved, not through great and good deeds, nor even through thought, however perceptive and enlightened, certainly not through sensations, however generated, nor what is called success, however glittering. The words are clear enough—*Blessed are the pure in heart: for they shall see God.*

To add to the macabre comedy of our situation, into the ribald scene of confusion and human inadequacy that I have been talking about, there break idiot voices prophesying a New Jerusalem just round the corner. One always, I find, underestimates the staying power of human folly. When poor old H. G. Wells breathed his last, having produced in *Mind at the End of its Tether* a final repudiation of everything he had ever said or thought, I fondly supposed, and said to myself, that no more would be heard in my time of men like gods. How wrong I was! A quarter of a century later a provost of King's College, Cambridge, was to carry the same notion to an even higher pitch of fantasy. No doubt, long after I am gone someone will be saying, on some indestructible BBC program like "Any Questions," a touch more abortion, another year at school, and birth pills given away with the free morning milk, and all will be well.

What are we to do about it, this crazy relapse into moral chaos and dementia? I never met a man made happy by money or worldly success or sensual indulgence, still less by the stupefaction of drugs or alcohol. Yet we all, in one way or another, pursue these ends, as the advertiser well knows. He offers them in Technicolor and stereo sound, and there are many takers. The politician likewise, often with a nondescript retinue of academic and clerical support, offers the same package in collective terms. Underneath, we all know how increasingly hollow and unconvincing it is—the

Great Society, mankind coming of age, men like gods, all the unspeakable cant of utopians on the run. Our very art and literature, such as they are, convey the same thing—the bad dreams of a materialistic society. Francis Bacon and Pinter tapering off into the sheer incoherence of a Burroughs and a Beckett, with the Beatles dancing on our grave, and Allen Ginsberg playing his hand harmonium, and that delectable old Hindu con man, the "Maharishi," throwing in his blessing. Communist utopianism produced Stalin; the pursuit of happiness, American style, produced Richard Nixon, and our special welfare variety has produced Harold Wilson. If that doesn't finally discredit all three, nothing ever will. As for the scientific utopia looming ahead, we have caught a glimpse of that, too, in the broiler houses, the factory farms, and lately the transplant operations, with still-warm bodies providing the spare parts for patching up others, and so *ad infinitum*.

So I come back to where I began, to that other king, one Jesus; to the Christian notion that man's efforts to make himself personally and collectively happy in earthly terms are doomed to failure. He must indeed, as Christ said, be born again, be a new man, or he's nothing. So at least I have concluded, having failed to find in past experience, present dilemmas, and future expectations any alternative proposition. As far as I am concerned, it is Christ or nothing.

To add a final touch of comic relief (because, you know, an ex-editor of *Punch* cannot help, even in the most gruesome situations, looking around for something comic), I might add that what I have just said is, I know, far more repellent to most of the present ecclesiastical establishment than any profession of scepticism or disbelief.

I increasingly see us in our human condition as manacled and in a dark cell. The chains are our mortal hopes and desires; the dark cell is our ego, in whose obscurity and tiny dimensions we are confined. Christ tells us how to escape, striking off the chains of desire, and putting a window in the dark cell through which we may joyously survey the wide vistas of eternity and the bright radiance of God's universal love. No view of life, as I am well aware, could be more diametrically opposed to the prevailing one today, especially as purveyed in our mass-communications media, dedicated as they are to the counterproposition that we *can* live by bread alone, and the more the better. Yet I am more convinced than I am in my own existence that the view of life Christ came into the world to preach, and died to sanctify, remains as true and as valid as ever, and that all who care to, young and old, healthy and infirm, wise and foolish, educated and uneducated, may live thereby, finding in our troubled, confused world, as in all other circumstances and at all other times, an enlightenment and a serenity not otherwise attainable. Even though, as may very well prove the case, our civilisation, like others before it, soon finally flickers out, and institutional Christianity with it, the light Christ shed shines as brightly as ever for those who seek an escape from darkness. The truths he spoke will answer their dilemmas and assuage their fears, bringing hope to the hopeless, zest to the despairing, and love to the loveless, precisely as happened two thousand years ago and through all the intervening centuries.

I finished off my filming in the Holy Land by taking with a friend the road to Emmaus. Those of you who still read the Bible will remember the details—how shortly after the Crucifixion, Cleopas, some sort of relative of Christ's family, and a friend were walking from Jerusalem to Emmaus and inevitably talking as they went along about the Crucifixion, which had happened so recently. They were joined by a third man who fell into step beside them and shared in their conversation. As my friend and I walked along like Cleopas and his friend, we recalled, as they did, the events of the Crucifixion and its aftermath in the light of our utterly different and yet similar world. Nor was it a fancy that we, too, were joined by a third presence. And I tell you that wherever the walk, and whoever the wayfarers, there is always this third presence ready to emerge from the shadows and fall in step along the dusty, stony way.

3. Living Water

It is a curious fact that today, as I have found, one is called a pessimist if one ventures to express a certain contempt for the things of this world and dares to entertain the truly extraordinary hopes about our human destiny which buoyed up the first Christians when, in earthly terms, their master had gone from them and their cause was lost. What a weird reversal, as I should have thought, of common sense! What a preposterous distortion of language! How, I ask myself, can it be pessimistic to call in question the transitory satisfactions available in our mortal existence, and to contrast them with the enduring ones offered us in the Gospels and Epistles? I wonder whether, in the history of all the civilisations that have ever been, a more insanely optimistic notion has ever been entertained than that you and I, mortal, puny creatures, may yet aspire, with God's grace and Christ's help, to be reborn into what St. Paul calls *the glorious liberty of the children of God*. Or if there was ever a more abysmally pessimistic one than that we, who reach out with our minds and our aspirations to the stars and beyond, should be able so to arrange our lives, so to eat and drink and fornicate and learn and frolic, that our brief span in this world fulfils all our hopes and desires.

Is it to be supposed that the woman of Samaria after her encounter with Christ—so exquisitely recounted by St. John—didn't remember, every time she drew water at Jacob's well, about that other living water she had been told of; that water which, once drunk, left one never thirsting again—a well inside one, and springing up everlastingly? In the same way, how can one who has glimpsed, however fleetingly, what King Lear calls "the mystery of things," that *life of the soul* to which Isaiah refers—how can such a one ever again be wholly serious about mere worldly pursuits like fame

Originally a sermon delivered at Queen's Cross Church, Aberdeen, Scotland (May 26, 1968). Reprinted from Malcolm Muggeridge, *Jesus Rediscovered* (Garden City, N.Y.: Doubleday, 1969), pp. 76–82.

and sensual pleasure and money, even though the color supplements, all the different manifestations of this dreadful Frankenstein of mass-communications media that we have constructed, aim ceaselessly to persuade us that these pursuits alone make life worthwhile! I may, I suppose, regard myself, or pass for being, a relatively successful man. People occasionally stare at me in the streets—that's fame. I can fairly easily earn enough to qualify for admission to the higher slopes of the Internal Revenue—that's success. Furnished with money and a little fame even the elderly, if they care to, may partake of trendy diversions—that's pleasure. It might happen once in a while that something I said or wrote was sufficiently heeded for me to persuade myself that it represented a serious impact on our time—that's fulfilment. Yet I say to you—and I beg you to believe me—multiply these tiny triumphs by a million, add them all together, and they are nothing—less than nothing, a positive impediment—measured against one draught of that living water Christ offers to the spiritually thirsty, irrespective of who or what they are. What, I ask myself, does life hold, what is there in the works of time, in the past, now, and to come, which could possibly be put in the balance against the refreshment of drinking that water?

I ventured to cite my own case. Let me cite another, infinitely more impressive. I can never forget reading, when I was a young man, in Tolstoy's *Confession*, of how, working in his study, he had to hide away a rope that was there for fear he should use it to hang himself. To me at that time it seemed extraordinary. Here was the greatest writer of modern times, someone of whom, as a young aspiring writer myself, I thought with the utmost veneration, whose work seemed (and seems) to me so marvelous that if in the course of my life I managed to write something even a hundredth part as good as the shortest and most desultory of his short stories, I should be well content. And here was this man, of whom Gorky said that as long as Tolstoy lived he could never feel an orphan in the world; here was this man of incomparable gifts and greatness—rich, courted, with a large family, a loving wife, every worldly blessing that anyone could possibly aspire to—unable to endure the sight of a rope because it reminded him of how he might end a life which had grown insufferable. Why insufferable? Because he was assailed by the hopes and desires of the world—even more desolating, as he well knew, in realization than in aspiration. Because he seemed to be alone and afraid in an alien universe. Then, as he recounts, he lost himself in Christ's love, from which, St. Paul tells us, nothing can separate us if we hold fast—not tribulation, not distress, not persecution, not famine, not nakedness, neither peril nor sword. Tolstoy, as we know, did hold fast, becoming, not only the greatest writer, but also one of the greatest Christians, of modern times. He earned thereby, inevitably, the relentless hostility of his country's Church and its hierarchy, but he had the incomparable satisfaction of devoting his sublime genius, not just to diverting his contemporaries, enriching himself, and feeding his own vanity, but to keeping alive the sweet truths Christ died to teach us—of forgiveness, of brotherliness, of love of God and of our fellows, dying to this world and being reborn as new men with new values, new hopes, and a new, inexpressible joy in the destiny Christ came on earth to reveal to us.[1] He could repeat with a steady voice St. Augustine's prayer—so infinitely touching to anyone who, however unworthily and inadequately, has tried to communicate in the spoken or the written word: *Let me offer you in sacrifice the service of my thoughts and my tongue, but first give me what I may offer you.*

We must look, it seems to me, for comedy in all things; the builders of our medieval cathedrals knew what they were doing when they stuck grinning gargoyles on their majestic edifices, and, as Chesterton pointed out, the Fall of Man is only the banana-skin joke carried to cosmic proportions. Now here's a funny thing! If I'd been talking in this sort of strain in this Scottish pulpit a century ago, there would have been nothing surprising or out of the way in the sentiments I expressed, though some eyebrows might, admittedly, have been raised at such excessive praise of a Russian writer who, whatever other merits he might have, was emphatically not a Scottish Presbyterian. Today it is otherwise. Many of the leaders and clergy of the various Christian denominations are insistent that Christ's kingdom, contrary to what he said, *is* of this world, and that treasure laid up on earth in the shape of an endlessly increasing wealth to be distributed ever more lavishly to the citizens of an affluent consumer society is of the greatest possible moment. Anyone who suggests that happiness—which usually means pleasure—as an end or pursuit runs directly

[1] In his book *A Third Testament*, Muggeridge admits that, "Tolstoy's quest for God was a lonely and solitary one, and, in the sense of providing him with a sure faith, unrealized. He struggled on doggedly and bravely, but he never found the enduring serenity and harmonious relationship with his family he so longed for."

Muggeridge also recognized that Tolstoy was a controversial figure and that he held many unorthodox beliefs that clearly conflicted with the teaching of his church.

contrary to the Christian way of life as conveyed in the New Testament is sure to be condemned as a life-hater, one who blasphemously denigrates God's world and the creature—man—made in his image.

Unspeakable clergymen twanging electric guitars denounce him; episcopal voices cast him into outer darkness; from without, and sometimes within, the churches comes insistence that to be carnally minded is life; that it is the flesh that quickeneth and the spirit that profiteth nothing. I speak here, I may add, about what in some small degree I have experienced myself. It was from the Roman Catholic chaplain of Edinburgh University and a number of his associates that there came the bitterest denunciation of myself as Rector and of my Assessor and friend, Allan Frazer, for having resigned rather than seem to countenance a demand for the indiscriminate distribution of contraceptives to the students. To the best of my knowledge no Church dignitary (with the honorable exception of a spokesman for the Free Church of Scotland) spoke up in public on our behalf, though one or two wrote to us privately in sympathetic terms. There are many other and much more important instances of the same sort. These induce me to say in all honesty that, in my opinion, the church leaders and clergy have made such concession to prevailing permissive *mores* and materialism that, unless there is a quick and dramatic reversal of their present attitudes, I personally shall be very surprised if a decade or so from now anything remains of institutional Christianity—an outcome which quite a number of them openly hope for. Here, at least, their hopes are likely to be realized.

If, indeed, the Christian religion rested upon the word of these leaders, and the ostensible Christian consensus they are struggling to achieve, I should long ago have abandoned all faith in its survival. In fact, of course, Christianity's validity lies in its own inherent and everlasting truth. What the Living Christ signified and signifies to men will endure even though the Vatican is another ruin with the Coliseum, and tourists are poking about the debris of Lambeth Palace as now they do about Herod's. No doubt a racy foreword by the Emperor Tiberius would have helped to popularize St. Paul's Epistles, and if the apostles had adjusted their teaching to current depravity they might have reached a larger audience. Their practice was the precise opposite; asking everything on Christ's behalf—a total surrender of the ego, a putting aside of the preoccupations of this world, a death to be followed by a rebirth—they were accorded everything. On the other hand, experience shows that those who ask little tend to be accorded nothing—a saying which may well be the epitaph of twentieth-century institutional Christianity.

When one comes to the social application of this newfound sanguine attitude to man's earthly circumstances, one enters upon a scene of pure fantasy, so outrageously ribald as to defy satire itself. If the directors of the vegetarian movement were to petition the Worshipful Company of Butchers for affiliation, it would not be nearly as funny as the spectacle of the Church's involvement in the notion of material progress, political liberation, and the realization through the exercise of power and the creation of wealth of a kingdom of heaven on earth. How I envy the historian who, like Gibbon, will look back across the centuries at the hilarious spectacle of Marxist/Christian dialogues attempting to find common ground between the brutal atheism of the Communist Manifesto and the Sermon on the Mount, of pious clergymen attaching themselves to enraged mobs shouting for Black Power or Student Power or some other crazed shibboleth, of an Anglican bishop in gaiters recommending *Lady Chatterley's Lover*. Such lunacy, I assure you, is the despair of professional comedians.

The trouble with earthly causes is that they, alas, are liable sooner or later to triumph. Turn your minds for a moment to the unhappy plight of those so-called Christian Socialists who identified the rise of the Labour Party with the coming of Christ's kingdom. What must be their feelings today? Or those others who saw in Soviet Communism the fulfilment of Christian hopes. What must they feel as the full villainy of Stalin's regime becomes manifest? All purely human hopes are fraudulent, as their realization in purely human terms must always prove deceptive. As the Magnificat so splendidly puts it, the mighty are put down from their seats and the humble and meek exalted; but never forget that these same humble and meek, once exalted, become mighty in their turn and fit to be put down.

Fantasies like these belong to the half-light before night falls. I have no wish to luxuriate in apocalyptic prognostications, yet it would seem obvious enough that the last precarious foothold of law and order in our world is now being dislodged. We may expect the darkness. Such were precisely the circumstances in which the Christian religion was born; they may well provide for its rebirth. In the Holy Land today one is confronted on every hand with the debris of the great Roman Empire and world order, which in Christ's time seemed so strong, widespread, and dominant. Who could have foreseen in those days that the words of an obscure teacher in a remote outpost of the empire would provide the basis for a new and most glorious civilisation—the two thousand years of Christendom now drawing to a close; that his squalid death by execution would inspire the noblest thoughts, the most sublime art, the most disinterested dedication and exquisite love the world has yet known. Likewise today, who can tell what comes after us—who have made ourselves so strong and feel so weak and helpless, who have become so materially rich and spiritually impoverished, who know so much and understand so little! I think of a man in the fourth century, Paulinus, about whom I have read. Foreseeing the darkness ahead, he decided to light a lamp and keep it burning in a Christian shrine. I should dearly love to do just this—a little lamp to signify that whatever the darkness, however profound the sense of lostness, the light of Christ's love and the clarity of his enlightenment still shine, and will continue to shine, for those that have eyes to see, a heart to love, and a soul to believe.

4. Unto Caesar

I see that I've been billed to speak to you about Christianity and world problems. Let me explain straight away that I don't believe there are such things as world problems, but only a problem of man and his existence in this world; furthermore, that if there were world problems, I am extremely sceptical as to whether there is, or can be, a specifically Christian answer to them. The relevant incident in the New Testament here is, of course, the putting of the question to Christ whether it was lawful to pay tribute to Caesar. His reply—highly ingenious and, I should suppose, partly ironical—to the effect that we should render to Caesar the things that are Caesar's and to God the things that are God's, neatly evaded the point at issue: Jewish nationalism. There is, I know, a school of thought, by no means without clerical support, which sees Christ as a sort of Che Guevara, and I fully expect yet another translation of the New Testament to be produced soon in which it is made clear that previous ones have erred in not indicating that Christ was a militant Jewish nationalist. The Caesars to whom Christ said tribute was due have long ago disappeared, and today, two thousand years later, Jewish nationalism is at last triumphant in Jerusalem. Neither circumstance, as far as I'm concerned, has the slightest bearing on the message Christ came to deliver, the life he came to live, and the death he came to die.

What, then, is our brief existence here on earth about? The media—I mean television, the color supplements, the magazines, the newspapers; all the different organs of this immense apparatus of persuasion which has been developed in our time—answer the question with the utmost clarity and gusto. It's about being successful in terms of money, sex, and fame, with violence thrown in for kicks. As trendy, sexy, affluent children of our time we may consider ourselves as living to the full. By the same token, if we are

Originally a sermon delivered at the Chapel of Hertford College, Oxford (November 3, 1968). Reprinted from Malcolm Muggeridge, *Jesus Rediscovered* (Garden City, N.Y.: Doubleday, 1969), pp. 82–88.

out of the swing, physically unattractive, and poor, we must consider ourselves as outcasts and deprived. Anyone who has lived at all in the real world must have understood that this fantasy of the media is a total absurdity. This is not a happy age, even—perhaps particularly—for its greatest ostensible beneficiaries. The parts of the world where the means of happiness in material and sensual terms are most plentiful—like California and Scandinavia—are also the places where despair, mental sickness, and other twentieth-century ills are most in evidence. Sex, fanned by public erotica, underpinned by the birth pill and legalized abortion, is a primrose path leading to satiety and disgust; the rich are usually either wretched or mad; the successful plod relentlessly on to prove to the world and to themselves that their success is worth having; violence, collective and individual, bids fair to destroy us all and what remains of our civilisation.

These judgements are not, I assure you, theoretical ones. I have worked in the media for the last forty years; I know how they function, the men who operate them, and the motives that govern them. I have even held in my hands some of their prizes. If I say to you that these prizes are worthless, that, far from enriching life, they impoverish it, I am speaking from direct, personal experience. You will, of course, not believe me; as Pascal points out, it is part of the irony of our human situation that we ardently pursue ends which we know to be worthless. Why, even at my age, and utterly convinced of the truth of what I have just said to you, I can still aspire after applause and public recognition, when it has been demonstrated to me again and again in the most emphatic and unmistakable manner that such satisfactions only create a deeper, more agonizing hunger than the one they are meant to allay. Even the great Augustine, with years of sanctity behind him, with one of the finest minds of his own or any other time, so passionately enrolled in the service of his God and his Saviour—even he could still be dragged with a silken thread into the blind alleyways of the senses. I think of him looking out of his window at Hippo on the Mediterranean, marveling at its grandeur, at—as he puts it—the changing colours it slips on and off like robes, and reflecting that if such beauty as this is for us unhappy, punished men, what will the rewards of the blessed be like? It is so vivid, so human, so splendid.

Is there an escape route? Many are recommended today. For instance, what is called protest, an escape through mere destructiveness and lawlessness—down with everything and everyone, including us! Then, again, escape on the plastic wings of narcotics and erotica. Or escape through inertia—just refusing to join in; lying inert in the bottom of the boat with the bilge water, indifferent as to where it's going and who holds the tiller. I feel a certain sympathy with, or at any rate understanding of, all of these escape routes, but I have to say to you that they're all cul-de-sacs. They lead nowhere. When the lawlessness and destruction have been achieved, the choice is between chaos and tyranny, and, faced with such a choice, the great majority of human beings will always choose tyranny, or have it imposed upon them. The plastic wings soon break, and those who relied on them to be lifted into the sky fall, a dead weight, onto the ground; the dropout in the end becomes a bore to himself and to everyone else.

A seemingly more promising escape route is through the notion of social or collective regeneration. We are to agitate for a juster, more equitable, more brotherly society in which the wicked things like war, racialism, economic exploitation, all forms of unnecessary human suffering, are eliminated. This is where the world problems come in. We march through the streets chanting in unison, "Ho! Ho! Ho Chi Minh!" thereby, as we fondly suppose, helping to promote his victory in the Vietnam War and the defeat of American imperialism. We barrack politicians with whom we disagree, like Mr. Enoch Powell, when they try to explain what they are getting at, thereby, we persuade ourselves, striking a blow against *apartheid* and segregationists everywhere. And so on. This sort of virtue has the great advantage, from the point of view of many clerics and secular evangelists, that is a soft sell. How difficult, how desperately difficult, to curb one's so-insistent ego, to put aside pride and vanity and follow the way of the Cross! How easy, how really almost fatuously easy, to support Ho Chi Minh and be against Mr. Powell!

Perhaps because it is so easy, the pursuit of collective virtue, ardently pursued over the last half century, has been singularly disappointing in its results. Two world wars, numerous revolutions, much political endeavor directed towards humanizing our economic and social arrangements, have not resulted in a kinder way of life for Western man, still less for mankind as a whole. Who that is honest surveying the happenings of recent decades—the millions and millions who have been killed or uprooted from their homes, the wanton destruction, the almost inconceivable cruelties of a Hitler and a Stalin, the crazed quest for wealth and excitement—can seriously maintain that we are moving forwards spiritually, morally, or even materially? This has been the century of the Kingdom of Heaven on Earth; many and varied have been its prophets and its guises—the

American Way of Life, the Welfare State, the New Civilisation which people like Shaw and the Webbs detected in the monstrosities of Stalin—but what has come to pass, I fear, is better described as the Kingdom of Hell on Earth, soon, I should suppose, to pass into oblivion, its piled-up radioactive dust one more monument to the folly of man when he supposes that his destiny is in his own hands.

Utopianism, I am glad to note, is decidedly on the wane—though some dons and half-baked students continue to traffic in it. Thus, few any longer suggest, as the flower of our intelligentsia did up to quite a short time ago, that paradise has been regained in the USSR. Immigrants to the United States go there nowadays in search of a more affluent, not a better, life; our own Welfare State finds its only heralds—such as they are—among sociologists and statisticians. Even the protesting young feel constrained to fix their hopes on Mao Tse-tung, because he is a long way away and little is known about him, rather than on more vulnerable saviours nearer at hand. The trouble with all earthly causes, however admirable they may be in intent, however earnestly promoted by their advocates, is that they are liable to triumph. Hugh Kingsmill, a writer whom I greatly admire, puts it like this: "What is divine in Man is elusive and impalpable, and he is easily tempted to embody it in a collective form—a church, a country, a social system, a leader—so that he may realise it with less effort and serve it with more profit. Yet the attempt to externalise the kingdom of heaven in a temporal shape must end in disaster. It cannot be created by charters or constitutions, nor established by arms. Those who set out for it alone will reach it together and those who seek it in company will perish by themselves."

Turning aside, then, from delusive prizes and utopias, which have been found wanting, what are we left with? Only our Christian faith. Let me conclude by trying to tell you, as briefly and simply as I can, what this means to me. I speak as someone unlearned in theology and philosophy. The various dogmas of institutional Christianity—like, for instance, the doctrine of the Trinity, or of the Immaculate Conception—just do not impinge; I neither believe nor disbelieve them, and feel no inclination to defend or denounce them. I find them perfectly comprehensible, perfectly harmless, and—as far as I'm concerned—totally without significance. Nor does the historicity of the Gospels' account of Christ's birth, life, and death worry me at all. If, tomorrow, someone were to unearth another Dead Sea scroll proving that, in earthly terms, the traditional Christian story just didn't happen in that way at that time, it wouldn't disturb my attitude to Christianity at all. Legends, in any case, seem to me more relevant to our human situation, and in that sense more "factual," than history, which is really only the propaganda of the victor. Thus—by way of example—I find the Book of Genesis, considered as legend, infinitely more prescient on the subject of the origins and subsequent unfolding of our human story than, say, the theory of evolution, considered as fact.

I see Christianity as a very bright light, particularly bright now because the surrounding darkness is so deep and dense; a brightness that holds my gaze inexorably, so that even if I want to—and I do sometimes want to—I can't detach it. Christ said he was the light of the world, and told us to let our light shine before men. To partake of this light, to keep it in one's eye as the Evangelist told Bunyan's Pilgrim to do, is Heaven; to be cut off from it is Hell—two experiences as recallable and describable as was getting up this morning and driving to Oxford. Away from the light, one is imprisoned in the tiny, desolate dungeon of one's ego; when the light breaks in, suddenly one is liberated, reborn; the shining vistas of eternity open before one, with all mankind for brothers and sisters—a single family with a father in heaven, all, in the truest sense, equal, and deserving of one another's abiding love and consideration.

Words, just words! I can hear you saying. Well, yes, words; but there's something else—a man who was born and lived like us, whose presence and teaching have continued to shine for generation after generation, just as they did for his disciples and for all who knew and listened to him in Galilee all those centuries ago, a man who died, but who nonetheless, in some quite unique way, remained, and remains, alive; a man who offered us the mysterious prospect of dying in order to live, who turned all the world's values upside down, telling us that it was the weak, not the strong, who mattered, the simple, not the learned, who understood, the poor, not the rich, who were blessed; a man whose cross, on which he died in agony, became the symbol of the wildest, sweetest hopes ever to be entertained, and the inspiration of the noblest and most joyous lives ever to be lived.

And now? Well, all I can say is, as one aging and singularly unimportant fellow man, that I have conscientiously looked far and wide, inside and outside my own head and heart, and I have found nothing other than this man and his words which offers any answer to the dilemmas of this tragic, troubled time. If his light has gone out, then, as far as I am concerned, there is no light.

5. Men Like Gods

I want to speak to you today about what I regard as the one vital question of our time. This, put very simply, is: Is God in charge of our affairs, or are we? A great, and growing, body of opinion, some of it ecclesiastical, much of it in worldly terms powerful and influential, takes the view that *we* are now in charge. Whereas formerly it was considered man's highest aim to understand God's purpose for him, and his highest achievement to fulfil that purpose, now we are urged to dispense with God altogether and assume control ourselves of the world, the universe, and our own collective individual destiny. God, we are told—if he ever existed—has died; as a concept, he is not needed any more. We know enough now about our environment and circumstances, have sufficient control over them, to take over. Our apprenticeship is served; mankind has come of age, and the time has come for us to assume command of ourselves and our world in our own right.

Let me say at once that I regard this notion as nonsensical, and, if persisted in, as likely to have disastrous consequences. The image of man puffed up to imagine himself a god occurs frequently in legend and literature and history. Even in the Garden of Eden the serpent tells Eve that if she eats of the forbidden tree she and Adam *shall be as gods*. The Roman emperors in their folly insisted on being worshipped as deities; and in our own time a whole succession of squalid dictators have arisen claiming an authority beyond reason, and even beyond sense. Far from becoming gods, Eve's disobedience led to her and Adam's expulsion from the Garden of Eden—she in sorrow to bring forth children, he to till the ground from whence he was taken. The deified Roman emperors are remembered, if at all, not as deities but as figures of absurdity and fantasy in the pages of

Originally a sermon delivered at St. Aldate's Church, Oxford, (December 1, 1968). Reprinted from Malcolm Muggeridge, *Jesus Rediscovered* (Garden City, N.Y.: Doubleday, 1969), pp. 88–94.

Gibbon, and we have watched our contemporary dictators go one after the other to their unspeakable and ignominious ends. Was it not Icarus who thought to fly into the sky on his wings of wax and feathers, only to have them melt as he approached the sun, so that he fell like a plummet into the sea? Christ would not even allow the disciples to call him good, because *there is none good but one, that is, God*, and at Lystra, when the priests of Jupiter wanted to offer sacrifices to Paul and Barnabas, they rent their clothes and said: *Sirs, why do ye these things? We also are men of like passions with you, and preach unto you that ye should turn from these vanities unto the living God.*

None of these instances is likely to deflate the pretensions of a twentieth-century scientific mind, with its extraordinary blend of knowledge, dogmatic arrogance, and infantile credulity, though one may note with a certain pleasure that even so ardent an upholder of men like gods as Dr. Edmund Leach, has lately been voicing a certain anxiety about the human take-over. "Unless," he writes, "we teach those of the next generation that they can afford to be atheists only if they assume the moral responsibilities of God, the prospects for the human race are decidedly bleak." Bleak indeed!

Science has seemingly achieved so much: We can travel with the speed of light; we shall soon be visiting the moon and exploring the Milky Way. We can send our words, and even our smiles, flying through the air to be picked up ten thousand miles away; we can turn back rivers, plant our deserts, and abundantly and effortlessly satisfy every human requirement, from potato chips to skyscrapers, from face cream to giant computers. All this has happened in one lifetime. Is it surprising, then, that those who have brought it about should see themselves, not as mere mortal men, but as very gods? That they should take on the functions of a god, claiming the right to decide whose life is worth protracting and whose should be cut short, who is to be allowed to reproduce and who should be sterilized; reaching with their drugs and psychiatric techniques into the mind, the psyche, and shaping it to suit their purposes; re-sorting the genes, replacing worn-out, derelict organs with new ones freshly taken from living flesh, fancying, perhaps, that in the end even mortality will be abolished—as an old-vintage car can be kept on the road indefinitely by constantly putting in new sparking plugs, dynamos, carburetors, as the old ones wear out; even redefining the moment of death to suit their convenience so that we are to be considered dead when Dr. Christiaan Barnard says we are?

Is it not wonderful? And, of course, that is only a beginning. Writers like Aldous Huxley and George Orwell have imagined the sort of scientific utopia which is coming to pass, but already their nightmare fancies are hopelessly out of date. A vast, air-conditioned, neon-lighted, glass-and-chromium broiler house begins to take shape, in which geneticists select the best stocks to fertilize, and watch over the developing embryo to ensure that all possibilities of error and distortion are eliminated. Where is the need for God in such a setup? Or even for a moral law? When man is thus able to shape and control his environment and being, then surely he may be relied on to create his own earthly paradise and live happily ever after in it.

But can he? It's precisely here that the doubt arises. Let us take a quick, cool look at the world these men like gods have so far succeeded in bringing to pass. It's a world of violence and destruction unparalleled in human history. Who can estimate the lives that have been lost and uprooted in the ferocious conflicts of our time; the buildings, the treasures of art and learning which have been wantonly destroyed; the misery and privations, the degradation of standards of truth and humanity which have accompanied these upheavals? And what about our present situation? Is it worthy of men like gods—with one part of the world glutted and surfeited with an excess of everything they need, or can be persuaded to need, and the rest of the world getting hungrier and hungrier, more and more deprived of their basic necessities? With vast resources of wealth and research devoted to making ever more potent engines of destruction, while in Asia and Africa and Latin America what we call in our Orwellian Newspeak the underdeveloped peoples of the world lack the very minimal medical requirements and personnel? I could go on and on. I tell you in all seriousness that in my opinion posterity will find the utmost difficulty in believing that people belonging to a technologically developed civilisation like ours could possibly have tolerated such a situation in the world; still less that their affairs were in the hands of men like gods. Men like apes, they'll prefer to believe, and even that will seem rather hard on the apes.

Let's imagine some future historian looking back across thousands of years at us and our fantasies, follies, and credulities. What will he make of it all, I wonder, seeing us imprisoned in a fantasy of our own making; in a dream, like Caliban's, full of sounds and sweet airs, so that when we wake (if we ever do) we cry to sleep again. A dream presented in innumerable ways and guises: in the written and the spoken word, in sound and vision and color; above all, of course, on television, that mysterious image of ourselves, that gigantic exercise in narcissism, piped into our homes, first two-dimensional in black and white, then (as one of the American networks puts it) in "living color"—whatever that may mean. The grass, I should explain, is not green enough for television, nor, for that matter, is the blood red enough. They both need reinforcement. Greener than green, redder than red—a dream indeed. I noted down some words of Machiavelli which seemed to me very much to the point: "For the great majority of mankind are satisfied with appearances, as though they were realities, and are often more influenced by things that seem than by those that are." The same notion is expressed by Blake in one of those couplets of his so packed with meaning, so luminous, that you can go on contemplating them to the end of your life without ever exhausting their significance:

> They ever must believe a lie
> Who see with, not through, the eye.

He might have had television in mind; the camera is the most potent instrument for seeing *with* the eye that's ever been devised, and just think of the lies—the lies upon lies upon lies—that it's been able to induce belief in!

Looked back at across the centuries, it will all seem even more hilariously comical than it does today, though I imagine our historian being somewhat at a loss to understand what lay behind the plunge into sheer fantasy that his researches reveal. They can't really have believed, he'll say to himself, that this notion of Progress they bandied about meant anything; that happiness lay along motorways, and well-being in a rising Gross National Product; that birth pills, easy divorce, and abortion made for happy families, and sex and barbiturates for quiet nights. There must, he'll conclude, be some other explanation; a civilisation must have been possessed by a death wish which so assiduously and ingeniously sought its own extinction—physically, by devoting so much of its wealth, knowledge, and skills to creating the means to blow itself and all mankind to smithereens; economically, by developing a consumer economy whereby more and more wants have to be artificially created and stimulated in order to take up an endlessly expanding production; morally, by abolishing the moral order altogether and pursuing the will-o'-the-wisp of happiness through satiety; spiritually, by abolishing God himself and setting up man as the arbiter of his own destiny. A big laugh there for our historian, I should guess, as, looking back, he notes how our generation of men proved the least like gods, the least capable of coping with the complexities and dilemmas of their time, of any that ever existed on earth.

Am I then concerned to say that there is no possibility of deliverance from this world of fantasy that we have created? Is the endlessly repeated message of the media—that money and sex are the only pursuits in life, violence its only excitement, and success its only fulfilment—irresistible? Are the only available escape routes all cul-de-sacs? Not at all. There is a remarkable passage in Pasternak's *Doctor Zhivago* in which the hero reflects that in a Communist society freedom exists only in concentration camps—in other words, that the only way to be free is to be imprisoned. The same notion is to be found at the very heart of the Christian religion—that the only way to live is to die. There *is* a way of deliverance, after all, but it lies in the exactly opposite direction to the one so dazzlingly signposted by the media—out of the ego, not into it, heads lifted up from the trough instead of buried in it, the arc lights pale and ineffectual in the bright light of everlasting truth.

This is the way Bunyan's Pilgrim took from the Wicket Gate to Mount Sion, the way that opened up for St. Paul after the Damascus road. It is, of course, open to everyone at all times and in all circumstances. I think of St. Augustine watching from his diocese at Hippo in North Africa, first the fall of Rome (and, incidentally, there were plenty of enlightened people then to contend that Alaric was a fine fellow, and that hope lay in a dialogue with him) and then the barbarians moving towards Hippo itself. It looked like an end, but really, as we know, it was a beginning.

The way begins where for Christ himself its mortal part ended—at the Cross. There alone, with all our earthly defenses down and our earthly pretentions relinquished, we can confront the true circumstances of our being; there alone grasp the triviality of these seemingly so majestic achievements of ours, like going to the moon, unravelling our genes, fitting one another with each other's hearts, livers, and kidneys. There, contemplating God in the likeness of man, we may understand how foolish and inept is man when he sees himself in the likeness of God.

6. Am I a Christian?

The subject that has been chosen tonight is one that to me is of immense seriousness. Am I a Christian? I don't think it's merely of seriousness to me. I think that many people who might in their normal habits of thought and ways seem very remote from any connection with the Christian religion might well be putting that question and putting it sometimes with great disconcertment. Am I a Christian? It ought to be the easiest question in the world to answer. A Christian is a follower of Christ, and I'm quite sure that the early Christians, from whom it all began and in whose honour this edifice and millions of others like it were erected, would have had no difficulty whatever in answering that question. To them it was abundantly simple. They followed a man of whom they'd known or heard at first hand, and who told them that His Kingdom was not of this world; and therefore the problem to them was an infinitely simple one. They didn't feel bound to relate their thoughts and their conduct to the permissive morality of the Court of the Emperor Nero. That was something that had nothing whatever to do with them. They didn't feel bound to associate themselves or attach themselves to political causes; they belonged to another world. Their cause was their love and loyalty to this Man. Even Peter on that tragic occasion when the cock crew knew exactly what he had done—denied an allegiance, an allegiance which was terrifically simple and meaningful.

Now of course today the situation is different. Two thousand years have passed. Churches have come and gone, theologies have been discussed and drafted and abandoned and re-discussed. In this Church today a creed will have been recited; a creed to which I myself could assent to barely one single proposition in honesty, and I still think and feel sufficiently a Protestant

Originally a sermon delivered at Great St. Mary's Church, Cambridge (May 7, 1967). Reprinted from Malcolm Muggeridge, *Vintage Muggeridge* (Grand Rapids, Mich.: Eerdmans, 1985), pp. 7–15.

to believe that the worst thing that any man can do is to say he believes something which in fact he doesn't. You will gather from this how utterly unfitted I would have been to be ordained in the Anglican or any other church. Yet there remains—and this, to me, is the extraordinary part about it—a sheer enchantment in the Christian religion; in the personality around which it is built, and in the Gospels and the Apostles from which it has been derived—an enchantment which has miraculously (one can only use that word) survived through the centuries. What other document is there extant which can still be read and have this unbelievable enchantment about it? There is, in this story, in this Man, some incredible living message which one still senses, and then one tries to relate that message to the edifice of institutional religion, whatever it may be, and somehow the two don't connect.

I spent three weeks recently in a Cistercian Abbey for the banal purpose of making a film about an enclosed order. But, of course, one did live there; one did get some idea, a feel of what this way of life amounted to. One of the occasions which sticks in my mind as illustrating what I mean about the extraordinary enchantment of the Christian faith, was talking to a lay brother; one of those men that you rarely meet in younger generations who combined an utterly simple and certain faith with an enormously practical and sagacious and amusing disposition. He was in charge of the farming; the monks farmed about a thousand acres. It was the lambing season, and he was very, very keen on these lambs. He was sitting, talking and looking lovingly at them, and suddenly I grasped the phrase 'Agnus Dei' which I had heard in the chapel in the morning—'the Lamb of God'. And I thought: surely this was perhaps the most extraordinary moment of all in human history, when men for the first time saw their God in the likeness of a lamb, instead of, as heretofore, in the image of power or wealth or sensuality or beauty; God was presented to them in the form of a lamb. And I told this to Brother Oliver, and somehow, in a way that I can't fully explain to you, I understood what was meant by the Incarnation; somehow this basic doctrine took on life as Brother Oliver and I contemplated together the sheer stupendousness historically of this moment.

Now I could go through the story and illustrate again and again this enchantment; this drama which pulls one up. I could relate it to the Crucifixion; itself another fantastic moment, when the sick joke of some Roman soldiers that led them to write a ribald legend above a dying man's head, 'King of the Jews', and to dress him up in a purple robe and put a crown of thorns on his head—that sick joke abolished for ever the validity of earthly authority. It was a most stupendous thing to happen and it lives on in the Cross, in this symbol of the Christian religion which has been spread to every corner of our world.

Similarly with the miracles. I was thinking about the miracle of the feeding of the five thousand, and suddenly I realised this: there was this Man preaching, this extraordinary Man, and there these people had collected to listen, and some of them had brought refreshments—you know how people do—and felt rather superior because they had something to eat, and thought how they'd bring their packages out and munch them. And then the words that this extraordinary Man was saying made it totally impossible for them to do that. They couldn't eat the food they had brought with that man speaking, and so they passed it round to be shared with all the others. Of course that might not be true, but if it were, it would be so much the more miraculous, because in point of fact a man whose words overcame the terrible imprisonment in our egos and greed which make life for us personally, and for the human race, such hell, would be performing an almost inconceivable miracle![1]

Then I was enormously interested in the temptations in the wilderness. The first of them was the temptation to turn stones into bread. Now that would be a terrific temptation to Oxfam and all the different charitable organisations, and to all the different political parties and institutions dedicated to improving human conditions. What a monstrous thing to refuse to turn stones into bread, if it were true that what's the matter with us is that we haven't got enough bread. But if what's the matter with us is that we don't understand, then how infinitely wise to resist the temptation! Again, the miracle of jumping off a building and not being hurt is almost like space travel; the same sort of thing as the so-called wonders of science. Why not do that and dazzle mankind, so that they fall down and worship? But that too was a temptation to be resisted, because, after all, the wonders of science are not so very wonderful, and only deserve worship if the infinitely more wonderful wonders of God—which include and transcend them—are overlooked. Finally, the most important of all, the temptation to take over the kingdoms of the earth.

[1] Muggeridge's interpretation of this miracle is in contrast with the traditional faith of the Church, which accepts the story at face value and believes Christ himself multiplied the loaves. Cf. the *Catechism of the Catholic Church*, nos. 107, 126, 548, and 1335.

This is what all good progressive people are always trying to do—to take over the governments and make them good. What a monstrous thing from the point of view of, say, Canon Collins, to refuse to accept the government of the world! But, you see, at the same time, what an alluring and enchanting thing to do, because how awful it would be if it were really possible to make human life acceptable by simply making governments good! And how absolutely essential it was to demonstrate that merely having righteous government doesn't in itself, constitute living righteously.

I've said enough to show what I mean, I hope, about the incredible and inexhaustible enchantment of this religion. Now there is the question I have to go on to if I am to ask myself, Am I a Christian? How is it that something so enchanting, something that seems to fit so perfectly into the situation in which human beings find themselves, should have become, on the one hand, a collection of remote and, to me, incomprehensible and unbelievable theological propositions, and, on the other, a sort of package of progressive and humane and enlightened sentiments which I call sometimes, when I find myself on the BBC's Meeting Point programme, 'soper opera'. As far as the theological propositions are concerned, it's not really for me to speak. I don't understand them, I don't see their importance, they mean absolutely nothing to me. It may be, of course, that, for instance, a concept like the Trinity is tremendously important, but anyway not to me, and I have just to put that aside. But the question of the Kingdom of Heaven on earth and the Kingdom of Heaven in Heaven does seem to me an absolutely crucial one. The appeal of Christianity, as I understand it, is that it offers man something beyond this world. It says to him that he must die in order to live, an extraordinary proposition to put before him. It tells him that he can never create peace or happiness for himself merely by perfecting his circumstances on this earth. It presents him, in other words, as a creature who intrinsically requires salvation. Now it would seem to me that the churches and those who present the Christian religion to us have moved entirely away from this attitude, and increasingly tell us that it is possible to make terms with this world.

Take one of my favourite characters, Bunyan's hero in *The Pilgrim's Progress* which is a superb image of human life. He is hurrying on through his mortal life. If you'd said to Bunyan, "But surely your Pilgrim ought to stop in Vanity Fair and ensure that it's turned into a co-operative enterprise, or that 'one man one vote' is introduced there before he hurries on," Bunyan would surely have thought that you'd taken leave of your senses. The essence of his Pilgrim is that he is pushing on. I would suggest to you that Western Man has for the last hundred and fifty years lived through a period of utopianism, collective utopianism; that, from the time of Darwin particularly, he has believed that it's possible to construct for himself a Kingdom of Heaven on earth. When I was young, we believed that that Kingdom of Heaven on earth had been constructed in the USSR. There are those good earnest people who believed that that Kingdom of Heaven on earth could be constructed by means of a Welfare State through the Labour Party. (I would hope and believe that the present Prime Minister has effectively put paid to [ended] those hopes!) The people who crossed the Atlantic to America went with the idea that they were going to find a Kingdom of Heaven on earth in America.

Now what has happened, it seems to me, is that these utopian hopes—and it was perfectly human that they should have been entertained—have been completely demolished, and we are confronted with a sort of emptiness. The very material success of our world adds to that effect. We have everything that we want materially, and it ought to make us happy, but for some reason it doesn't. It should be the case that the places where all these material things are most available, and where the pursuit of happiness (that absurd and ironical phrase) is most ardently undertaken, should also be the places where human beings are most happy and most purposive and most zealous in their lives; and in fact it's not so. Something has gone wrong. It hasn't worked. The idea that human beings can achieve fulfilment on earth by satisfying their fleshly appetites and their egotistic impulses has simply not worked, and where it's most possible to satisfy them is precisely where it's worked least. This situation is of course enormously intensified by virtue of the fact that, at the same time, we have created like a Frankenstein monster an enormous apparatus of persuasion such as has never before been known on earth.

Now I've spent the last forty years working in this apparatus, and I know exactly how it works. I know the people who operate it and the aims it pursues; and what is the effect? The effect of it is simply this, that it says to those whom it influences—and its power is fantastic—it says to them in effect, 'Satisfy your greed, satisfy your sensuality, that is the purpose of life.' You have a situation which is so fantastic that it would be difficult to believe in it if one didn't know it existed, and which posterity will certainly find difficulty in believing in, if there is any posterity. You have in a small area of the world an economic system which only works in so far as it constantly increases its gross national product. This is our golden calf, and year by year it must get bigger. In order that its getting bigger shouldn't create chaos, people must constantly consume more and want more, so that we must dedicate some of our most brilliant talents and a huge proportion of our wealth to making them want what they don't want. It's the most extraordinary state of affairs. At the same time, while this is going on in one part of the world, in another part of the world people are getting poorer and poorer and hungrier and hungrier.

When I was in Detroit, Mr. Reuther said to me that every year they must sell nine million new automobiles in the United States or the place goes bust. Imagine it, you must persuade nine million people to want a new automobile in order to survive. This is a completely crazy situation, and the sense of its craziness is precisely what is creating in human beings so tremendous a spiritual hunger. They know that it's not true that if you satisfy all people's material and physical wants you will make them serene and happy. They know that it's not working out, and so this produces in them a sense of total lostness and bewilderment. It seems to me absolutely clear that either they must recover a sense of what those early Christians had when they too found themselves in a world which was running into destruction and ruin, or the process goes on and produces catastrophe.

It's a perfectly simple choice, and the problem before us is how to present this Christian answer in such a way that people see how apposite it is. I don't know how that can be done. I see a world which is sailing under completely false colours, whose fantastic technological achievements have produced for it both plenty such as has never been known before and means of destruction such as has never been known before and boredom such as has never been known before. The only conceivable alternative to this materialist view of life is in some form or another the Christian view, but, as I have tried to indicate, this Christian view itself in the course of its presentation has got hopelessly caught up with the other.

Now what can one do? What can an individual do, faced with such a situation? I have one hero, a man called Paulinus who was born in the fourth century, and who came to realise that his civilisation was crashing to destruction. He decided that the only thing he could do was to keep alight a lamp in a particular shrine, and that's what he decided to do. It seems to me that that's all one can do, and that, in answer to this fantastic materialist view of life with this fantastic machine of persuasion behind it, the lamp should say to people that the opposite is true, that as the Christian religion taught originally, so it remains true that men can't live by bread alone, that men have to die in the flesh to be reborn in the Spirit, that men are not creatures of production whose existence can be measured by what they can produce or by what they can learn, but a family with a father in Heaven, and that the relationship between men is the relationship of brothers, and that each of them, in that he is loved by the father, must be in all senses the equal of every other, however he might differ in capacity or intelligence or beauty or anything else. All these things the lamp would say.

It might be just a forlorn enterprise; it might be that a materialist view of life will work out; that with the birth pill and nuclear weapons and the possibility of the gross national product endlessly increasing and of people endlessly able to satisfy all their desires, a sort of happiness could be produced. If it were so, it would seem to me the most pessimistic and terrible conclusion that could possibly be reached. And if it's not so, then my lamp, like Paulinus's, would continue to shine when a darkness had fallen and a darkness which would be even deeper if it were to be associated, as it might be, with increasing technological development and efficiency. Such is the conclusion to which I've come, and whether it involves being a Christian or not I still don't know. It seems to me absolutely clear that there is only one answer to the deepening dilemma of contemporary materialism and that is essentially the answer set forth in the Christian religion namely, that men can never become natives of this earth, and that if they ever succeeded in so doing, then only would the light of divinity be finally put out in them.

PART THREE

INTERVIEWS

1. How Does One Find Faith?

MR. BUCKLEY: I propose on this occasion with Malcolm Muggeridge to do something a little unusual. We will devote the hour to exploring the phenomenon, if that is the right word for it, of religious faith. The conversation will be exploratory in nature and probably not adversary, and with very good reason it will focus much more heavily on the views and meditations of Malcolm Muggeridge than on my own. There is every reason for this decision, most prominently the superior wit, learning and experience of Mr. Muggeridge; but it is also true that in recent years he has emerged as perhaps the most eloquent English-speaking lay apostle of Christianity, and this he accomplished by encountering faith. When he turned against the Devil, the Devil was outnumbered.

In order to impose a little structure on the hour, I shall first be asking Mr. Muggeridge to give us an idea of how he came himself to God. After which, I propose that we examine the major sources of difficulty experienced by others who have not found faith, either because they reject it or because they are indifferent to it.

I suppose it is appropriate to add that we are taping this hour in the private workroom of Malcolm Muggeridge at his home deep in Sussex, sixty miles from London, where he and his wife have lived for the past twenty-five years, after as hectic a life abroad as that lived by any man of letters. He is currently at work on the third volume of his autobiography and co-operating in the production of an eight-hour series of television on his professional life.

To set out then, Mr. Muggeridge, tell us what it was that happened to you?

MR. MUGGERIDGE: This sounds a very simple question, but actually it's a very difficult question to answer. Of course, my evangelical friends are always rather disappointed that I can't produce a sort of Damascus road experience—you know, that I was such a person and then

An interview with William F. Buckley Jr., *Firing Line* television show (1978). Reprinted from Malcolm Muggeridge, *Vintage Muggeridge* (Grand Rapids, Mich.: Eerdmans, 1985), pp. 109–36.

suddenly this happened, and I was such another person. But I can't. That isn't something that happened to me. This has been for me the unfolding of an enlightenment which is full of doubt as well as certainty. I rather believe in doubting. It's sometimes thought that it's the antithesis of faith, but I think it's connected with faith—something that actually St. Augustine said—like, you know, reinforced concrete and you have those strips of metal in the concrete which make it stronger.

Mr. B: Well, is doubt the dialectical partner of faith?

Mr. M: I would say so.

Mr. B: That it forces continuous re-examination, which is why it is assumed that all the saints—or is it?—doubted.

Mr. M: If it's not assumed, it's certainly true that they did; and I would agree absolutely with that. The only people I've met in this world who never doubt are materialists and atheists.

Mr. B: But the doubts that they express are hardly theological.

Mr. M: I think that they have a sort of ludicrous certainty that there is nothing transcendental to know, you see, but for me, at any rate, doubt has been an integral part of coming to have faith; nor has there been as I've said, any dramatic moment, any time when there it was, like has happened, for instance, to Pascal—people like that—or to Augustine. It's a process which I am quite sure will certainly continue until I depart from this life, which I shall fairly soon, and which maybe goes on into the next life for all I know, but an integral part of belief is to doubt. Now, why did this longing for faith assail me? Insofar as I can point to anything it is to do with this profession which both you and I followed of observing what's going on in the world and attempting to report and comment thereon, because that particular occupation gives one a very heightened sense of the sheer fantasy of human affairs—the sheer fantasy of power, and of the structures that men construct out of power—and therefore gives one an intense, overwhelming longing to be in contact with reality. And so you look for reality and you try this and you try that, and ultimately you arrive at the conclusion—great over-simplification—that really is a mystery. The heart of reality is a mystery.

Mr. B: Even if that were so, why should that mystery lead you to Christian belief?

Mr. M: Because it leads you to God. The mystery—and I think the best expression for it I've ever read is in a book I'm very fond of and I'm sure you know, called *The Cloud of Unknowing*; and it's when you are aware of the cloud of unknowing that you begin to know, and what you know—to simplify and put it very simply, is God. That's the beginning of faith for me.

Mr. B: But that informal Christianity requires grace, but you seem to have described a purely deductive process.

Mr. M: The deductive process is the means, but faith is the motive force that takes you there.

Mr. B: In other words, if as an observer you cease to observe, then you don't have that motive force that grace contributes?

Mr. M: Absolutely right. That is the grace. It's exactly like falling in love. You see another human being and for some extraordinary reason you're in a state of joy and ecstasy over that person, but the driving force which enables you to express that and to bring it into your life is love. Without love, it's nothing; it passes. It's the same with seeking reality, and there the driving force we call faith. It's a very difficult thing to define, actually.

Mr. B: Well, why is it that scientists who devote themselves at least as avidly professionally as journalists to seeking out the truth, so many of them don't stumble on this mystery?

Mr. M: The greatest ones do, incidentally: Einstein, Whitehead, people like that. The very highest names in science do stumble on it and for precisely the same reason because the knowledge that they have through their researches is so limited, so fragile, and so inadequate that they, too, are forced to find some absolute.

Mr. B: Now, the use of the word "mystery" has been much disdained by sceptics as a too easy way to account for some of the hideous anomalous tortures of history: The Holocaust, to take something on a macrocosmic scale; the six-year old girl who dies of leukemia at another scale. Isn't it probably the case that such anomalies as these do more to encourage scepticism than anything in the divine order?

Mr. M: I don't think they encourage scepticism. On the contrary, I would say that they encourage credulity as a matter of fact. What they do is they present a dilemma to which reason provides no answer.

Mr. B: Yes.

Mr. M: And you can only find the answer through what is called mysticism, or indeed through what Blake called the Imagination, which is art.

Mr. B: Now, what did Blake mean by Imagination?

Mr. M: He meant, putting it in one of my favourite sayings of his when he says—because it's so like this very medium we're working in now—he says, "They ever must believe a lie who see with not thro' the eye." He meant by Imagination seeing through the eye—seeing into this meaning of things rather than seeing things.

Mr. B: How would Blake have seen through to such a phenomenon as I mentioned—the death of a six-year old child?

Mr. M: Because he would see in it—there are some lines of his which I can't quote exactly from memory, but: "Joy and woe wove fine clothing for the soul divine." In other words, suffering, affliction, disappointment, failure—all these things—are an integral part of the drama of our human existence, and without them there'd be no drama. Let me tell you what will be a simple parable which I've often thought of. Some very humane, rather simple-minded old lady sees the play King Lear performed, and she is outraged that a poor old man should be humiliated, so made to suffer; and in the eternal shade she meets Shakespeare, and she says to him, "What a monstrous thing to make that poor old man go through all that," and Shakespeare says, "Yes, I quite agree. It was very painful, and I could have arranged for him to take a sedative at the end of Act I, but then, ma'am, there would have been no play."

Mr. B: Well—

Mr. M: See my point?

Mr. B: Yes, I see your point. On the other hand, I'm not sure that King Lear wouldn't have preferred that there should not have been a play than that he should have lived through Acts II and III.

Mr. M: But then he would have been a cowardly man and, of course, he did in fact have to go through that suffering in order to understand why there had to be a play: and of course, in that marvellous speech of his—one of my favourite things in all Shakespeare—when he, to Cordelia says, "We two will go to prison,"—you know—"and take upon's the mystery of things." It's a beautiful phrase, isn't it? It expresses exactly what I mean. This affliction has to be, and that is of course why one is drawn irresistibly as a Western European to the Christian faith and to Christ, because this is the central point: the cross. There's another parable I've often thought of. When St. Paul starts off on his journeys, he consults with an eminent public relations man: "I've got this campaign and I want to promote the gospel." And the man would say, "Well, you've got to have some sort of symbol. You've got to have an image. You've got to have some sign of your faith." And then Paul would say, "Well, I have got one. I've got this cross." The public relations man laughed his head off: "You can't popularise a thing like that. It's absolutely mad!" But it wasn't mad. It worked for centuries and centuries, bringing out all the creativity in people, all the love and disinterestedness in people, this symbol of suffering; and I think that's the heart of the thing. Of course, it's what has been lost and why the faith is languishing; because it cannot take in that truth that we can learn nothing: and you know, as an old man, Bill, looking back on one's life, it's one of the things that strikes you most forcibly—that the only thing that's taught one anything is suffering, not success, not happiness, not anything like that. The only thing that really teaches one what life's about—the joy of understanding, the joy of coming in contact with what it really signifies—is suffering, is affliction.

Mr. B: Well, you may recall the closing passages in The Life of St. Francis, *in which Chesterton remarks that whatever tortures he suffered as his life came to an end from whatever cause, one thing only one could know is that it was a happy man dying. Now the paradox—and I've witnessed it twice, people suffering agonies but who were spiritually serene—is: it may be easier for people who suffer through experience than for people who see them suffering.*

Mr. M: Certainly. I'm sure it is. I think because, first of all, there is an element you could almost call decency in us which says, "Well, I haven't had to suffer that myself and therefore it ill behoves me to point to it as a blessing."

Mr. B: Yes.

Mr. M: But of course, that would eliminate this idea of the cross, which was for everyone. Actually, in every time and in every age, this is demonstrated to us, and I think in our time it's been marvellously demonstrated by Solzhenitsyn and the other heroic people from the Soviet labour camps, all of whom say the same thing—the ones that have achieved spiritual perception through it—that there they learned this point, that it's through the affliction that you can see reality and that, therefore, as Solzhenitsyn himself says in his Gulag book, "Thank you, prison camp, for bringing this illumination into my life which otherwise I would have lost."

Mr. B: Well, a reductionism of that point, however, you wouldn't applaud, namely that Stalin was God's prophet.

Mr. M: No, but he might be God's instrument. In fact, he was, because in history it's impossible for anybody to function except as God's instrument because history is the scenario that God's written and the parts—all the parts—are necessary, just as the part of Judas was necessary for the Incarnation.

Mr. B: If one indulges in that kind of predetermination, one strips that drama of spontaneity that, for instance, was shown by King Lear, doesn't one?

Mr. M: But the thing is, it's not—

Mr. B: How do you handle that paradox?

Mr. M: It's freedom within the context of God's will, which is God's drama, and therefore anything that happens to us is in some degree God's will. We are participating in the unfolding of God's will. Supposing it's true, for instance, at this moment—which I think it probably is—that what we call Western Civilisation is guttering out to collapse. If you take that in purely human historical terms, this is an unmitigated catastrophe. You and I must beat our breasts and say that we lived to see the end of everything.

Mr. B: But not quite the end of everything, because the gates of hell will not prevail against—

Mr. M: Right, but also, historically speaking, what we love is coming to an end.

Mr. B: Christendom.

Mr. M: Christendom finished.

Mr. B: It probably has finished.

Mr. M: I think so. Why, certainly. But the point is, that is a catastrophe of God's purposes. I tell you, a thing I often think of as I beat my breast over what's going on in the world is St. Augustine receiving the news in Carthage that Rome had been sacked. Well, I mean, that's an appalling thing. He was a very civilised Roman, and it was a dreadful thing that the barbarians should have come in there and have burned the place down.

Mr. B: And he had been there for ten years.

Mr. M: Absolutely. Now, what did he say to his flock? He said, "This is grievous news, but let us remember if it's happened, then God has willed it; that men build cities and men destroy cities, that there's also the City of God, and that's where we belong." To me, that's the perfect expression, and I think—

Mr. B: Well, he said that's where we belong, but this is what we will never achieve.

Mr. M: Right, but it's insofar as we're citizens of the City of God that we can be Christian in the City of Man.

Mr. B: We can bear it.

Mr. M: We can bear it.

Mr. B: All right now, but this is in no sense a counsel of submissiveness, is it?

Mr. M: Not at all. Not at all.

Mr. B: All right, how do you distinguish between the mandate that says acknowledge all adversity with a spirit of compliance and that counsel which says you are meant to struggle for your own livelihood, for your own principles, for your own country, for your own family?

Mr. M: Well, again you see, I think—and this is another great part of the realisation of reality in transcendental terms—that both those things are true, just as our Lord said to the people who were questioning him—cunningly, he said, "Yes, we owe things to Caesar, and we owe things to God." We are living in our time and it is our duty to acquit ourselves in the context of that time as truthfully, nobly, lovingly as we can.

Mr. B: Well, how does Caesar feature, for instance, in the struggle of the individual against physical adversity? You have, on previous occasions, spoken of the requirement—the ethical and religious requirement—that one struggle to live as long as one can. Your war against euthanasia is the extreme example of this. How does Caesar figure here in that struggle against submissiveness?

Mr. M: It simply means that you are not in a position—you're not competent—to decide that your own life should come to an end or that other lives should come to an end, that you must be engaged on the side of life and the sacredness of life in its earthly version—in its earthly terms—as you are a citizen of the earthly city. But, of course, your eyes are cast and, as you get to the end of your life more and more cast, in the direction of the City of God.

There are the two things, you see. I think one of the terrible difficulties we have in discussing these matters is this; that rooted in our minds is what Kierkegaard calls the either/or proposition. I mean, either we have free will or it is determination. This is not so. We have got free will, and not a sparrow can fall to the ground without God's will—or God willing it.

Mr. B: There's a complementarity somewhere?

Mr. M: Absolutely, and that is essential to know, and the scientific idea of either/or is a very disastrous proposition.

Mr. B: Now wait a minute. You're not denying the principle of contradiction, are you?

Mr. M: No.

Mr. B: You cannot be and not be at the same time.

Mr. M: But you can be, as the Incarnation showed—God can exist as a man and a man can be God. Why the terrific power of that drama, why it sheds such a light on the things we're talking about—that Christian drama—is precisely because it exemplified that. Jesus had to suffer. Otherwise, what's the cross? There's no sacrifice. At the same time, he had to be God because he was perfect.

Mr. B: "Christ without the crucifixion is liberalism," said Whittaker Chambers.

Mr. M: Yes, it's very good, that.

Mr. B: Well, these false disjunctions are probably the principal blocks, are they not, to a more universal acceptance of God?

Mr. M: They are, but we can't elucidate them in terms that the twentieth century wants.

Mr. B: No, because the vocabulary is wanting, isn't it?

Mr. M: Absolutely.

Mr. B: It requires either a vocabulary so sophisticated as to be elusive except to the very few, or intuition, which is why the Russian illiterate kulak in Gulag understands, right?

Mr. M: Yes, this is true, but at the same time, if you take the case of Pascal—it always interests me very much—who was the greatest mind of his time and leading scientist of his time, it was through his science and through his intellect that he arrived at the conclusion that the mind itself was sort of a cul-de-sac, and that he could only fulfil his life and grasp what it was about and relate himself to its true reality through faith. And that is the point. That's a marvellous definition of faith, you know, in the Epistle to the Hebrews, where it says, "Faith is the substance of things hoped for and the evidence of things not seen." In other words, it gives a shape to this marvellous hope that grows in us.

Mr. B: Why wouldn't it also if it were illusory?

Mr. M: If it were illusory? Well, I mean, yes, it could be so, but then we have to assume that with grace we can distinguish between illusory things and real things, that the mystery comprehends both.

Mr. B: Your approach to God and to Christianity is through—to use a paradoxical term—the understanding of mystery, and yet—

Mr. M: The acceptance of a mystery, Bill, is the way—

Mr. B: Acceptance of the mystery.

Mr. M: I don't understand it, because nobody ever will by its very nature.

Mr. B: That's why I said paradoxical.

Mr. M: Yes, but still, it is the acceptance of it. I bow my head in humility, I hope, and would wish to do and to say, "Thy will be done," meaning I accept totally the mystery of these circumstances.

Mr. B: How, then, do you handle—or do you bother—the Thomistic argument that the existence of God can be proved by a series of formal, logical propositions?

Mr. M: It has no interest to me.

Mr. B: No interest to you.

Mr. M: Not at all.

Mr. B: In other words, you wouldn't even bother to acquaint yourself with those propositions?

Mr. M: I might, as a mental exercise, amuse myself with it, but the one thing that I'm quite sure could never happen is that human reason could prove a transcendental truth. It can be compatible, as Newman showed again and again; it can be compatible with a transcendental truth.

Mr. B: There again, if you're using the word rigorously, "transcendental" is above reason.

Mr. M: Absolutely.

Mr. B: But on this programme a few months ago in an hour that was widely noticed, Mortimer Adler spoke his thesis, at the end of which he concluded that the existence of God was proven by ontological reasoning, and he did so by a very elaborate and active intellectual virtuosity which was rather arresting. However, he declined to go on so far as to say that it proved anything at all about the attributes of God. These, he said, were perhaps deducible by other means—revelation, for instance—so that he is prepared to say that the intelligent man must believe in God, but he need not expect to know what it is that is part of God's design. For instance, he need not affirm human immortality. This is, however, central to your belief, isn't it?

Mr. M: Again, you see—I have nothing but respect for Mortimer Adler, and I think that he should exercise his wits in the direction of God is much better than that he should exercise them in the direction of nuclear fission or something like that. That's all so, but at the same time, what appeals to me much more is the attitude of the founder of the Christian religion who said that, of course, it was children—it was simple people—who would understand what he was saying, and that when he was confronted with someone like Nicodemus, who was a sort of Adler—

Mr. B: He who seeth not and yet believes.

Mr. M: That appeals to me more, but I wouldn't for one moment detract from any effort that any human being should make in any capacity to reach out to this reality which is unattainable.

Mr. B: Well: you've studied and written about people who have searched after that reality, many of them using different modalities: Blake, Pascal, Bonhoeffer. . . .

Now let me ask you this, which is a question at the root of much current Christian concern: how far may a society go to defend itself against barbarians? In terms of formal instruction, the Catholics recall a statement made by Pope Pius XII—I think the year was 1948—in which he said, "Certain things are so valuable"—by which he meant, of course, divine institutions: the family, the church—"that they can rightly be fought for through the use of all one's resources." It was widely interpreted as baptising the use of nuclear fission for defence, and indeed during the past twenty to twenty-five years there seems to be a bifurcation: those Christians who say, "In no circumstances ought there to be a nuclear defence," and others who say, "Yes, because to treasure biological life so fiercely that one cares not at all about the circumstances within which it is lived is the ultimate profanation—not Nagasaki." Have you thought your own way through to that conclusion in these terms?

Mr. M: I, like anybody else at this age, have thought much about it, and to me, I go back again to this saying of our Lord that we have duties to Caesar and duties to God. Our duties to Caesar require us, as for instance in 1939, to deal with a worldly situation that has arisen and risk our lives and—

Mr. B: Suppose one were to say, "I'm not willing to do it for Caesar. For Caesar I'm not willing to be the man in the bomber that presses the fateful button and eliminates the town of Leningrad but I am willing to do it for my family or for the survival of the Christian idea."

Mr. M: Bill, each man has to work this formula out for himself.

Mr. B: But have you worked it out?

Mr. M: Insofar as it's possible for me to do so, yes.

Mr. B: And you would understand yourself to be working for Caesar as you did when you fought in the second World War?

Mr. M: I would say there are circumstances in which I recognise my duty to Caesar. I admit to you that romantically—I've often longed for it—I would have loved to have been a monk, because if you're a monk, what you owe to Caesar is minimal—you have no family, you have no home, you have no possessions, all these things that involve us in Caesar's world. But we can't kid ourselves. If we have those things, we are involved. We have to weigh up the situation that arises and ask ourselves, "Does my duty to Caesar require me to do this?" In 1939 I had no doubt whatever that it did, and that duty to Caesar has to be fulfiled in all circumstances. It's quite useless to say that I can do my duty to Caesar with a crossbow, but I can't do my duty to Caesar with a nuclear bomb, because you're exerting power—force—in order to maintain an earthly position. But there is also duty to God; and the duty to God offers its own responsibilities; and we are left to decide for ourselves where those two duties lie: what we owe to Caesar; what we owe to God.

Mr. B: Well, "We are left to ourselves to decide," is a little atomistic, isn't it? Are you now anticipating a statement which you might make later that you recognise no teaching authority in Christianity?

Mr. M: I wouldn't say that I recognise no teaching authority at all. I think that particularly the historical Church with certain things that it has laid down—like its opposition to usury, its present opposition to birth control and so on—these things serve the greatest importance. But what I'm saying is this: that the Christian of modern times believes that a table of conduct can be derived, and you say, "This is the Christian programme. Vote for it. I'm in favour/I'm not in favour." There's no such thing. This life we have to live between the earthly city and the City of God, between time and eternity, between ourselves and our Creator; and we have to deal with the circumstances that arise in our individual life and in our collective lives on that basis.

Mr. B: Well, I think most people grant that: that, for instance, there isn't a Christian means of organising a society. There are Christian socialists, there are Christian individualists and so on. Where the duty of informed Christianity becomes relevant is primarily in the act of exclusion. Certain things you can't do, right? You can't kill people because you don't like the colour of their skin or their religious beliefs.

Mr. M: In certain circumstances, though, you are required to kill them.

Mr. B: Under certain circumstances you're required to kill them, but those circumstances are rather rigidly specified.

Mr. M: Even that requires a decision in the light of—for a Christian—in the light of his faith. I personally happen to believe that there are circumstances in which capital punishment is perfectly legitimate and desirable.

Mr. B: Well, join the Bible.

Mr. M: Yes. But that, again—I'm equally prepared to accept that a very devout Christian might reach a different conclusion.

Mr. B: Sure.

Mr. M: And I don't believe that there's a rule of thumb that you can say, "My dear fellow, you're not being a Christian because you believe in capital punishment," or that, "You're not being a Christian because you don't." In other words, we are required in our existence here to work this out, to relate ourselves—We're in the extraordinary position that our Lord was in as incarnate God. We are living in time. We belong to eternity.

Mr. B: So therefore the obligation of the Christian is simply to search out his conscience as rigorously as he can and make the decision that he deems appropriate.

Mr. M: That's right. It is to keep our eyes fixed—and that is what, as far as I know, all the mystics and saints have said, and many a theist says today, just as clearly. We have to find God, and keep our eyes fixed on Him.

Mr. B: Okay. Now, let me ask you this: there are few people more experienced than you in many fields—in literature and journalism and so on. What have you found to be the principal obstacle to a conscious search for spirituality? It seems to me that you see a world in which people reading books, seeing plays—whether current plays or plays written five hundred years ago—recognise the dimension of spirituality. They know that it's true. They know that it's extremely important. And yet they resist any search for it. They think it's unmodish, they think it's anachronised, and certainly they aren't willing to talk about it. It strikes me as odd in the same way that it would be odd if people knew about the existence of sex, but for some reason never exerted themselves in such a way as to stimulate that appetite.

Mr. M: Well, I see exactly what you're asking, and one can only speak of one's own personal life here. If there's one statement in the whole of the New Testament that rings true in the light of my own experience, it is that to be carnally minded is death, and to be spiritually minded is life and peace; and therefore, one of the agonies of living has been the eternal effort on the part of the collectivity in which I live—

Mr. B: To mortify the flesh.

Mr. M: (laughing) Yes. You see, that's one thing. Then, of course, even more basic is this ego which we have built into us and the overcoming of which is really the essence of life. I mean, it is to the degree to which you overcome it—the degree to which you eliminate this eternal dragging of every thought and inspiration you have to the core of your ego—that you could be said to live spiritually. So pride, carnality, egotism, cupidity—in fact, you know, it's a funny thing when you sit down to think this out, you arrive at, sort of, the case of our old friends, the seven deadly sins.

Mr. B: Well, I know, but those are temptations. What I don't understand is this: I can imagine a swinging dinner party—by which I mean one at which the participants are intellectually curious, culturally diverse—in which you can bring up, let's say, an invention—some scientific discovery announced in that morning's paper having to do with splitting genes—or you can discuss the politics of Pakistan or you can discuss the latest play or the latest fashion or you can be curious about what it is that goes into the process of senility; you can talk about the pleasures that are taken from almost anything except the discovery of God. And I really, honestly don't understand, but I think you would agree it's true, that if you were in the middle of a dinner, to say, "I'd like to tell you about somebody who was dying from cancer and in the course of his racking torture, he picked up the Bible, and in the course of several days he discovered something that transported him into serene circumstances," I think conversation would stop, and people would think, "Oh God, St. Mugg has spoken up again. Let's not invite him next time around."

Mr. M: Well, let me answer this with the utmost candour that there have been times when, in such circumstances, I have felt that I ought to speak about God and I haven't. Right, but on the other hand, there have been circumstances I'm happy to say where I have and it's never failed to work. That's what's so extraordinary.

Mr. B: Yes, but usually—and I've observed you—usually when you do it, it's when you are addressing a thousand people or two hundred people or five thousand people and they have to submit to your oratorical architecture because they have no alternative, and you can then make it work. But although you can, as I say, do it in formal circumstances in informal circumstances you have not regularly done it.

Mr. M: Well I have. I have.

Mr. B: Well, you have because you have developed a certain audacity in this respect.

Mr. M: Yes, but I soon discovered that, far from being a kind of deflating social occasion such as you mentioned—sitting around a dinner table—the strange thing is that in ninety-nine cases out of a hundred it's an enormous stimulant.

Mr. B: I don't doubt your figure, because you've obviously experimented, but I have never experimented with it. I've been to a thousand social occasions at not one of which was the subject brought up.

Mr. M: But you could have brought it up.

Mr. B: No, I never could have brought it up because of the sense of the social situation.

Mr. M: What I would like to think is that one day you will, greatly daring; and I will make a bet with you here and now for a moderate sum of money that you will be surprised by the degree to which all these worldly people—as they seem to be worldly people or very much agnostic people and so on—how fascinated and attracted and interested they are by your proposition, and, of course, it depends in some degree how you put it out. I mean, the very simple Christian, probably an infinitely better Christian than I am, but who is a tremendously dogmatic person—we'll say Billy Graham, someone of that sort—this might be put in a way which would abash people. But I have discovered the opposite, that if you indicate in sincerity and truth that in the most wretched, inadequate way you have decided that there's absolutely no purpose in life except relating yourself to God and that on the Christian side there's only one way of doing that effectively and that is through the Incarnation, that the interest is quickened and that hostility which you expect to meet with, in fact, you don't.

Mr. B: Well, this may be the one point on which we are going to disagree, or else you move in much more sanctified company than I do. The term, a "Christer," is a pejorative term as socially used and in order to earn the reputation of being one, you have only to mention Christ, I would say, three times. Once per year might be permissible. Twice per year is tolerable. Three times per year is overdoing it. You become, a "Christer," and people think of you as not quite focused on the important things.

Mr. M: Well, I agree that of course people—the judgements that they might express—but I have never succeeded in expressing the heart of the Christian message with faith that it hasn't proved to be a stimulant rather than a depressant on conversation and has been responded to sympathetically rather than with hostility. But all the people sitting at that table, like yourself, have been mesmerised by this terrific consensus that Christ is out-moded; nobody is interested in Christ; he's a bore. But they've only been mesmerised, and you can break that mesmeric effect by simply refusing to accept it.

Mr. B: At least you grant that this is social pioneering.

Mr. M: Oh, it requires a certain effort, I quite agree, and I've often failed to do it. I've often joined in the rather shallow gossip that's going on.

Mr. B: But I also have some of your speeches and very, very often they are highly allusive in their reference to—for instance, I remember a speech—you were called in several years ago to substitute for President Johnson or somebody to speak to the newspaper editors in Washington, and it happened that I addressed them the next day and they were still reeling from the impact of your performance, and so I rushed and read your speech—I think we published it, as a matter of fact and it was only in the very last sentence or two that the spinal column of the whole speech became evident when you made reference to "the most brilliant light that ever shone in this world, you continue to believe, shone in Bethlehem."

Mr. M: Those tactics might be wrong, but they're not based on any lack of faith in what I'm trying to say.

Mr. B: No, no, I'm not saying they are.

Mr. M: No, no.

Mr. B: They're procedural.

Mr. M: Yes, it's procedural.

Mr. B: Tactical.

Mr. M: Tactical. And I think that certainly at a gathering of that kind I may have overdone it, you know, in—

Mr. B: Underdone it, you mean.

Mr. M: Well, overdone it in the sense of delaying the, as it were, the denouement—the unfolding of the denouement—but it would seem to me tactically necessary to lead up, rather, to it, than to plunge into it.

Mr. B: In speaking to the nation's newspaper editors, I suppose it would be a little bit like going to Plato's Retreat and talking about monogamy.

Mr. M: (laughing) It might be. Actually, there again, the response to that astonished me. Actually, it's been often my memory of dealing with American editors.

Mr. B: I've encouraged you.

Mr. M: Very much so, very much so.

Mr. B: All right, take the experience of Solzhenitsyn. The impact of Solzhenitsyn is so palpable that nobody can make him or it go away. It would be like attempting to live through Elizabethan England as though Shakespeare didn't exist. He is that much of a pressure. Now, having gone through what he's gone through, having probably had a more significant effect than anyone in this century in turning around political philosophical sentiment in Western Europe, there is a residue; and that residue is that he concluded that God is King, that Jesus Christ was the Incarnation. Now that terribly pains a great number of people who cannot deny the importance of Solzhenitsyn, but are horrified at the lengths to which he takes his own analysis, and they seek to pull the one Solzhenitsyn away from the other and they find that this is an impossible job.

Mr. M: Yes, it's very amusing to watch.

Mr. B: Yes, it is nonfissionable. Now, have you noticed that particular struggle?

Mr. M: Very much so. Very much so, and I tremble for him because I think that the pack is after him and because what he says is unbearable: that the answer to dictatorship is not liberalism, but Christianity. I mean, that is an unbearable proposition from their point of view, and it is where he stands. I've observed him, and I tremble a bit for his future because, as a foreigner living in an alien country, he's very much vulnerable. The rest of us can sort of lie low and keep quiet at times and so on. But still, it has been something wonderful to watch and, to more people than you might think, enormously heartening: that that is what this man should have to say instead of a lot of claptrap.

Mr. B: Sure, and the fact that he should go to Harvard and say exactly the same thing there he would say anywhere else. Do you remember on one occasion, you and I and Bernard Levin watched the famous interview by Solzhenitsyn that lasted about a half hour conducted by Mr. Charlton—I think it was—of the BBC? And then we discussed it in the balance of an hour, and Bernard Levin, who began by saying, "Let me make myself plain. I consider Solzhenitsyn the most important living human being and the most ennobling; however, I wish to disassociate myself entirely from his theological conclusions." Now, is that disassociation increasingly hard, do you think?

Mr. M: Well, I think it's being increasingly exploited, you see, and when you can tear it in a hundred ways. They started off by never mentioning that he was a Christian. I mean, for a long time, he was made a hero of the cause of freedom, but it was never mentioned that an integral and essential part of it was his Christian belief. Now that he's so stressed that—quite sort of specifically stressed it—they attack from another direction, that we can't have this idea that only Christians can—why not Buddhists?—and all that sort of stuff.

Mr. B: Then they go on also to say that he's a theocrat which I don't think he is.

Mr. M: Not at all, not at all. Oh no, he's in some ways very similar. I found this last book of his—what is it called? *The Oak and the Calf*—I found that the best of all his books in a way because it describes him in very simple terms in the conclusions that he's reached and his relations with authorities in the USSR before he left.

Mr. B: Yes, it is his odyssey and an account of the pains required to save those invaluable literary properties.

Mr. M: Absolutely. Awfully touching for a writer, that he had the courage to go on writing, writing, without seemingly any possibility that he would be published.

Mr. B: Yes. Now, would you say that his presence has weighed heavily on the scale in respect of the search for God? Are many more people, as a result of Solzhenitsyn's writings, concerned about the theological alternative to secularism?

Mr. M: It would be awfully difficult to answer that, actually, because he's been, on the whole, interpreted very inadequately in the press and on the media, so that it's hard to say that; but I would think that perhaps more people than we think have been comforted. To me, as a person who was a journalist in the USSR in 1932, the idea that all these years later, one of the kind of favourite sons of the regime could emerge, speaking in these accents—and when I say, "favourite sons," I mean who emerges as an absolutely celebrated author for a time—

Mr. B: Yes, well, he was sort of the intellectual complement of Svetlana. The notion that the only living child of Stalin should become a Western Christian, it must be terribly discouraging to the engines of Marxism.

Mr. M: (laughing) The most extraordinary moment of my life, I got a two-page—two full-scale pages typed—fan letter from Svetlana, and I thought to myself, "If there's one thing that would have seemed to me utterly inconceivable in this world, it would be if Stalin's daughter were to write to me."

Mr. B: (laughing) A fan letter from Stalin's daughter.

Mr. M: And a very charming and perceptive letter.

Mr. B: This was in reaction to one of your books?

Mr. M: Well, it was in connection with Christianity, and particularly a book called *Jesus Rediscovered*, which she'd read. Life has such extraordinary surprises. It produces such amazing contradictions. That was certainly one of them. No, but I agree. I think that Solzhenitsyn—what he's done and his loyalty to his fellow prisoners in the Gulag and his tenacity with which he's gone on stating these deep truths about good and evil will seem in posterity one of the most amazing things of our time without any doubt. And don't forget—which people do forget—that Solzhenitsyn, after the coming out of *One Day in the Life of Ivan Denisovitch*, he could have just settled down to be the most famous writer in the USSR and just by keeping off a few delicate subjects could have had a life of Riley just like Maxim Gorki. And he wouldn't do it because he was determined to go on saying what he had to say.

It's a wonderful parable of our time.

Mr. B: Yes. Well, in the last couple of minutes, let me ask you this. You decline to generalise on the basis of your own approach to faith, the likely approach of other people. Is this because yours is idiosyncratic, or is it because you are convinced that it always comes individually?

Mr. M: Basically, I think it is the latter, that I'm absolutely sure that the ways to God are infinitely diverse, depending on temperaments and circumstances and hundreds of things; and one of the things that is, to me, off-putting in a certain amount of otherwise very creditable Christians—a manifestation in our time—is the idea there is a standard procedure that you're going to go that way, almost as though Bunyan had written in his pilgrimage that unless you actually took that path—you know, mark that on the map—you've had it. And I would, also in utter humility—because I don't in any way regard myself as in any way a good Christian or one who will approach the Pearly Gates other than in the most craven state of mind as to the record that will be in the hands of whoever keeps the gate—

Mr. B: Well, to say that you are an imperfect Christian is, for one thing, to acknowledge a congenital flaw in human nature, but to say that you approached God in a distinctive way is not to discourage, obviously, other people from seeking him out according to their own inclinations and temperament, right?

Mr. M: It's a terrible thing, you see, that as you get this idea of what being a good Christian is and you become stricken with your own inadequacy, your sense of yourself as a sinner—as a hopeless person—is magnified. I used to think it was an affectation in someone like St. Francis or St. Paul to say, "I am a prince of sinners," you know, but I see that—or Mother Teresa who was always the one to say, "I'm not worthy, I'm not worthy,"—but it is to the extent that you can conceive this fulfilment, this spiritual fulfilment—

Mr. B: It becomes true. Thank you very much, Malcolm Muggeridge.

2. Do We Need Religion?

MR. BUCKLEY: Recently from these quarters I spoke with Malcolm Muggeridge on the subject of the search for religion, his encounter with it, and the desolation of abomination that came from it. What we did not get into, and propose to do in this hour, is the question of denominationalism. Is he a member of a particular communion, and if not, why not? What is the role of the institutionalised church? Who and what are the enemies of the institutionalised churches? Why is it that the call to evangelism comes so embarrassingly, even to those whose belief in God is the central point of existence and claim on sanity? These questions, together with a few of the aphorisms collected by Mr. Muggeridge on the occasion of his seventy-fifth birthday, we explore in the study of Malcolm Muggeridge, author of over twenty books, a journalist with few, if any, peers, who, in his retirement, is working on a third volume of his autobiography. This he is doing while the BBC puts together an eight hour special on his professional life. He says he has visited America for the last time, and if this is indeed the case, we can be grateful, as we seldom have been before, for the benefits of television.

I'll begin, then, by asking what I suppose is the most obvious question, particularly inasmuch as I am one myself: why are you not a Catholic?

MR. MUGGERIDGE: It's not altogether easy to answer that actually, Bill. I've, believe it or not, longed to be a Catholic. It's something that I've longed for as though it were the most marvellous thing, but I've never been able to feel in honesty that I could present myself for instruction, and it's extremely difficult to know why. The truth is, I think, that I take a very pessimistic view of the Catholic Church, despite the very brilliant Pope you've now got. It seems to me that it's dropping to pieces;

An interview with William F. Buckley Jr., *Firing Line* television show (1978). Reprinted from Malcolm Muggeridge, *Vintage Muggeridge* (Grand Rapids, Mich.: Eerdmans, 1985), pp. 137–65.

and of course it had a severe blow after the Vatican Councils. Therefore, I would be joining something of which I was enormously critical, and this isn't really an honourable thing to do.

Mr. B: That's never bothered you before.

Mr. M: I've never contemplated anything so serious as joining a church. I mean, even if you were to turn to mundane things—joining a club—if you were to join it quite confident that you were going to challenge all its rules and have rows with all its members, it would be rather a foolish step to take.

Mr. B: You once called yourself an imperfect Christian. Is this a sign of pride?

Mr. M: I don't think so, because I would have no troubles if I felt that I could go as a sinner into the Church. I'm sure many people have. It's a feeling that I would go there in some degree under false pretences. I don't know. There was an incident which, trivial in itself, played quite a part in my decision not to become a Catholic. The time when I was nearest to going and asking to be instructed—and I'd planned that I would go to Father D'Arcy because I had a great love for him—it was when I was rector at Edinburgh University, and I ran into a row there which you might have heard of when I was asked, as rector, by the students—

Mr. B: To supply contraceptives.

Mr. M: That's right—to recommend that they should be given, unquestioningly, free supplies of contraceptives by the University medical unit, and I refused to do this and there was a hullabaloo. And I thought to myself, you see, "Well, there are a thousand Catholics in the University, and they'll be on my side anyway. I've got a thousand men on my side." What happened was that the first big blast against me was a letter in *The Scotsman* by the Roman Catholic chaplain at the University saying what a monstrous thing this was that I had done.

Mr. B: Excuse me, but why was it monstrous?

Mr. M: It was monstrous, according to him, because it accused the students of wanting to be promiscuous; but in a letter I wrote in answer to it, I said I wondered what the Reverend Father thought they wanted the contraceptives for? Was it to save up for their wedding day? He offered no answer to that. But then I thought that somebody would give him a very big reprimand. But no such thing happened. Then I thought he'd almost certainly become a bishop. But that didn't happen either. What has happened is the perfect payoff of the whole episode: he's now rector of Edinburgh University (laughter).

Mr. B: And did they get their contraceptives?

Mr. M: Oh yes, oh yes. But there was nobody who reprimanded him. One Jesuit monk wrote to me and said that he thought it was monstrous and that he'd written to this Father and suggested that he should apologise to me, but nothing came of that. Anyway, it was a small episode, but it gave me the feeling that—one of the things I admired the Church for so much was *Humanae Vitae*. I think it's absolutely right that when a society doesn't want children, when it is prepared to accept eroticism unrelated in any way to its purpose, then it's on the downward path. So I admired it so much, and then I realised that since I was involved in this row, their adherence to it was very, very ceremonial rather than actual. They didn't really believe in it themselves, and I don't—I mean, I think the figures of population and so on in some places like Quebec show that they don't believe it, and they haven't practised it.

Mr. B: Well, I'm, to put it lightly, stupified that you would make a decision whether or not to extend your loyalty to an institution based on the behaviour of some of its communicants. I can't imagine any time in history when anybody would have become a Catholic if he had been so easily put off.

Mr. M: That's true. That obviously wasn't a major thing, Bill, but what it did was kind of crystallised certain feelings I had that these things that I so enormously admired—and of course the same thing is true of the Mass. The happiest time I ever had in terms of worship was when Kitty and I were staying in a village behind Nice and there was an old-fashioned priest there and we went to Mass in the church there every morning, and I absolutely loved it and I never felt more sort of happy spiritually. But—

Mr. B: You're not saying that the Church isn't clubbable?

Mr. M: No, not at all, but that the things in it that hold my admiration are the very things that it's turning its back on—that I would be involved in endless controversies connected with them.

Mr. B: Well, you would be the millionth Catholic who was.

Mr. M: (laughing) Yes, I suppose so. But can't you see that perhaps it's an excuse I've invented myself. It's quite possible.

Mr. B: You have no problems, then, I take it, with the Apostles' Creed?

Mr. M: None at all.

Mr. B: Or with apostolicity?

Mr. M: Not at all. I assent to it. Or the infallibility of the Pope; that doesn't worry me at all. I can see the purpose of all those things, and I see the context of people that I so admire—like St. Augustine and St. Francis—who were ready to accept all that; and the idea that I would come forth and say, "No, I couldn't possibly be in a church when the Pope claims to be infallible—"

Mr. B: Well, of course, that was some time after—

Mr. M: It was after, of course, but things of that sort, you see? None of that has ever presented any difficulty. On the contrary, it's the feeling that the Church itself is moving from these basic beliefs that is distressing. Or maybe it's just some kind of instinct.

Mr. B: But there can't have been a more resonant re-affirmation of them than by the present Pope. I'm not here to try to convert you. I'm just exploring.

Mr. M: No, no, no. I know. This is absolutely true, and of course, it has given great joy to many people because of that, but it still remains the case that I can't join it; and I'll have to meet my Maker not having joined it. Probably I'll get a frightful pasting in purgatory for it, but I can't help it. No.

Mr. B: Now, what about the intra-Christian community quarrels? What importance do you attach to them?

Mr. M: Well, I think there's only one quarrel in the institution of churches that seems to me to be serious and vital—and of course, the Roman Catholic Church is not equally, but also involved in it—and that is the quarrel between those who accept our Lord saying that his kingdom is not of this world and those who believe that they can construct a kingdom of heaven on earth. That is the basic quarrel.

Mr. B: Utopians, yes.

Mr. M: Yes, Utopians. And I, you know, with all the feeling I have in the world, I am against the Utopians and on the side of the—

Mr. B: And you see the Utopians as figuring primarily in which sect?

Mr. M: Well, I think that they figure more in the Protestant sects, especially perhaps the poor old Church of England which I technically belong to, but which is an appalling—probably the most awful shambles that's ever existed, even in the history of institutional Christianity. But it's becoming very noticeable in the Catholic Church in certain sects and particularly, for instance, in Latin America I would have said, without knowing a great deal about it. Anyway, that is the big row, and, of course, the body that I once described as the *pons asinorum* of all Christian endeavours—the World Council of Churches—is a kind of classic example of it which I think does immense and unbelievable harm to the Christian faith. And I greatly respect the Catholic Church for keeping out of it, even though it sends an observer there.

Mr. B: Is your quarrel with the World Council of Churches based on its accent on secularism and secularist achievements?

Mr. M: Yes, and plus its devastating attacks on places like South Africa and total acquiescence in places like the USSR, which is represented there by clergy from the stooge Russian Orthodox Church.

Mr. B: What role has the community—the flock—to play in intensifying the Christian experience? It is by various denominations thought of as a shared experience—right?—a joint experience. You are not only your brother's keeper, but you are in a sense your brother's companion. The notion of congregation is theological in its derivation, I think.

Mr. M: Yes.

Mr. B: Do you have a special attitude towards people who say, "I don't need a church. I don't need other communicants. I'll just go out in the fields and communicate with my Maker?"

Mr. M: (laughing) I don't particularly like that, but I can't very well criticise it because I could be said to be in it myself. Why I don't think I'm really in it is because there's nothing I long for more.

Mr. B: Well, let me ask you this question: would you, in the spirit of Immanuel Kant, universalise your own experiences? That is to say, "For the reasons that I do not join, I counsel others not to?"

Mr. M: No, I wouldn't dream of doing that. I mean, as a matter of fact, it happens sometimes people who are about to become Roman Catholic for some reason come and see me, and I always give it my blessing. I think it's marvellous. It just is something I can't do myself. There's one other thing in it I haven't mentioned that it is not very important, but it's worth mentioning. Now, of course, I'm thought of as a person who is an aspiring Christian or a Christian or at any rate whose heart is in the Christian position. And as, through television, a number of people recognise my aged mug, it quite often happens that people come up to me as fellow Christians might come up and sort of just shake your hand and you go to a restaurant and—it once happened to me, a waiter comes padding along behind you and you think, "I haven't given a big enough tip," and he wants to say, "I'm a Christian too."

Mr. B: So in that sense you are already a member of a community, even though it's not a formal communion.

Mr. M: Right, and also I've a feeling, first of all, that I would never want to ask these people, "Which denomination do you belong to?" And therefore, in a way, to identify oneself, even with something so marvellous as the Catholic Church, would be in a sort of way letting some of those people down.

Mr. B: I understand what you mean. To belong to any organisation is in a sense an act of exclusion.

Mr. M: It is.

Mr. B: And it is once again a paradox that that which is considered to be incorporative of society should also be, in a sense, exclusivist.

Mr. M: Absolutely.

Mr. B: After all, the rites, which I take it you will never submit to, require you to abjure a whole series of things that are read out, and you say, "I do abjure them, I do abjure them"—all the famous heresies and so on. Well, having—I won't quite say disposed of that question—

Mr. M: Yes, it's too big.

Mr. B: Let me try out on you, because I think I see a line that connects them, a series of rather provocative answers that you gave to The New York Times *when, on the occasion of your seventy-fifth birthday, they asked you to formulate some of the conclusions you've arrived at.*

Mr. M: I remember well.

Mr. B: Okay. No. 1—this is you speaking—"When mortal men try to live without God, they infallibly succumb to megalomania or erotomania or both: the raised fist or the raised phallus, Nietzsche or D. H. Lawrence. Pascal said this and the contemporary world abundantly bears it out." Isn't that a bit exaggerated?

Mr. M: I don't think it is, actually, because—I see why you say it's exaggerated, but I—

Mr. B: It's because you say, "infallibly". That's the operative affront.

Mr. M: Yes, well, certainly Western society bears it out, doesn't it? It is megalomania, the absolute insistence that the only thing that matters is the ego, the individual person. . . .

Mr. B: Well, the theologian Robert Fitch wrote a wonderful book ten or fifteen years ago called The Odyssey of the Self-Centred Self, *in which he says that—we now call it the "me" decade—that man, who used to be concerned with God, is now concerned with himself, but there were these intermediate phases: he was concerned with nature at one point; he was concerned with science at one point. And he sees this evolution as having come to megalomania. But is it not possible that you would be concerned with something other than God or yourself?*

Mr. M: Well, of course, you have many other preoccupations, but I would contend that those occupations themselves run into the sand unless they are related to God, the ultimate reality; that we can't find anything even to occupy our time effectively if we leave God out; and that it simply is true that man cannot exist in the universe, in time, on his own steam. It doesn't make any sense. It can't be.

Mr. B: All right. Now let me ask you this: when you use the word "erotomania", do you use it literally, or are you using it as a comprehensive term for sensuality in general, which would include, for instance, eating and drinking?

Mr. M: I suppose you could take it as both really. I must say that I think that as our society is increasingly preoccupied with one single appetite—namely the sexual appetite—that I perhaps did mean erotomania mainly, but it should equally take in the others, which are part of the same thing. Perhaps the better word should have been "carnality".

Mr. B: Carnality, yes.

Mr. M: Would have been a better word. But of course, we see it in this preoccupation with sex, and I must now say this: that recently, I've had occasion to read through a lot of old diaries that I'd forgotten, and reading through them has been particularly disagreeable because it shows how preoccupied I was myself with Eros—how much of my time and hope and pleasure seemed to be connected with that. And I look back on it as a kind of servitude, really. And I'm sure it's true when the history of the twentieth century is written it will be seen, as was true of course of the last stages of the Roman Empire—this utter preoccupation with, not reproduction, but with the mere excitements accompanying reproduction.

Mr. B: In what category would you put the satisfaction of aesthetic appetites?

Mr. M: Obviously, a very high level of this. Indeed, the aesthetic appetite is moving into the field of mysticism, which is precisely where we meet God, so that I would include—as we said in our previous talk—Blake's concept of the Imagination as part of man's mystical life.

Mr. B: Let me skip then to your Proposition No. 4, because it's related to what you've just finished saying: "A God who chose to generate genius capable of producing a Missa Solemnis *or a Chartres Cathedral would surely be unwilling to confine his creativity to so banal and mechanistic a procedure as natural selection. It would be as though* King Lear *had come off a conveyor belt* or Paradise Lost *out of a computer." Are you saying quite directly that God was the animating genius behind great art?*

Mr. M: Most certainly.

Mr. B: What about great art that is totally secularist in its conception?

Mr. M: I don't think it's great. I know this is a dogmatic statement, but I don't think it is. I don't think there's any great art which does not have in it some sort of transcendental significance.

Mr. B: What would you say about The Tempest?

Mr. M: I would put *The Tempest* in the whole realm of Shakespeare, and I would say that in Shakespeare there is an enormous contribution towards this awareness of man's destiny which is an expression of transcendentalism.

Mr. B: Have you a thesis as to why Shakespeare never accosted the point directly?

Mr. M: Yes. I think he was treading on a hot plate in the Elizabethan Age, and although he ridiculed the Puritans and things like that, I think that to embark upon any kind of theological basis would be something that, first of all, would not have appealed to him personally, but equally, would have had great dangers. People were being bumped off, weren't they, at that time?

Mr. B: Yes. Well, he lived in pre-Cromwellian times, but religious controversies were heated. But can you explain the singular absence of religious metaphor in Shakespeare?

Mr. M: I wouldn't say religious metaphor. I would say there was an absence possibly of Christian metaphor, but not of religious metaphor. In fact, it's absolutely bristling with it, particularly the great tragedies.

Mr. B: I should have said Christian metaphor.

Mr. M: Yes, I think there is an absence of that, and again it was a troubled time, wasn't it? The metaphysical poets were coming along, but that was a different age.

Mr. B: Well, what you've just said in fact relates to another of your opinions. Shakespeare died in 1616, which is approximately halfway through a period of thirty or forty years when, it can roughly be said I suppose, that the knowledge of the physical universe doubled, trebled, quadrupled, ending with the Principia. *It was an age in which human beings were urged to cultivate knowledge. Along you come four hundred years later with the following put-down: "Accumulating knowledge is a form of avarice and lends itself to another version of the Midas story, this time of a man so avid for knowledge that everything he touches turns to facts; his faith becomes theology; his love becomes lechery; his wisdom becomes science; pursuing meaning, he ignores truth."*

Mr. M: Well, I stand by that.

Mr. B: Okay, let's examine that. You're saying that the exploration of knowledge leads to kind of an arid accumulation of it.

Mr. M: Yes, and to feeling that knowledge has value in itself, apart from its relation to truth, which is something quite different. Incidentally, again talking of Blake, you know what he wrote across his copy of Bacon's *Advancement of Learning*—which was, of course, a very important book in history. He wrote, "Good news for Satan's kingdom." Now, I think, he's absolutely right. It doesn't mean that men mustn't seek knowledge, but they seek knowledge in order to understand truth better. But there's no knowledge itself apart from truth, and it's a different thing from truth. It's not just worthless, but harmful. And it's very much the case now. It's what our universities are largely doing, and therefore they're producing people—

Mr. B: Nihilism.

Mr. M: Yes, absolutely.

Mr. B: Well, a search for knowledge is not—or is it?—an invitation to invincible ignorance if the search becomes more important than the discovery?

Mr. M: Yes, I think it can be that, and there are many people—I'll name no names—among the more famous dons of the age who illustrate that to perfection. Again, you have, of course, in Pascal the opposite trend, in which he, who had acquired so much knowledge, saw it as absolutely worthless in itself. What we are concerned with is truth; and knowledge can be part of truth, but it is not truth.

Mr. B: In what dismissive way did you use the word, "theology," when you said, "His faith becomes theology?"

Mr. M: Well, it becomes stating certain dogmatic propositions which, though they may play a part in building up a concept of faith, detached from faith are quite worthless.

Mr. B: You are using the word as one might use "scientistic", as distinguished from "scientific".

Mr. M: Precisely, precisely, precisely. But I'm not against knowledge, you know. I mean, I think every single thing that men do can be done because God has equipped them to do it and, therefore, in doing it, they can be serving God's purposes; but they can also use it in such a way that it negates God's purposes.

Mr. B: Mightn't it be said with some confidence that the search for historical and sociological knowledge teaches us what in fact you have formulated in one of your propositions? The way you put it is as follows: "There can never be good governments that are less bad than others. The quest for a perfect government ends infallibly in anarchy or the Gulag Archipelago." Now, that is an anti-Utopian conviction of yours that I happen to share, and it once again, using the Christian metaphor, distinguishes the City of Man from the City of God, does it not? But isn't it true that a pursuit of knowledge teaches us the limitations of government?

Mr. M: It should, but it doesn't always. In that it's done for itself alone, it tends to increase people's arrogance rather than teach them humility, which is of course the condition of all awareness of truth. Simon advises that the only purpose of seeking knowledge through education is to make men realise the inadequacy of their knowledge and, in realising that, of course, then they are brought nearer to God. But when you make knowledge an end in itself, then it's destructive of truth.

Mr. B: Let's examine this in concrete terms. Suppose you were to encounter someone who, at age thirty, determined to consecrate the whole of his life and all of his energies to the search for the causes of cancer. Are you implying that the consecration is going to strip him of his capacity to put cancer in proper focus?

Mr. M: No, because I think that he would be actuated by love, by humane feelings, by a desire to deliver—

Mr. B: It might be vanity.

Mr. M: It might be vanity, but if he were to be effective at it, you would find that vanity wouldn't get him very far actually. It's the quest for something that will deliver mankind from one of their scourges that makes such a quest near to God; otherwise, if it were purely vanity—and I think you see that in the development of things like heart transplants where the vanity of surgeons to show that they can do these things is evident.

Mr. B: It becomes exhibitionism.

Mr. M: Yes, and it is very noticeable. That's only an extreme example. But you could go further and say that the dreadful dilemmas which doctors have created for themselves through the development of their knowledge are due to the fact that that knowledge has been sought for self alone, and it has been sought for self alone by regarding human beings as mere carcasses, bodies, leaving out the dimension of the soul. That's the explanation of the dreadful plight into which they've got through the very brilliance of their discoveries. It's an amazing parable for us to watch and meditate upon.

Mr. B: The injunction to seek out perfection while recognising that you can never achieve it, to seek the company of the saints—the standard term is "the counsel of perfection"—encourages absorption with the end in mind. I cited the case of the man who wants to find the causes of cancer. Let us change the example to the man who seeks to make the most beautiful music. Toscanini was an intolerable human being and a great genius as a conductor. We are all used to reading about how difficult it is to get along with genius. There are, of course, fabulous exceptions. Bach was a cozy family man, but for every one like him there is the Napoleon or the Alexander or whoever. Now, in attempting a Christian understanding here, what is it that goes slightly wrong? Looking for something for the sake of gratifying yourself rather than of serving something?

Mr. M: The ego.

Mr. B: The ego.

Mr. M: Same old ego, you see. One thing to be this famous conductor on whom all eyes are cast, not in utter humility—and I go back to the word humility, which is the key word, which is wanting to produce in the best possible way this marvellous music which would carry men away from their egos, away from their mundane existence, into the spiritual world. That's the point, so that we always come back to it: that it is what they are doing it for that matters. Of course the Christian says that essentially we do it for the glory of God. I think of the people building Chartres Cathedral, say, and doing it for the glory of God. We don't even know who they were.

Mr. B: No, but we certainly know they made enormous sacrifices because there was a kind of residue—

Mr. M: Yes.

Mr. B: —in the twelfth century—

Mr. M: But a man who builds a great skyscraper so that everybody says, "That's his skyscraper. He built that." That's the opposite thing. And in that the twentieth century has produced self-interested endeavour, it has spread ugliness through the world, because egotism is very ugly. Man thinking of himself as one of the great marvels of creation is an ugly thing. Man thinking of himself as one single, tiny figure in the whole creation of God—one member of this enormous family that God has created—that's when he's near to truth.

Mr. B: No, but man is entitled to think of himself as not only all-important in the sense of his supreme mission of pleasing God and achieving immortality, but also as the paradigm by which he understands the injunction to love others as oneself. Is that not correct? If one despised oneself and one's love of others were equal to that of oneself—

Mr. M: You would have to despise others.

Mr. B: —it would be insufficient.

Mr. M: That wouldn't be right at all.

Mr. B: No.

Mr. M: But if you are aware of yourself as a fallen creature, which you are told to be—

Mr. B: Then you love others in the knowledge of their imperfection.

Mr. M: That's right.

Mr. B: *Okay. Now, one of the things that Christianity suffers from is its association with asperity and desiccation. Mencken's redolent put-down that, "A Puritan is somebody who is afraid that somebody somewhere is happy," influenced the attitudes of an entire age. The pleasure of Christianity can be very intense, you have specified, and in one of your propositions to* The New York Times, *you wrote: "Mystical ecstasy and laughter are the two great delights of living, and saints and clowns their purveyors, the only two categories of human beings who can be relied on to tell the truth; hence, steeples and gargoyles side by side on the great cathedrals." Now, are they telling the same truth or are they giving you a dialectic form from which truth emerges?*

Mr. M: Well, I think a bit of both, but let's think of the steeple and the gargoyle. The steeple is this beautiful thing reaching up into the sky admitting, as it were, its own inadequacy—attempting something utterly impossible—to climb up to heaven through a steeple. The gargoyle is this little man grinning and laughing at the absurd behaviour of men on earth, and these two things both built into this building to the glory of God.

Mr. B: *Now, he's not laughing at evil, is he?*

Mr. M: No.

Mr. B: *He's laughing at pomposity.*

Mr. M: He's laughing at the inadequacy of man, the pretensions of man, the absolute preposterous gap—disparity—between his aspirations and his performance, which is the eternal comedy of human life. It will be so till the end of time, you see.

Mr. B: *And what is it that is the principal source of laughter? The difference between human nature and human performance.*

Mr. M: The difference between human nature and human performance.

Mr. B: *Human aspiration is not laughable, is it?*

Mr. M: Well, it is, because it's—

Mr. B: Only when it's excessive. Why?

Mr. M: Because of always aspiring to do more than they can actually do. That's why—

Mr. B: But to aspire to do good is not to aspire to do too much.

Mr. M: No, but—

Mr. B: Mother Teresa aspires to do good and does.

Mr. M: Well, actually she doesn't aspire to do good. She's the first person to say that what she does is simply to love her neighbour as herself. I mean, the idea of aspiring wouldn't really occur to her. When people aspire—and I've used it of myself in this talk, actually, as an aspiring Christian, and it's slightly fraudulent in this context really, because it means that you're hoping to be a marvellous Christian—

Mr. B: Well, if you aspire to please God, you're not necessarily ridiculous, are you?

Mr. M: You're on the path. You're on the path. You're on the right path.

Mr. B: One of my favourite short stories is the one of "Our Lady's Juggler." You recall that? Anatole France's.

Mr. M: I don't remember it, at any rate.

Mr. B: Well, you have a recently arrived monk at a monastery of very learned men, and on the feast day of Mary, each of them performs that at which he is a virtuoso. There is the organist, there is the composer, there is the poet. And this poor little man, what he was before he entered the monastery was a juggler, a common juggler who went around the little towns of France and a few people threw a few pennies at him and he lived that way. So when the turn came for him to perform, he passed on the grounds that he had no qualification to serve. But then, at ten o'clock that night, when all of his companions had gone to sleep, he tiptoes into the chapel with his old balls—

Mr. M: Does his act.

Mr. B: —and he does his act.

Mr. M: I like that.

Mr. B: And at that moment, the statue of Our Lady comes to life and she smiles.

Mr. M: I like that.

Mr. B: It's an exquisite story, and it's the nearest thing to egalitarianism that I can think of in much of Christian literature. But here is somebody who aspires to please about whom you can hardly say that what he did was laughable.

Mr. M: No, no. It's beautiful. It was also a bit funny, but rightly so.

Mr. B: Objectively, it was funny.

Mr. M: Yes, and that funniness is a beautiful thing in it.

Mr. B: Yes.

Mr. M: Which I'm sure he would have rejoiced over also. But what I think—perhaps this aspiring business, I carried it too far, but aspiring means that one—I love this idea of humility—of the recognition that with the best will in the world and the most ardent love of God, we still are utterly, hopelessly inadequate in our performance. When we try to write about eternity and we try to write about truth, what we're doing is simply the scribble of children before they've learned their alphabets.

Mr. B: But that simply isn't true. The people who built Chartres did not do anything except create something very beautiful.

Mr. M: Yes, but when they look at Chartres in eternity, it seems like a piffling little monument compared with what it's celebrating.

Mr. B: Well, it can only be that if you assume an imagination great enough to think of it as trifling, but it is very hard to imagine a context in which Bach's B Minor Mass *is trifling.*

Mr. M: I think Bach, now, in eternity, you would find that he would eagerly agree with me that it's the most ridiculously inadequate piece of music ever written. I mean, that's what is marvellous.

Mr. B: I think you certainly strain credulity, because on the one hand, you begin by saying only God could have created something so beautiful, and then you say this trifling—

Mr. M: It's because when a man is actually with God, then he sees that what he's tried to do, and in our terms done so marvellously, amounts to something which is utterly inadequate. That's what I'm saying: that what the steeple is reaching up to is so far, far away, that the steeple, beautiful as it is—let's say one of the English—Salisbury Cathedral is a beautiful steeple, but what is it compared with the sky into which it is reaching? And it's in the realisation of that comparison that this awareness of, on the one hand, the absurdity of our efforts, and on the other, the inadequacy of them.

Mr. B: In pursuit then of tolerable pleasure—from which we have excluded vanity, erotomania, gluttony—you touch on happiness, and you write: "Another disastrous concept is the pursuit of happiness, a last-minute improvisation in the American Declaration of Independence substituting for the defence of property. Happiness pursued cannot be caught, and if it could, it would not be happiness."

Mr. M: Well, that's true.

Mr. B: Well, there are a lot of paradoxes there.

Mr. M: But it's true.

Mr. B: It's true if you say that the pursuit of happiness has to be asymptotic—you can never quite get there. You can get closer and closer and closer, but you never quite get there. However, the pursuit of happiness is supposed to bring happiness.

Mr. M: But it's a wrong approach.

Mr. B: It's the pursuit that brings the happiness, not the acquisition of it, isn't it?

Mr. M: I think the pursuit is a misguided concept because I think the thing about happiness is that it happens—it comes to us. It comes to us mysteriously. Again, when our relations with God are harmonious—

Mr. B: But spiritual exercises are a form of pursuit, aren't they? Prayer.

Mr. M: Prayer is not really a form of pursuit. The purpose of prayer—of all spiritual exercises—is to get nearer to God. To be near to God is to be happy, and suddenly happiness floods your being; but if you were to pursue that, say, "I must get near to God in order to be happy," you wouldn't get near to him and you wouldn't be happy. That's what I'm trying to say.

Mr. B: It has to be providential.

Mr. M: Unchased.

Mr. B: It has to be providential.

Mr. M: Yes. It has to come about as part of a state of mind, and a state of mind which, in my opinion, insofar as it can be defined at all, is based on this relationship with God, this readiness, this preparedness to say, "Thy will be done." It's an incredible thing the joy that comes of being able to say and mean that.

Mr. B: When you say, "Thy will be done," what you are really contracting to do is to accept that which happens, right?

Mr. M: Yes, to say that it is your—

Mr. B: And therefore you are disciplining yourself—

Mr. M: Right.

Mr. B: —to a kind of abjection which is in harmony with what Providence ordains.

Mr. M: And then suddenly you're happy.

Mr. B: And suddenly you're happy.

Mr. M: You're happy. You're not happy when you say, "There is happiness. I must go after it." And of course, unfortunately, what it's amounted to—and had to amount to—particularly in our world today is the pursuit of pleasure, which of all the things that men go in for is the most fatuous and the most, ultimately, agonising.

Mr. B: Was Sisyphus happy?

Mr. M: Sisyphus—he was the man that pushed the stone, pushed up the stone—

Mr. B: Only to have it come down.

Mr. M: —and have it come down. Well, I—

Mr. B: Camus wrote, "Il faut supposer Sisyphus heureux."

Mr. M: Fair enough.

Mr. B: But I once quoted that and was reprimanded by a correspondent who said, "You missed the whole point. Sisyphus was condemned to unhappiness." Now Camus groped with this and came really around, in a sense, to your—in this case, rather hopeful—conclusion—

Mr. M: Yes.

Mr. B: "Il faut supposer Sisyphus heureux."

Mr. M: Yes, but I think this is right. I mean, I think you could roll a stone to the glory of God. You know, there's a beautiful poem of Herbert's about how one of the most happy people is a woman who brushes out a room to the glory of God. That's happiness. Everything can be done, even probably poor old Sisyphus's job, recognising it as part of his destiny. Camus was right. We must assume that he was happy doing it.

Mr. B: Was the Flying Dutchman happy?

Mr. M: (laughing) It's difficult for me to put myself in that position of the Flying Dutchman. I don't know whether he was happy or not, but there's no reason—I mean, I can imagine a happy Flying Dutchman, you see, depending on his attitude of mind to himself and what he was doing. The pursuit of happiness—why I was suggesting that it had the most devastating consequences is because it presupposes, indeed, I suppose it was meant to, that there are things: "That is happy. To sleep with that girl will make me happy. To have this money and to be able to do this, that, and the other thing, will make me happy. To be able to be eloquent and applauded will make me happy." None of these things make us happy. They are wretched things. But then, there is this extraordinary happiness, and the happiness lies in being aware that, as a human being created by God, one is fulfiling God's purpose, and that therefore, this extraordinary happiness overwhelms one. And that's what I meant by mystical ecstasy. Mystical ecstasy is the awareness of that happiness.

Mr. B: I take it too, then, it is an awareness of the transience of our experience on earth, because in one of your final propositions, you put it this way: "I have never doubted that our existence in this world has some sort of sequel. It would seem to me preposterous to suppose that this universe was set up solely to provide a mise en scène *for the interminable soap opera of history with its stock characters and situations endlessly repeated." Now, because you think it preposterous, you think there is life everlasting or do you think there is life everlasting because we were told by Christ that there was life everlasting?*

Mr. M: Well, both.

Mr. B: And the knowledge of it shows how preposterous the soap opera of history is?

Mr. M: Absolutely. That's what the Incarnation did.

Mr. B: So you would deduce heaven from the study of this world and deduce the nature of this world from a study of revelation?

Mr. M: I would deduce heaven from all the things in this world—hints, tiny hints of heaven—from all the things in this world that are beautiful and loving and good, you see? And those things all contain hints of heaven, especially, of course, love.

Mr. B: Notwithstanding that, under the aspect of the heavens, they are trivialised?

Mr. M: They are, because realising that they contain hints of heaven, you realise how miserably and wretchedly inadequate they are. But still the hint is there, you see.

Mr. B: Divine intimation.

Mr. M: Yes, that's exactly it. Wordsworth's poem "Intimations" is exactly the same sort of idea. That's how I see it, and the idea that man's achievements are in themselves superlative: they're only superlative because they contain that hint. Take away that, and they're nothing. Nothing at all. And that's why when people haven't got that, they tend to build a building that goes miles and miles into the sky, thinking, "If only I can make it as high as that, it will be the wonder of the world." It won't be the wonder of the world because it doesn't contain that special hint of what heaven is like. Time contains hints of eternity, and it's only through those hints of eternity in time that we can bear time.

Mr. B: Otherwise, time would be endless.

Mr. M: Time would be endless and unbearable.

Mr. B: Finally, you frame what you call the most important happening in the world. "It is," you say, "the resurgence of Christianity in the Soviet Union, demonstrating that the whole mighty effort sustained over sixty years to brainwash the Russian people into accepting materialism has been a fiasco. In the long run, governments, however powerful, fall flat on their faces before The Word, which two thousand years ago came to dwell among us full of grace and truth. In other words, absolute power collapses when confronted with absolute love." You deduce or do not deduce from this extremely hopeful phenomenon, i.e. the failure with all the mechanisms of modern totalitarianism to extirpate Christianity from Russia, that the Soviet regime is doomed to fall on its face—to fail?

Mr. M: Well, every—

Mr. B: It's failed already.

Mr. M: Yes, completely failed, because it has not succeeded in producing human beings on its terms.

Mr. B: The Marxist man.

Mr. M: Yes, that's right. It hasn't come about and never could anybody have had a better opportunity. Of course, it made this enormous impression on me because I would have considered it absolutely inconceivable in Russia—

Mr. B: Fifty years ago.

Mr. M: —in the early thirties when I was there and saw that every single thing anybody read, everything they heard, everything they were taught at school, every conceivable hint that there would be anything else except man, and anything else except man exerting power to create perfect circumstances for himself, that despite that—the refusal to allow anything else—this extraordinary survival of the opposite proposition spread, not through the agencies of propaganda, but through the Gulag Archipelago.

Mr. B: From which you deduce that it is something that resides in the human spirit that cannot possibly be extinguished?

Mr. M: Exactly. Nothing can extinguish it. Till the end of time it shall be there, and it will always manifest itself. And men must never lose heart because of that. That's the reason they must never, not because they think, "If we can just rearrange our currency, we'd get a better gross national product," or "We could invent some source of energy that would be inexhaustible." All the difficult ideas that they have are absolutely worthless. The great guarantee that human life is always worth creating, always worth bringing into this world, always worth living, is because there is built into it this indestructible awareness that it belongs to eternity and not to time.

Mr. B: Then the worldly challenge is to struggle for a society that permits the fertilisation of that instinct.

Mr. M: Yes, but the funny thing is, you see, that the societies in which the fertilisation has been permitted are the ones that are—

Mr. B: About to commit suicide.

Mr. M: Yes, and that where it seems to be shining with an incredible brightness is the one place in the world where you wouldn't, under any circumstances, expect to find it surviving.

Mr. B: The Catacombs. Thank you, Malcolm Muggeridge.

3. Peace and Power

MR. BUCKLEY: In the relatively long history of this programme, entering its nineteenth year, only one guest has appeared seven times, and he is Malcolm Muggeridge. One programme, in which he explored the search of faith, is regularly shown in Christmas week. I hope it is shown well after I am departed, perhaps even after he has departed. He had for many years spoken of himself as an old man, which at eighty-two he technically is. When reminded that at age ninety Harold MacMillan was made an earl, Mr. Muggeridge responded that now he knew for sure that he had nothing to live for.

After almost four years we are back in the home of Mr. and Mrs. Muggeridge in Sussex. The last programme done here inquired first into the search for faith, and in the second hour, to the question of denominationalism. He asked, in fact, that we call the hour, "Why I am not a Catholic." Twenty-six months after the programme was shown, he and his wife went to a neighbouring church and were baptised. He was asked why by a press always fascinated by their most distinguished living alumnus, and he spoke of, I quote, "a sense of homecoming, of picking up the threads of a lost life, of responding to a bell that has long been ringing, of finding a place at a table that has long been left vacant." I suppose we should touch on what it was that he now heard in the tone of that bell, before moving on to explore a relatively recent phenomenon, namely the rise of Christian pacifism: particularly, or so it would seem sometimes in America, within the Catholic Church.

So: I begin by asking the question directly. What, Mr. Muggeridge, did you now hear in the tintinnabulations of the bells?

MR. MUGGERIDGE: Instead of the bell sounding as something that I couldn't respond to, now I hear it with joy because it means that I go

An interview with William F. Buckley Jr., *Firing Line* television show (February 19, 1983), and later televised on PBS. Reprinted from Malcolm Muggeridge, *Vintage Muggeridge* (Grand Rapids, Mich., 1985), pp. 167–92.

to Mass, and this has been, in old age, a wonderfully fulfiling thing. I think it's just partly good fortune because the little chapel in which we were received, and where we now go is packed with children, and I love to have Mass with all these little children around, and come away feeling enormously happy.

Mr. B: Well, but why was it that this could not have been anticipated earlier? I ask this question not to tease you, but out of a genuine curiosity. You said four years ago that you were afraid of entering into any discipline in which you would find yourself instantly in the rôle of a critic more so even than a communicant. What was it that altered that criterion?

Mr. M: It is because of the experience itself, Bill. That is all I can say, is that it's one of the things in my life. Worship is a beautiful thing and a thing that I missed for many years, and now I enjoy it very much. This morning, for instance, well, thinking of you, as a matter of fact, and of this, Kitty and I went off to Mass, and obviously it is this ancient ritual. I read somewhere in a book recently, which perhaps shed a little bit of light on it, that since the Last Supper, an hour has never passed in which there is not someone in the world receiving—giving and receiving—the sacrament, and it's an amazing thought, that. All the terrible things that have happened and the confusion, and yet this is something that has gone on and on, and now I can participate in it.

Mr. B: Well, you mentioned in our discussion last time around a second point, namely that the resurgence of faith behind the Iron Curtain reminded one of the special stimulus of catacomb life. Do you reiterate that, now that you still live on the correct side of the Iron Curtain and have an opportunity to worship and receive the sacraments? Do you feel that you are missing something, for instance, that the Pole has got, or the Ukrainian Christian or the Czechoslovak?

Mr. M: I don't think so, no, although what I said then has been only strengthened in what I've heard and read and, in a very limited way, experienced that, strangely enough, the Christian religion is disintegrating in the Western world, without any question, but that it is, in some mysterious manner, growing in power and influence where you would perhaps least expect it, which is in these labour camps. In a conversation that I had with Solzhenitsyn recently, who, of course, is very well versed in what goes on in the Gulag, he makes this point very strongly. In abolishing the Christian faith, the regime has really restored it and that where this suffering takes place, where people are utterly cut off from everything that would normally be thought of as making life worth living, there this amazing hope is reborn.

Mr. B: Well, there is, of course, a temptation to find a divine purpose in everything. I think that temptation should presumptively be resisted. But the phenomenon to which you allude tempts one to ask whether we might be in fact heading towards apocalypse. It has struck me that the recognition of the world's end is a cliché in Christian doctrine, and yet it strikes me that as that possibility becomes increasingly vivid, there is a fear of it that is inconsistent with that philosophical detachment in which it was accepted two thousand years ago. Does that strike you also?

Mr. M: I think there's a tremendous lot in that. I mean, God knows, the necessary forces and scenario is available for such an ending. It's the first time in human history that men have in their hands the means of bringing the world to an end. I mean, they might think they had—

Mr. B: No, I don't want you to predict it—

Mr. M: No, no, no.

Mr. B: —any more than I would want to do so.

Mr. M: No, but I don't think that. I think that it is part of this experience of living that you see this potential of an end, but that actually there can't be an end and that the circumstances which would bring the end could also bring about the beginning. In other words, putting it in very simple terms, imagine that we do have the lunacy of a great atomic explosion, a nuclear explosion. All right, enormous destruction will take place and enormous numbers of deaths will occur, but also, somewhere or other, somebody will just suddenly be prostrating themselves before some coloured stone or something and it all begins again.

Mr. B: Yes, as that hack Russian writer once wrote, that when all the world is paved in concrete, somewhere a blade of grass will come through. However, let's look at it a bit more totally, if you don't mind—

Mr. M: Please.

Mr. B: —on the understanding that this is an abstract exercise. Carl Sagan, the American scientist, has recently popularised, if that's the right word, the intuition that in fact if three thousand whatever—megabytes or unmegabytes or kilobytes or whatever—go off, it will cause a cosmic winter, which will make survival absolutely impossible. When he told me this, I gave perhaps the wrong reply. Spastically, I said, "Well that's very good news because I should think that would be the ultimate deterrent to that kind of trigger being pressed." But in any case, you began by saying, and I think it's correct, that technically the means do exist to blot out life, including the blade of grass. Now, why should we resist, as our churchmen seem to have done, an attempt to integrate that hypothetical contingency in Christian doctrine?

Mr. M: Well, largely for one reason and one reason alone, which, to me, is absolutely decisive, and that is that ultimately the only prayer there is to say is, "Thy will be done." In other words, if something can happen and if that something happens, it can only be part of the purpose of our Creator for His creation, and that it might seem to be utterly destructive and hopeless, but out of it would come continuation, and this is—even if the whole thing were to be obliterated, still that would be God's purpose. Otherwise, it couldn't happen.

Mr. B: Well, here wouldn't a theologian insist that God's purpose be defined as giving to man the will which can mischievously be exerted to the end of suicide?

Mr. M: Yes.

Mr. B: All right. If somebody commits suicide, it's not God's purpose that he should commit suicide, is it?

Mr. M: No, no, but the fact that it happens means that God willed it to happen.

Mr. B: God willed that we have the power to have it happen?

Mr. M: Yes.

Mr. B: Yes.

Mr. M: And if we had that power, He also willed that in certain circumstances, we might use that power, and a resultant situation would be, in that sense, what He conceives should be brought about.

Mr. B: But the proximate pressure would be the Devil's rather than God's, would it not?

Mr. M: The pressure might be the Devil's and, to some extent, will be the Devil's, but, you see, even the Devil's purposes are ultimately turned into God's purpose. It was the Devil's purpose that our Lord should be crucified, but in His Crucifixion lay everything that's wonderful in a civilisation that you and I belong to. If that is now going to destroy itself, it can only destroy itself with, not necessarily with God's approval, but with God's consent; and therefore, out of it will come something which is impossible to foresee. Some life far away or some life in the wreckage will suddenly manifest itself, and the whole process will begin.

Mr. B: A transmutation of life into something different?

Mr. M: Yes, could be.

Mr. B: Okay. Well now, let's focus on the phenomenon of the end of the world and ask whether it has had an unhealthy bearing on a number of priests and theologians of every Christian denomination who seem to be approaching Christian pacifism, which was never a traditional position in Christianity. Do you find that the bishops' statement, for instance, in America that made so many headlines a year or so ago, that that sometimes had a taste of idolatry for life in this world in the sense that it was given a priority which it was never intended to have?

Mr. M: Well, I think that is so. There is a lack of humility in quarters where there should be no lack of humility. It's saying that this is the most appalling thing and if this happens, then everything is lost. But everything can't be lost because we are part of the Creation and what happens to us is in some degree, in some particular, the fulfiling of God's purpose for His Creation, and I think that these bishops have been infected with what is the great sickness of the twentieth century, which is science. They've caught that illness, and a lot of the things that they've done which are distressing if you look into them is because they've caught that illness, or this idiotic thing of evolution, which I'm sure will amuse mankind or whoever succeeds mankind for centuries to come—this idea that, you know, there was an amoebic mess and this amoebic mess became Bertrand Russell or somebody like that.

Mr. B: I can believe that.

Mr. M: (laughing) Yes. That this is a sort of craziness that science has fed into life, and produced an inanity which no previous supposition has. The hierarchy are disgracing themselves quite often by falling into that trap.

Mr. B: Well, as I understand it, here is the distinction that they attempt to make. It is correct that Christianity has never adopted pacifism, certainly not the Catholic Church. It has accepted the notion that some things are worth dying for, in pursuit of. Not suicide, but in pursuit of, let's say, of safety for your family, you may venture out and expose yourself to the possibility of death. Now, what's different now, say many of them, is that the corporate decision, of which I gave a particular example, is one that holds hostage the survival of the human race, and that the stakes, therefore, are too great to justify going out to protect the safety of the hearth, which means going out with hydrogen bombs and perhaps this three hundred megatons or whatever it is that's sufficient to destroy the earth; this, they say, is a quantum jump away from the conventional understanding of Christian hierarchy, and for that reason, some of them are finding themselves uttering pacifist pieties, which really call for unilateral surrender. Now, do you see anything in the fact of the bomb that invalidates preceding thinking as it touches on Christian pacifism?

Mr. M: No, I don't. You see, I think that part of the fallacy of their position is seeing this bomb as a unique threat.

Mr. B: Why is that a fallacy?

Mr. M: Well, because it's not a unique threat. I mean, because mankind has been under attack in various ways throughout his history. In the Latin Council in the twelfth century, a resolution was taken that the crossbow was such an evil, monstrous weapon that no Christian should use it.

It could, however, be used against heathens, but not against Christians, this diabolical weapon. Multiply that by a billion billion billion, and you have the atomic bomb.

Mr. B: But do you? You see, they say that's not true. They say you're using a synecdoche when you talk about one man with a crossbow; but, say they, when the target is life itself, you've got to usher in more sophisticated rules. Now, I'm anxious to hear your analysis of why that isn't so.

Mr. M: Well, it isn't so because in fact it's not a difference in kind; it's a difference in degree. You see, for instance, because my memory goes back a long way now, and in all the prognostications about the '39–'45 war were that "the airplanes will always get through, saturation bombing will take place, we're all going to be destroyed." In fact, they, as human beings always do, produced some very bizarre ideas. One was that there should be an enormous store of coffins available—and this sounds as though I'm making it up, but I'm not—and there wasn't enough wood for all the coffins that would be required by this holocaust, so they had cardboard coffins.

Mr. B: But they were more nearly right than wrong, weren't they? The deaths in World War I were fifteen million. In the Second World War, fifty-five million, leading up to Hiroshima. So wouldn't you say that there was a certain amount of prophetic validity in what they—

Mr. M: Not really, because I think that it presupposes that this miserable, ridiculous, little creature, *homo sapiens*, will be able totally to destroy God's creation, and he won't. That's all. I mean, Hiroshima, again, is a very good example. It so happened that I went there very soon after the end of the war in a train with the emperor because General MacArthur told the emperor that he wasn't a sun god any more; he was an ordinary king and he must wear a hat and raise it and so on.

Mr. B: He was just a dumpy, frumpy and banal king?

Mr. M: Absolutely. Well, then we got to Hiroshima, this place of doom. But of course it wasn't a place of doom. And you know, the only man I ever met who actually lived through the bomb in Hiroshima was the late head of the Jesuits, Arrupe.

Mr. B: He was there?

Mr. M: He was a priest there.

Mr. B: I didn't know that.

Mr. M: And I asked him about all these things, a sort of black rain and all these things that were built up in the picture, you know, in that single issue of *The New Yorker*—

Mr. B: Yes, John Hersey's.

Mr. M: —that brought it all out. And of course, it was a very, very bad explosion, a very destructive explosion.

Mr. B: Mr. Muggeridge, I don't—you don't intend to communicate—or do you?—that we are exaggerating the apocalyptic powers of the existing inventory of weapons. If whoever it was who counted is correct, we have six-hundred million times the explosive power of the Hiroshima bomb in our current inventory.

Mr. M: Yes. Bill, I don't take those figures. I mean, they are true, but the implications of them are not true. If there is a nuclear bomb, a nuclear explosion that destroys everything, if there's one single black man in the middle of some huge jungle still alive, then it hasn't destroyed mankind. It'll begin again. It'll go on. I mean, it's the idea that this thing we've got will in fact obliterate the human race, and that, too, again, is only obliterating the occupants of one very small, little feature in the universe, and to regard that as the end of everything is the mad ego that develops.

Mr. B: Well, it may be just a little acre, but it's our planet's little acre, isn't it?

Mr. M: It is our planet, and I'm very fond of it in a way.

Mr. B: You seem to resist, for reasons that aren't plain to me yet, the notion that in fact it is written that the end of the world will come.

Mr. M: It could come. I doubt if it could come in human terms. I don't think that it could come in God's terms because the whole idea is built not upon God's purposes, but upon man's purpose; and man's purpose is always wrong.

Mr. B: Well, it was certainly wrong in crucifying Him, but in fact, people seem to be arguing, even people whose roots are in Christian thought, that although the New Testament does speak about the end of the world, such a thing is really inconceivable, and that, under the circumstances, all policy should be written around preventing that possibility and that the shrewdest way to do that is to destroy, even unilaterally, our nuclear inventory, which, to me, is lunatic and heretical in its implications. But I don't want to argue with them that they may in fact be right that the next time around not even one black man in Africa will survive, or one blade of grass.

Mr. M: Well, of course, we can't really decide, you know, exactly what's going to happen, but there is an element of scientific egotism and pride built into the idea that having invented this thing, life's over, if it's used. This is absolutely typical madness of the scientific mind. I don't think that is at all what the end of the world, as envisioned by people like the Apostle Paul, was.

Mr. B: What did he have in mind?

Mr. M: What he had in mind was the coming again of our Lord. That was the essential thing, and that would be more important and more sublime than anything that human beings could do. I mean, that was what the end of the world was—the end of the reign of man and that Christ would come again and life would be quite different. Now, this is a dream, but it's a very beautiful dream; and I don't think that it can be equated in any way with the use of an ultrapowerful nuclear bomb, which would, of course, do enormous damage. The other day the Pope said something. He's a good man, that Pope, and he now and again says terribly good things. And he said the trouble with this nuclear thing is not really the bomb; the trouble is that there should be men who would use the bomb; that's the terrible thing, and that's the Devil's thing. I quite agree. I think he's absolutely right.

Mr. B: Well, I think he's absolutely right, and I think he's correct that people forget that. James Burnham pointed out years ago in his seminal book that a rifle is no more deadly than a broomstick in the absence of the will to use it as a rifle. But we do know that there are people alive who would not cavil at the use of the bomb if in fact it could be guaranteed to bring about what it was that they sought to bring about. Now, is there in the net dialectical situation an argument for throwing away our atom bombs? On the Christian principle?

Mr. M: I don't think at this moment that there is. There could be. There could come a time when it might seem right to do it, but now I think that the one hope of preventing this, not apocalypse, but the total destruction of everything we call Western Civilisation is this. Let me go to a sort of frightfully small point really. I happened to be in America when the Cuban crisis was going on, and there was Khrushchev and John F. Kennedy meeting together, and you could see exactly that each of them was thinking, you know, "Well, he's got this and we don't want him to have it." In other words, they didn't want a nuclear war and there wasn't a nuclear war. And you could have, of course, a situation in which the person who's Khrushchev does want it because he thinks that, owing to all this peace business that is being stirred up, that a decisive victory could be won by the Communist powers. That is possibly true. But I don't think that if you have two relatively equal nuclear force potentials, that is a situation which is terribly dangerous. It becomes dangerous if one of them becomes so weak that the temptation to the other to use its superiority would be to use it over there.

Mr. B: Is that the imaginary situation in which you said you might make the point that Christian duty prescribed throwing away your nuclear arsenal?

Mr. M: I didn't think that it implies that.

Mr. B: Well, what did you have in mind when you said under some circumstances that might be—

Mr. M: Well, it might be the case that—

Mr. B: —recommended.

Mr. M: It might be the case that there could be an agreement, a real agreement, not a faked agreement, but a real agreement, to get rid of this in exactly the same way that at a much lower level the danger of poison gas, the danger of bacteriological war—

Mr. B: Yes, but that's not unilateral, if there's an agreement, is there?

Mr. M: No, it's not, but it is—

Mr. B: So you're not really anxious to specify a circumstantial situation in which you would recommend, as a Christian, that we unilaterally do away with—

Mr. M: In the present set up of the world, no. I think that it's absolutely a foolish notion, which has been largely stimulated by people who want to make sure that the East is the strong side, and those people are working away like beavers. We have a local Monsignor here who lends himself to this. It's one of the few changes that take place, because before it was the Dean of Canterbury, an Anglican, but now we have a Monsignor who says that the Communists, for instance, are men of peace.

Mr. B: Sort of like the Red dean twenty-five years ago, Hewlett Johnson.

Mr. M: That's right, he reappears as a Monsignor.

Mr. B: Well, I suppose to say you're a man of peace in the generic sense is not to commit an empirical error, but if you point at Stalin and say, "This was a man of peace," it's extremely difficult to carry the metaphor, isn't it?

Mr. M: Bill, there is a peace, and funnily enough, in meditating on all this business, it came to me rather vividly because a rather strange thing happened. When we were trying to get the Nobel peace prize for Mother Teresa, which we had to do several years in succession to get, and then she finally got it, and the question came back from Oslo, which is where the thing is settled by these rather sombre Norwegian senators who decide who is the person of peace, that—the question came back, "What does Mother Teresa do for peace?" In other words, where does she sort of march and recite slogans and hold hands around missile sites and so on and so on; what has she done for peace?

Mr. B: She gives it a sense of priority.

Mr. M: Yes, well, the point is that she lives in the opposite proposition.

Mr. B: That's right, right.

Mr. M: I mean, those two great forces in our existence of power and love. She is the one who lives in terms of love. Now, that is really working for peace. That is really overcoming the menace of people who are going to totally destroy our world and ourselves. But it struck me as very humorous in a way that somebody should want to be given some point in her activities which you could say, "That is definitely in the direction of peace," and I suppose, for the people who put that question, if she had actually joined this so-called peace movement that would have met the case. But of course it's much more than that.

Mr. B: Yes.

Mr. M: In her, one can see why the Christian can confront the danger of a nuclear holocaust without undue fear.

Mr. B: Well, surely in the case of Mother Teresa you have an example of somebody who is carrying out so explicitly the injunction that she should love her neighbours as to entitle you to say, "If everybody loved their neighbours as she loves her neighbours, you would not crank up the kind of hostility that would bring on belligerence."

Mr. M: Exactly.

Mr. B: Well, do you acknowledge or not the following line of reasoning, namely that if in a nuclear exchange, the victim of the first strike, in this case, the West, were to proceed to fire back, although it's too late, according to my accounting, to prevent that first strike, you don't necessarily repeal the doctrine of deterrence because you have accomplished something in virtue of firing back and ridding the world of such aggressors as committed the first strike. Do you have a moral justification, in other words, in firing back with the sole purpose of ridding the world of such aggressors? That's the question.

Mr. M: Yes, well, I think that it's a matter which I couldn't in advance say.

Mr. B: But you would have to if you were president, wouldn't you?

Mr. M: Yes, you would have to envisage the possibility of that.

Mr. B: We intend to run you, you know.

Mr. M: Yes, you would have to do that, and it's certainly very important that the people who are going to send the first shot know quite well—that this one is coming back because that is the best of all deterrents—

Mr. B: Right, right, right. And in the absence of that certitude there's an attrition of the deterrent factor.

Mr. M: It increases enormously the danger of the thing being precipitated from one quarter. That is indeed true.

Mr. B: Yes.

Mr. M: And so that pacifism in the sense of saying that, "We will get rid of all our weapons," well, yes, if you are prepared to have no authority in the world, no influence in the world, no importance in the world; to wind up your role as a country, as a people. That is one sort of pacifism, and it's one that I couldn't bring myself to respect. But the idea that you would give up your nuclear weapons and then whoever gets over his illness and can function in the Kremlin would then say, "Well, it's not much good us having nuclear weapons if these people have given them up," that is pure drivel, isn't it?

Mr. B: Yes, C. S. Lewis said that the pacifists have a vested interest in losing their campaign.

Mr. M: Yes.

Mr. B: Because the belligerents would not permit them to be pacifists, and under the circumstances, they can only continue to be pacifists for so long as they lose the popular campaign. Pacifists are not tolerated in the Soviet Union. Under the circumstances, the sure way to guarantee that you would end your pacifist existence would be to surrender to the Soviet Union. So although that point sometimes sounds a little too trim and neat, I think it is a profoundly interesting point.

Mr. M: So do I.

Mr. B: Now, when you speak of the disintegration of Christian life, do you mean exclusively among the laity or also among the clergy?

Mr. M: Well, I mean both, actually.

Mr. B: So is there not visible a resistance to that disintegration among the organised clergy?

Mr. M: I suspect there might be. I haven't actually come across it myself, but I suspect there might be because the clergy are subject to the fantasies of human beings, and that's one.

Mr. B: I know a scholar who a year or so ago said, "You know, I've been dying to become a Catholic for about ten to twelve years, but I can't get anybody interested enough to tell me about it," and I thought that was extremely interesting.

Mr. M: Very interesting, yes.

Mr. B: The notion that religious evangelism should have a very low social priority, is really quite new, or is it? Is that a twentieth-century phenomenon?

Mr. M: I'm not quite sure what you mean by that.

Mr. B: Well, in most centuries people had what they called "fighting faiths," and although they were often stupid about how they attempted to evangelise, the Inquisition being a notorious example, still they cared. And the question arises whether in the twentieth century people care enough to bother, for instance, to preach the word of Christ, even at the risk of being boring. Is that a part of the disintegration that you isolate? That lack of zest?

Mr. M: I would think it probably is, but I still am not quite sort of clear myself as to exactly what's in their minds over that. I think that it could be regarded as a sort of deterioration, as a loss of faith, in a way. I feel the ultimate faith of the Christian religion is that God is responsible for Creation, and God is a God of love, not of hate; God is all the qualities that we want to see in the world, and that nothing can be settled except in relation to that. Man can make an inconceivable mess of anything, and I would say that he's putting up a tremendous performance at this moment, partly by this utter acceptance of the idea that this bomb makes nothing worthwhile.

Mr. B: Well, when we pray that we be delivered from temptation, might it be correct to say that a temptation in having a nuclear arsenal is to use it, even if your motives are defensive rather than aggressive, and that under the circumstances, it is prudent to remove such a temptation from yourself—yourself, of course, being a country?

Mr. M: That would be quite a good idea provided the people who put it forward will recognise exactly what that would mean. If they would get rid of all their weapons, they would then count for absolutely nothing in the world. They would be of no importance whatever. They would have no influence whatever upon what happens. After all, there are countries that have reached that point, small countries like Scandinavian countries who haven't really got any defences, and who seem to get along all right for the time being. I think that the notion that we must get rid of all these weapons at all costs, and that if we do we shall live happily ever after, is a great fantasy, and one that is planted on us to some extent by pressures that are really quite different but don't admit to being so.

Mr. B: Now, those pressures. Do they emanate from people who simply are unrealistic, or do they emanate from people who are sentimental about the Soviet Union? Somebody said about you that the only sense in which you have been feveredly consistent is your opposition to Communism ever since you discovered it in Moscow in 1932. Is this consistency of opposition to Communism by you something that derives from a special knowledge of Communism, or is it generally communicable among people who haven't had your experience?

Mr. M: Well, obviously it exists because of that experience, which, for me, was a great sort of turnover of views about life, and it was intensified by this spectacle, which I still think is one of the strangest of all that one's experienced, which is the spectacle of the choice intelligentsia of the Western world prostrating themselves before Stalin and his setup there.

Mr. B: And how do you account for that?

Mr. M: I can't yet. I mean, of course there are different features of it, but I think that a lot of the people who went there and some who were known to me, even related through marriage, that what they wanted to feel was that they could have power, absolute power, without going through all the rigamarole of being elected and making their views acceptable.

Mr. B: But why did they want the power?

Mr. M: Because they love power. Because people who have not realised that the basis of human life is love, do love power and pine for power.

Mr. B: Well, do they in some cases pine for power because they feel that they can genuinely make a better world through the exercise of it?

Mr. M: They persuade themselves of that.

Mr. B: Yes.

Mr. M: It's rather like someone attempting a seduction and saying that, "After all, this will do you good," you know. I mean, they are absolutely avid for power for power's own sake. This is something that's in human beings, and it is enormously evident in ideologies, and they may see this setup in the USSR and where, you know, everything can be done because you are completely free to do what seems to you right.

Mr. B: Basically the urge for power is a very dangerous one. It's one that Jesus Christ declined to have.

Mr. M: Yes, but certainly if you were, let's say, being tormented by Hitler in the '30s, you would welcome power sufficient to resist, wouldn't you?

Mr. B: That's what a war's about, isn't it?

Mr. M: Yes. But you're, let's say, a contender. A political contender for office in 1932 would desire power perhaps for the best of reasons. He would think they were the best of reasons.

Mr. B: But it would corrupt?

Mr. M: Yes, and it would also be something that appealed to him. In other words, instead of having to argue with a lot of difficult people and address a lot of meetings and things, he would be in a position to do what he thought was the right thing on his own strength. At least that was the only explanation I could see for all these extraordinary people coming there because everything in the regime and in the way in which it operated was contrary to what they believed in and liked. But it still had the marvellous point in its favour that it gave you absolute power. I mention a very small example. We were taken down to the Dneprostroi Dam when it finished, and there was an American colonel who had been building it, and I asked him, purely as sort of conversation, "How do you like it here?" expecting some marvellous tirade, and he said, "Oh it's absolutely superb." And so I said, "Why do you think it's superb?" And he said, "Well, because, you see, we never have any labour troubles." And that seems to me to embody the whole thing. I mean, from his view, it was perfect. You were building a dam, you wanted a thousand more people, telephone to the GPU and they come, no questions asked, no pay discussions.

Mr. B: What Michael Oakeshott calls "making politics as the crow flies."

Mr. M: Yes.

Mr. B: Well, but the scholastic Christian philosophy teaches us that government is a divine institution. What do you understand to be meant by that assertion?

Mr. M: I've never met a government that seemed to me to be a divine institution, I'm afraid. But it is true that power has to be exercised, which is presumably what Jesus Christ meant when he said, "We render unto Caesar the things that are Caesar's and unto God, the things that are God's."

Mr. B: So therefore there are some things that should be Caesar's?

Mr. M: Exactly.

Mr. B: For instance, a police force, right?

Mr. M: Yes. They're all dangerous, even then, but they're also necessary. But in answering that question about "Should we pay tribute to Caesar?" He does recognise that Caesar has claims upon us. If we enjoy the security—

Mr. B: That he gives you.

Mr. M: That he gives us.

Mr. B: Yes, and that would translate nowadays, for instance, in the right to conscript—

Mr. M: Yes.

Mr. B: —an army in England or in America.

Mr. M: To limit what's called freedom under certain circumstances.

Mr. B: Yes, yes. But the quest for power in democratic circumstances, you are saying, is self-governing; that is to say, you run less of a risk of accumulating as much of it as you would if you didn't have the democratic tribunal to pass judgement. Well, let me then finish in the last five minutes we have by asking you to sum up on this point. Is there anything that's happened in your lifetime which you think affects those priorities on the basis of which Christianity for two thousand years has told us that there is such a thing as a just war?

Mr. M: I think that is a question that I have a great difficulty in giving a sort of "yes" and "no" answer to, but in one's personal life, in 1939 it seemed to me right that we should fight Hitler, that, if we were to abandon Europe to Hitler, this would be an appalling thing. Afterwards, when it turned out that in fact by knocking off Hitler we simply abandoned ourselves to Stalin, I felt less enthusiastic about it. But it is true that there is such a thing as a just war. There are circumstances in which, if you are going to maintain your civilised way of life, you may have to defend it, and if not, all you can do is to say that, "I'm not prepared to defend it, I don't think that these weapons and things should be used, and therefore I recognise that I must give up every idea of being secure in my way of life and being looked after in any way."

Mr. B: As you may or may not know, there is a protocol in gambling houses, and that protocol is that you may not be given credit. Now, some people do anyway. The idea there is that you should put up only as many chips as you can actually commandeer through the exercise of your financial resources, because otherwise you end up gambling your house and your children's education money or whatever. Now, in a sense, that's something that invokes proportionality. There are people, Christian theologians, who are saying that the proportionality that governed the idea of the just war is now out of bounds, that the kind of credit, the chips, which you were given up until the discovery of the nuclear bomb were realisable, whereas you now have a dimension that would be the equivalent of total credit. You don't believe, for instance, in your right to gamble your own soul, or do you?

Mr. M: It's very good image, actually, of the whole thing. I see the difficulty.

Mr. B: But you're not pronouncing on it?

Mr. M: I'm pronouncing on it in this sense, that if a person is ready to say that, "Because this bomb and a nuclear war would be so terrible, I herewith give up all idea of securing my property, my family, of looking after anything. I give it up because it seems to me that the price to be paid, if it's nuclear war, is too great."

Mr. B: You as an individual or you as a corporate state?

Mr. M: Well, first of all as an individual.

Mr. B: Yes, yes.

Mr. M: And then insofar as you influence the state, yes, also as a state.

Mr. B: We call this Finlandisation in America.

Mr. M: Yes, but even that's a cheat because the Finns are not quite, utterly in the hands of the Communists.

Mr. B: But that's by sufferance of the Communists, isn't it?

Mr. M: Well, it is in a way, but they're also rather cunning themselves. I mean, I think that the Russians use it, of course. They have let it be like that, which doesn't matter to them one way or the other, in order that they can use that argument.

Mr. B: Sure, it's like China letting Hong Kong be as it is.

Mr. M: That's right, that's right.

Mr. B: But it is by sufferance. Now, if one were offered by some divine arbiter the exchange of life as it is lived in Finland, i.e., with as many freedoms as they have and none other, one might say, "Well, this is better than risking a nuclear exchange." On the other hand, there would be no guarantee, would there, that they would be able to—

Mr. M: No, and this is exactly what's happening actually. The next move in this game, unless there is trouble inside the USSR, is that the West Germans will say that, "After all, we've had a sort of Finland settlement," and call it a day, in which case the triumph of the Communist setup will be total, and probably the United Kingdom and the other small countries will be forced to fall into the same thing.

Mr. B: Sure. They always talk about what if the Soviet Union said to West Germany, "Pull out of NATO and disband your army, and we will allow you to unify with East Germany and you will have one Germany," which might look wonderful on Monday, but what happens on Tuesday is what we need to remind them, isn't it?

Mr. M: It's been a very clever move of the Communists to sit up and say, "Well, look at these people. They're quite happy, and so on." You see?

Mr. B: Yes. "What's so bad about Finlandisation?"

Mr. M: Exactly. Actually, we had a team here to ask about Orwell and—frightfully nice people—and I said to them, "Supposing I say that Orwell's account of things in *1984* and *Animal Farm* is based entirely on the arrangements in the Soviet Union. Would you allow that to be spoken?" And he said, "I'm afraid not."

Mr. B: Thank you very much, Mr. Malcolm Muggeridge.

Mr. M: Thank you.

4. A Loving God

ROY TREVIVIAN Malcolm, can you tell me first of all where were the seeds of religion planted in you? Were you brought up in a religious home? Was your childhood in any way surrounded by the idea of God?

MALCOLM MUGGERIDGE It is very difficult to know exactly what a religious home is. Let me tell you about my home. My father was a pioneer Socialist and Fabian, and, if he had a religion, that was it. We were brought up to regard Socialism as the one thing that mattered, and it is quite arguable that my very strong reaction against the idea of creating a kingdom of heaven on earth may be a sort of reaction to this, exactly as many people brought up in, say, a strongly Methodist home react the other way. But, of course, my father, like so many of the early Socialists, and, in my opinion, the best, was a spillover from the chapel. He was a very poor boy; he left school when he was thirteen, and he told me once when he was quite old—and I never forgot it—that from the age of thirteen there were always other people dependent upon him. Well, the chapel was everything. The chapel was his university. He went to mock parliaments, literary societies, and terrible things called mutual improvement societies. His socialism was derived from such activities as these, so he had a sort of Christian background, which I certainly absorbed.

R.T. You mean he expressed this form of Christianity in the home?

M.M. He expressed it in the sense that we were brought up to revere the person of Christ, but we were also brought up to ridicule the church and dogmas of all kinds, including the Crucifixion. My father sometimes spoke at religious meetings, and then he would always refer the Christian

A 1968 dialogue with Roy Trevivian. Reprinted from Malcolm Muggeridge, *Jesus Rediscovered* (Garden City, N.Y.: Doubleday, 1969), pp. 181–235.

gospel to his notions of a better world and a better society. That was the religion in which I was brought up and which I accepted.

R.T. But did it include going to church?

M.M. I did in fact go for a time to a Congregational church, though primarily, I confess, for social reasons; specifically for the mundane purpose of meeting girls. This may seem strange in the light of the present situation. We were a family of boys, and we never knew any girls, and one of the few occasions when I met girls in a vaguely romantic way was at chapel. Also there was a rather marvelous old clergyman there, a Congregational minister, a Scotsman called Sanderson. I can see him now—a remarkable old chap with a long white beard, who used to talk about the New Testament in a vivid and picturesque way, especially about fishermen. Having come from the Shetland Islands, he knew a lot about fishermen, and he would bring to his exposition of the New Testament a knowledge of fishermen which appealed to me very much. But that was not a very deep impression. I can also trace in myself, when I look back, another strain, and that was a feeling I always had as a child, and have now, of being a stranger in this world, of not being a native. I can remember it so vividly, as almost the first recollection of life—an overpowering feeling that this world is not a place where I really belong.

R.T. When you say this world, do you mean the universe, or do you mean the way man is in the universe?

M.M. I mean my physical existence in time. I couldn't have put it that way then, but I know the inconceivable poignancy with which I first heard the phrase in the Bible "a stranger in a strange land." I don't think any phrase I have ever heard gave me such a sense of poignancy.

R.T. Can you fill this out a little bit more, so that I can understand clearly what you mean?

M.M. It's not easy, because this is, I think now, the essence of mysticism and of a mystical view of life—this sense that man has of not completely belonging here. He doesn't belong here, because his soul belongs to eternity, whereas this is a place of time and bodies. It is the feeling out of which all art, all literature, all mystical concepts, all philosophy, anything like that, has come.

R.T. *When did this feeling first come to you?*

M.M. I tell you in all honesty, almost the first thing I can remember as a conscious child was this feeling that somehow or another I didn't belong here, that here is not my home. It was only afterwards, when I began to read writers like Blake and Pascal, the writers that I now think are the great luminaries of modern times—also Tolstoy—that I understood the relation between mysticism and feeling a stranger in a strange land. All this business of men's alienation, which is on every tongue now, seems to me to relate directly to this feeling of not belonging here. If I could point to one single basic feeling out of which the structure of my mind and thought and belief grew, it would be this—that I do not belong here.

R.T. *As a young person, did this feeling of estrangement in the world go hand in hand with a feeling that God loved you?*

M.M. Not till much later, because God didn't arise in my upbringing. But it did mean—and I have to make this clear immediately—that all the worldly things, essential things, like money and fame and success and sensuality, which even a child is aware of, even though I was greedy for them, decidedly so, perhaps even above the average, I never really liked them, I never thought they were any good.

R.T. *And yet at quite a young age you threw yourself wholeheartedly into supporting the Socialist movement.*

M.M. Oh, very strongly so—absolutely. But that was partly just love of my father. He was a most delightful man, and I loved him dearly. I not only loved him, but I completely accepted his view of the world. I was absolutely convinced that if my father and his friends took over, which I firmly believed they would, because it all seemed to me to be so reasonable, what they said, that everything was going to be fine. It was just a matter of time, and people would see that the capitalist system was useless, that everybody should stay at school until they were sixteen or seventeen, and that leisure time should be devoted to reading Shakespeare instead of going to race meetings, and so on and so on. All this seemed to me to be obvious, and it was just a matter of my father and his friends winning votes and getting into power. The whole thing was as clear as day.

R.T. *Where does your mother figure in all this?*

M.M. My mother played a very small part in my life, strangely enough. She was a terribly nice woman, straight working class, whereas my father belonged to the lower middle class. His father was an undertaker, who disappeared very early on, and his mother started a secondhand furniture business in Penge, but it was all in terms of the lower, lower, lower middle class. My mother's family lived in Sheffield, in back-to-back houses, and were all steel-workers. My father met her in the Isle of Man when he was on holiday. It was a sort of H. G. Wells episode—he a young clerk holidaying in the Isle of Man, and she a girl from Sheffield, very pretty, very pretty indeed, and he fell in love with her and brought her south. When we used to go and visit her family, whom we adored, the funny thing to me is, looking back, that theoretically, of course, they were the downtrodden and oppressed and we were the up-and-coming, but in actual terms of standard of life, we children always considered that we had a much better "blow out" with them, and that their house was warmer and their whole manner of life more lavish than ours—which it was, as a matter of fact, because they spent everything on these comforts.

R.T. *A big fire and plenty of food on the table . . .*

M.M. Absolutely—and of course in Yorkshire that meant plenty of home-made food of a very high order of excellence. For instance, at Christmas we would be fairly certain a hamper would come to us from Sheffield full of delicacies. Like so many lower-middle-class families with their belief in education and all that sort of thing, we lived really very abstemiously, relative to the working classes, who didn't give a damn about all that, but just wanted to be comfortable. And comfortable they were in those days.

R.T. *Your mother still seems very much a ghostlike figure. You didn't have very much to do with her?*

M.M. She wasn't exactly ghostlike, but she was utterly uneducated; she could barely write—I don't mean that she was a fool by any manner of means, but she could barely write, and all my passionate interest in life was centered on books. My father was really a very extraordinary man, and, having left school at thirteen, he taught himself French, and was very well read. He even taught himself to play the piano. He had a passion for learning that men of that type had. He went up to London at about eight o'clock from East Croydon station, and he would return at about six o'clock; he would then engage in several hours of municipal activity because he was a town councillor—committees, meetings, and on top of all that (and how the hell did he do it? one now asks oneself) he would educate himself, and continued to do so until the day of his death—to read and to think and to make notes. I have got one of his notebooks. On Saturday afternoon, which was his afternoon off, he would maybe go off and bicycle from Croydon to Tunbridge Wells and address a meeting, and then bicycle back. He had fantastic energy, and all my interest was centered on him.

R.T. What did your mother contribute, then?

M.M. She kept the house going; she washed and cleaned and cooked; we had no help of any kind.

R.T. Did she understand you?

M.M. No, not at all. I never had a conversation of mutual understanding with my mother at all. I used to read my father's books precociously, and she once found me reading Rousseau's *Confessions*, when, God knows, I must have been very young. I shouldn't think I knew what it was about really, but she gave me a frightful dressing down, and said that Rousseau was a bad man. I remember the phrase she used, very typical; she said "Rousseau was born with his blood boiling." I had no idea what she meant by this, but I realize now that it was a sort of primitive way of saying that he was sexually obsessed.

R.T. We both know enough about Freud for me to be able to ask: Could not this feeling of estrangement in the universe be due to the lack of a strong link with your mother?

M.M. It could be so, but I think, if it were, then all the Christian mystics would have had mothers from whom they were alienated—which is very much not the case. Take, for instance, the case of St. Augustine, who is a very sympathetic figure to me. His mother was a colossally strong influence on his life. I am exceedingly doubtful about all that psychological stuff, and I don't really believe in it at all. I think Freud produced one of the worst sorts of grotesque oversimplifications. After all, what he hit on was very simple and obvious—that sex, the procreative urge, is a basic urge, which can't be left out of account. Well, that's perfectly obvious, and it probably had been left out of account, but I think it now is taken too much into account. It has sometimes occurred to me that Freud and Marx were two Jews who punished us for all we had done to the Jews by, in effect, destroying the Christian religion. Freud destroyed it by taking away any sense of personal responsibility for wrongdoing.

R.T. I don't go along with you in what you say about being a stranger here. I would say that here I have no continuing dwelling place, but I feel at home in the universe. I feel that it is a friendly place; I don't think that I am alienated from the universe.

M.M. I love it. I love it. Every day I live in the world I love it more. Every time I look out of that window, I love it, every leaf, every color, and the more I feel myself a stranger the more I love it. Because I know that the whole of this has a much larger dimension than my eye can pick out.

R.T. I see, you don't feel alienated *from the* universe*?*

M.M. I feel only that I don't live here. I am visiting.

R.T. Oh yes, yes, but you can feel at home here?

M.M. Yes, I am having a delightful time, but I'm making a brief visit, and therefore all plans that are based on the idea that we live permanently here, and that this is the beginning and end of life, seem to me ludicrous.

R.T. When did this business about religion and the possible truth of what Jesus Christ was teaching, when did this come back to you in a big way?

M.M. I don't think there was ever a dramatic moment when it came back. I have often thought about this. It's something—well, put it this way—it has always seemed to me that the most interesting thing in the world is to try and understand what life is about. This is the only pursuit that could possibly engage a serious person—what is life about? And of course it is a continuing pursuit. As I have realized the fallacy of all materialist philosophies and materialist utopias, and of the politics of utopianism, so I have come to feel more and more strongly that the answer to life does not lie in materialism. In seeking the other transcendental answer I have inevitably and increasingly been driven to the conclusion, almost against my own will, that for a West European whose life and background and tradition are in terms of Western European Christian civilisation, the only answer lies in the person and life and teaching of Christ. Here, and here only, the transcendental answer is expressed adequately and appropriately. Now that is not the kind of conclusion that involves anything like a Damascus road experience. It is a process of continuing realisation. On the other hand, of course, one reaches a point when one comes out into the open about it. For me that was delayed because I felt it was necessary that my personal life should not be a disgrace to the Christian religion when I avowed it. There were certain things which I had to do about my personal life. In my particular case—and I am not laying this down as any kind of a rule—this involved abstemiousness and asceticism, and the mastery of self-indulgence.

R.T. Can you give me some instances?

M.M. The most trivial ones are drinking and smoking, both of which I indulged in fairly lavishly. These are obvious enough, as is overeating. The most important of all is sex—I mean indulgence in promiscuity. That is more difficult, because sex is, of all forms of self-indulgence, the one which makes the most appeal to the imagination. Greed, cupidity, and related pursuits are really rather vulgar and make very little appeal to the imagination, but sexual indulgence makes a considerable appeal. Therefore, it is the hardest to conquer, but in my opinion it is absolutely essential that it should be conquered.

R.T. You are saying to me that before you could avow that you were a Christian these things had to be renounced.

M.M. Yes. I felt very strongly that I couldn't take on something for which I had such a respect as I have for the Christian religion if I was liable to disgrace it. I believe that no moral proposition is worth propounding unless it is also expressed in terms of personal conduct. If I say that all men are my brothers, the first thing I have to be sure of is that I do veritably feel them to be so, and behave accordingly. If I don't, better not to say it.

R.T. And act on it.

M.M. And act on it. If I don't do that, better keep quiet. Thus, for instance, in the case of the racial problem in the United States, I feel in many ways more comfortable about it in the Southern states than in the North, because in the South the arrangement which prevails, vicious though it is, at least expresses the actual state of mind of people, and is therefore more bearable. Moral propositions without action are as sick as sex without procreation. That's precisely what's wrong with liberalism—the basic ideology of our society. So it seems to me that all moral feelings that one might have, and all moral propositions one might wish to propound, must be related to personal conduct. If you take the basic Christian view of life that one must die in the flesh in order to be reborn, then one must be master of one's flesh, and it is quite impossible to combine that with self-indulgence, especially sexual self-indulgence, whether outside or inside matrimony. I think it is also a base thing to seek to perpetuate sex once the actual urge is passed. So all this had to be dealt with. For me it was like a man who wanted to apply to join a particular club or, better, religious order. First of all he had to be sure that he could fulfil the requirements. That took me a certain amount of time and effort. It would be very wicked for any man to say that he had completely achieved mastery of his fleshly appetites, but I felt able to declare myself a Christian when I was reasonably sure that a scrutiny of my life would not disgrace the inconceivably high standards that Christians I admire—like Tolstoy and Pascal—have set.

R.T. But what about fame? You have more fame now than you have ever had. Isn't this a form of indulgence?

M.M. I suppose it would be if one cared much about it, but I don't. I think I am being genuine. I don't say that occasionally, if I know that people are aware of me, there isn't a sort of satisfaction—but there is also a sort of dissatisfaction. If tomorrow such fame as I enjoy were to be completely obliterated, it wouldn't worry me; it wouldn't worry me at all, it wouldn't cost me a pang. But I agree, of course, that it is a thing you have to watch, because one's ego is indestructible, and the Devil is always there working on this ego. The old-fashioned idea that there is a force in us of wickedness, which is the Devil, is, in my opinion, completely true. And of course, the ego, the Devil's instrument, is always there to his hand. But fame is not a thing to which I attach much value; neither to fame nor to money. I attach perhaps excessive value to being good at my chosen work—which is writing or communicating. If someone says to me: "That was a marvelous thing you wrote," or, "I was enormously impressed by what you said," this gives me a glow of pleasure, and I don't think a wholly unworthy one because, although it is connected with vanity, the pleasure in it is more, I hope and believe, the sense that one has communicated something to someone which was worthy. You know that marvelous saying of Christ's "Let your light shine"; well, when one feels that one has shone a little light, that is what gives satisfaction. I should still like to stress that I do not believe in asceticism for asceticism's own sake. In other words, I am not a Puritan in any sense. I don't think there is virtue in self-denial as such. If I want to do something, and I stop myself doing it, I don't think that is virtuous, though it may be wise or well advised. For myself, personally, I have found that I can only concentrate my thoughts and activities on Christianity and everything connected with it—which is the one object I care about in life now—if I don't indulge my senses. This applies even to overeating, which is quite a harmless thing.

R.T. What do you mean when you say overeating?

M.M. I simply mean eating a lot. Actually, I am a vegetarian nowadays and eat rather little. If I eat a lot, still more if I drink a lot, or smoke a lot, or indulge in sexual activities a lot, this means to me personally, with my sort of make-up, that I am shut off from the sight of God. The image which I use to myself is taken from driving. If it's too hot inside the car, if the temperatures outside and inside are ill adjusted, then the windscreen mists over and you can't see. In the same sort of way, if I allow myself to become preoccupied with my bodily appetites, my soul's window gets misted over and I can't see out. I do not in any way criticise people who don't feel similarly. I do not think that abstinence is essential to the pursuit of truth through Christianity, though I notice that the figures in the past whom I most admire, and whose writings and thoughts most appeal to me, usually did take that way. So there must be some connection. Even so, I would never preach abstinence to people as such; I would point out to them that my experience of life, such as it is, suggests that an integral part of looking at the spiritual reality of life is divorcing yourself as far as possible from involvement in the sensual or physical part. I make one exception to that: For me, in my life, there has been only one sensual experience which has carried spiritual undertones, and that is the ecstasy of physical passion when one is young and when it is associated with love. That is an experience which has, I think, spiritual undertones. It explains why in literature it is the only sensual passion which has produced great art. Other forms of indulgence have not; they have produced oddities of writing, or perversions of writing, but they have not produced great literature. That particular experience has, and it is the one exception. But I would emphasize the point that it belongs to youth, and that efforts to protract it and to apply it in middle age or old age usually produce horror and distortion. Money as a pursuit is, in my opinion, about the most contemptible of all. On the other hand we need money to live, and I don't think as a factor in life it is in itself either good or bad. After all, it is only a means of exchange. I have never pursued money; most of my life I have been relatively poor. In the years before the 1939–45 war, as a free-lance writer, I seldom earned as much as £20 a week. That, with a wife and four children, was certainly not affluence. Yet it is a time I look back on with great satisfaction. I think that people who are poor and have to live modestly and bring up children at considerable sacrifice to themselves are fortunate, not unfortunate. It is the others who are unfortunate. They are missing out on something very exhilarating and delightful.

R.T. Can you develop that a little bit?

M.M. Judging from my own friends, and people that I have known, those who escape these difficulties miss a great deal. Christians are often accused of being morbid when they talk of the joy of sacrificing. I think it is one of the deepest truths of the Christian religion. Far from being a source of sadness, sacrifice is a great joy and source of illumination—perhaps the greatest of all. I also think that to live modestly is always a richer experience, because you are living like the majority of people; the trouble with the rich, as I have known them, is not really that they are bad people, but that they are cut off from an essential experience. They don't understand. For ninety-nine per cent of human beings their lives are governed by the struggle to acquire the means to live. This is how the arrangement is, and, if you don't experience that, you miss a great deal. I don't think I ever had a bank passbook in black until I was well into my forties. With four children there were always unexpected expenses, and so one was always in the red.

R.T. Did this make you anxious?

M.M. I have been anxious about money, yes, and I think the bad side of poverty is the fear that it creates, but I would certainly think that the unreality of life for the rich, and ultimately the boredom of life for them, is a worse misfortune. Lately I have earned a lot, and I have had to confront the question of what I should do about it. Here, again, abstemiousness is a help. At least I can say that expenditure on myself is now minimal. The idea of a big house, servants, that sort of thing, would be in any case abhorrent; my own present personal scale of living is certainly no higher than it would be if I had retired on a small pension. This seems to me preferable to falling into the sort of ethical and financial shifts that Tolstoy's efforts to have no property or earnings at all involved. At the same time, of course, I have to recognize that whatever financial stringency I have known in the past, it has never been at all comparable with the grinding poverty which, to our shame, continues to exist in the affluent societies of America and Western Europe, still less with the ever-worsening poverty of Africa and Asia. Nor, I know, is my way of life, however abstemious, other than privileged by comparison with the great majority of my fellow men. I often wish it were otherwise; the only uniform I have ever looked at with envy is that of a lay brother. A phrase used by St. Francis of Assisi that I once read has continued to echo in my mind—"naked on the naked earth." So placed, even in this cruel and unjust world, one could live and sleep in peace.

R.T. Asceticism, as you have described it to me, is not an end in itself, but is a means of clearing the way for a deeper communion with God. Malcolm, what do you imagine about God? I know this is a ridiculous and impossible question, but up to not long ago people had an image of God, and then we were told we mustn't have images of God, that God was the ground of our being, God wasn't out there, God was in here, and so on. I find it almost impossible to pray to God, talk about God, imagine God, without imagining something. I would like you, if you would, to wrestle with this; when you are addressing God, or when the subject of God comes up in conversation, what happens in your mind? What do you think about?

M.M. I can answer that, because it is something that I think about a great deal. I may not answer it as definitely as many might hope, but I will answer it as truthfully as possible. How do I arrive first of all at the notion of God? For me the notion of God comes primarily from a sense, probably the deepest spiritual experience that I have ever had, of the oneness of life. Everything, I am profoundly convinced, is connected with everything else; the universe, my life, the past, the future, all this is a oneness, in which each part bears a relation to each other part. Now, it is inconceivable to me that there could be this oneness without a One, a unitary spirit behind it. I see in the world, the phenomenal world, in nature, which I love very much, in the achievements of men, which I admire very much, in myself, in my responses and reactions to the world, I see this mysterious connection, this oneness, which to me presupposes one being, a oneness behind all life. Nothing that could happen in exploring the universe, or finding out about life, affects that idea; on the contrary, each new discovery embellishes, enlarges, it. There is no conflict at all. I have also noticed that the greatest scientists, men like Einstein, are more than anyone else aware of this, because they see scientifically what we see intuitively: this fact that there is nothing which you can explore in the universe which is not related to everything else. As Blake indicated majestically, if we could understand perfectly a grain of sand we should understand the universe. That, to me, says "God." Now then, how do I see this God? If it were not for the Christian religion, I should see no more of God than that. I should content myself with saying that there is a oneness, a spirit, animating this universe.

R.T. You have talked about a God who unified, but this could be just an impersonal force.

M.M. The next step is one of faith, but one which, I contend, is borne out by the very shape and color and flavor of the universe, as well as by everything that has been experienced about it. That spirit is a loving spirit, not a hating spirit, or an indifferent spirit; a creative, not a destructive, spirit. We recognize its hand in all the creativity of men, and we recognize its opposite in all the destructiveness of men; we recognize its hand in art, because art is an image of this unity of the universe. So we now arrive at the point that there is a spirit, and this spirit is a spirit of love, not of hate or indifference, a spirit of creativity, not of destructiveness. Now, if it were not for the Gospels, there I should stop, and I shouldn't mind stopping there. Christianity is not something I needed in this sense, because I could perfectly comfortably and happily live and die on the basis of what I have just said.

R.T. How, before the Gospels, or in spite of the Gospels, or instead of the Gospels, did you come to the conclusion that this spirit was loving; on what evidence?

M.M. On the evidence first of all of the actual world itself, which I love. I mean its colors, its scents, its seasons, all the things that I find so enchanting; these are, to me, an expression of love. Then again, not always, but in one's highest moments, so are one's closest and truest human relationships. If you are capable, if a man is capable of this emotion of love, which we all recognize, as every civilisation has recognized, and as even savages recognize, as the highest impulse which we can feel about another human being, to the point that we prefer another human being's interests to our own, this suggests to me at once—more than suggests, involves the assumption—that the spirit which has created us partakes of the nature of this love, because it could only partake of the highest, not the lowest. I once read in a book by some Flemish mystic that hunger presupposes the existence of bread; similarly, I think that this longing that all men have had since the beginning of time, and in all circumstances, and will always have until the end of time, whatever may happen—that this longing presupposes the existence of what is longed for. But as I say, if it were not for the Christian Gospels, there the matter would rest, and there it would rest perfectly happily and contentedly, so far as I am concerned.

R.T. Malcolm, have you had what could be described as a present-day mystical experience of Jesus Christ?

M.M. I can't say "no" to that, although I wish to explain that I am by temperament an extremely sceptical person. I don't believe in a lot that people say about their religious experiences. I'm very sceptical about the fantasies of mysticism altogether. I don't believe in visions myself, since I have never had one, but on the other hand, as I have continued to think about the Christian religion, begun to read the Gospels and related literature, particularly contemporary writings, I have had a sense of the presence of Christ. Perhaps the particular moment was when I was making some films in the Holy Land for television; on the road to Emmaus I understood, in a particularly vivid and personal way, that there is someone else, a third man, who will join one and help one along the way. On his own, no human being can hope to overcome the wickedness and selfishness inherent in his nature. It's absolutely impossible. Yet Christians have been able to do this because there is this help available. I know that this help *is* available; I know I can call on it myself. To realize this is a very different thing from a Damascus road experience, or the kind of visions and voices that have been seen and heard. The person who put it best for me was the writer whose work, to me, is the most perfect expression of Christianity in our time—though she herself was not a Christian in any formal sense. I mean Simone Weil. Describing a moment of illumination, she says that Christ came down and took possession of her. I can understand that, because there is a point when the captivation of Christ, and of his teaching, is so great that it is exactly like being utterly obsessed with someone else. One is, as Simone Weil puts it, in the most literal sense possessed.

R.T. That is an interesting phrase—that Christ came down and captivated her. Do you believe that Christians are those people whom he has captivated, or those who have sought his captivation?

M.M. I would not be dogmatic about that, because I am absolutely convinced that there are many routes to Christ and his mercies. I think that all any man can do is to try to find his own way, and, if he is capable of communicating, perhaps to tell others about his adventures, so that he may conceivably help them. But I think there are an infinite number of ways, from the absolutely simple illumination that we associate with the saints, past and present, to the agonizing struggle of someone like Kierkegaard to attain the sort of understanding of Christ and relationship with him that he longed for.

R.T. *What triggers it off in a man, though? This is a wild generalization, but I think of the masses and masses of people who never give a thought to God or Jesus Christ or eternity, and then of the others that do. I know I am hovering here on a Calvinistic notion, but is it God who chooses a few, or is this something that can happen for all of us? What I am wondering about here is what starts it in a man, what awakens a man to the possibility that life is more than what he just sees on this earth?*

M.M. We don't know. We say that there are millions of people who never think of God, but we don't know; we can never really know. It appears like that, but we can never tell. One gets some very strange surprises. I firmly believe that there is a divine light in every human being ever born or to be born. I don't think any life can be lived in total darkness, but of course I agree with you that the actual gift of experiencing the light consciously, and still more of being able to convey the nature of that light, is a somewhat rare thing. This is part of the general mystery of our being, but I am absolutely sure that when we do understand we shall see that, first of all, the illumination was much more widespread than appears to us to be the case, and, secondly, that it was necessary for this light to shine through certain individuals whose particular role this has just happened to be. I have never myself met a soul in total darkness, except for those who are mad. Unfortunately, when people are mad—and our civilisation is ever producing more who are mad—then you have a feeling of their being in total darkness. Even with them, though, you never know. My eldest son, a dedicated Christian if ever there was one, worked for a while as a helper in an institution which cares for the incurably mentally sick. I asked him whether he was ever afraid, especially when dealing with homicidal cases. No, he said; they, too, were God's children. What could he do for them? I asked. He told me that he read the New Testament to them in the hope that a phrase, or even a word, some little glimmer of its light, might reach them. Surely, God would not let so sweet a hope quite fail. On that same visit to the Holy Land I came to feel quite certain that not even Judas had irretrievably cut himself off from the love of God.

R.T. *We come now to the Gospels and the incredible event of Jesus Christ.*

M.M. Yes. The Gospels, as I have grown to understand them, and this is a later thing ...

R.T. How late exactly?

M.M. I should have said that it was only in the last ten years that I have come to understand how, through the Gospels, we can see God in the shape of a man, and a man in the shape of God, thereby grasping what I think is the most wonderful concept of all—of God as a father and of the human race as a family; not equal, as political idealists like to pretend, not at all, but equal as brothers and sisters in a family are equal. Some are clever, some are stupid, some are attractive, some are boring, some are ugly, some are beautiful; all this is true, but the moment that you have a sense of a family and a father these differences become insignificant, as they do in a family, and all are equal. No one in a family would say that a plain sister is inferior to a pretty one; not inside a family, only outside. If this Christian notion is correct—and I am profoundly convinced that it is—then it answers the question of the relationship between man and man. From the Christian Gospels, and their presentation of Christ's captivating personality, then, I have been able to fathom the mysterious circumstance that he was God, and that in him God became man. These are assumptions that I find no difficulty over at all. They are not even particularly miraculous, certainly no more so than much else that we take for granted about the material universe. There is, in any case, a massive weight of evidence in support of them which one can read in the lives of people who have accepted their validity, and been transformed thereby.

R.T. What do you mean when you say that this man was God?

M.M. I mean that through the character of this man and the teaching of this man I may understand God, and I may understand what God wants for and from man.

R.T. What is it about Jesus Christ that convinces you of this difference in him?

M.M. The Jesus who emerges from the Gospels is this man who tells me, who explains to me, the ways of God, and, I also think, who explains to God the ways of man. In other words, he is an intermediary between God and men who reveals in his person and in his life the unity that we have sensed, and who translates it into individual terms.

R.T. What individual acts or attitudes of his show this?

M.M. Primarily, of course, his death. That is the essential thing; if that hadn't happened, then he would only have been one more wonderful teacher; but his death and all that followed from it seems to me clearly to establish the relationship between God and his creation.

R.T. Talk to me about his death. What do you think was going on at Calvary?

M.M. I think that men had to be shown that the way to revelation was through suffering, not, as they may have been inclined to think, that the way was through happiness. A great image revelatory of this was absolutely essential. They had also to be shown that what they must worship is, in earthly terms, defeat, not, as they thought, victory; that they must worship what in earthly terms is weak, not what has hitherto been thought of as strength; that this image of a man dying because of the truth that he embodied, established forever what truth is—something you die for.

R.T. The Cross was a great counterblast, then, against the view that this world is complete in itself or an end in itself?

M.M. That is why, coinciding as it did with that fantastic Roman Empire, and stating the exact opposite proposition to what that empire was built on—that is why it swept through men's hearts, why it had this incredible effect on them, as it still does, because it is a great illumination. You see, it's a natural impulse in man, the jungle man, to think that he must attach himself to power, because that would defend him; that he must accumulate wealth, because that will win him respect; that he must make men afraid of him, because then they will do what he wants. Now the exact opposite proposition had to be established—and Christ established it—that the exact opposite of the jungle man's assumption was the truth.

R.T. And this is how you understand the Atonement?

M.M. Absolutely. Absolutely.

R.T. You are quite sure there was a Resurrection?

M.M. I am sure there was a Resurrection, but I don't in the least care whether the stone was moved or not moved, or what anybody saw, or anything like that. I am absolutely indifferent to that. But there must have been a Resurrection, because Christ is alive now. Christ is alive now, two thousand years later. There is no question at all about that.

R.T. What do you mean when you say that he is alive now?

M.M. He is alive now in the sense that he exists now as a person who can be reached.

R.T. You believe you can have a personal relationship with Jesus Christ now?

M.M. I believe that Jesus Christ is alive now, that, as it were, his life is still valid, so that it is possible, not only to hear and learn, but *experience*, the truths that he propounded. Now you may say that this is not quite what Christians mean, and I daresay it isn't, but I really can't help that. I know absolutely, without any question, that you can derive strength and illumination from a relationship with the man in the Gospels which you cannot achieve, we'll say for instance with Socrates, who was a very wise and good man who also died.

R.T. There is a sense that Jesus is alive now, in a way that Socrates is not alive now?

M.M. Socrates is not alive now, although I can read Socrates and know his thoughts, which are very elevating thoughts, and read about his death, which was a very noble death.

R.T. But there is the very mysterious presence of Jesus Christ now?

M.M. Yes, and that is the Resurrection; that is what I, at any rate, mean by the living Christ. In some unique way the thought and teaching and persona of this man are still here, although there are plenty of people from whom, in an earthly sense, one might learn more, because they are more sophisticated and complicated. With Jesus there is some unique quality which has inspired our civilisation. If this inspiration ever dried up, then our civilisation would be over.

R.T. Does the element of the miraculous in the Gospels worry you at all?

M.M. Not at all. I don't find the miracles in any way puzzling. Christ used to say to the people he miraculously cured that their sins were forgiven them; in other words, he relieved them of their guilt. If you relieve people of their guilt, you also relieve them of their sickness, because physical imperfections are only a manifestation of spiritual imperfection. I find the miracles much more realistic than much modern medicine, and than all modern psychiatry. I think that Christ was a great healer because he was a man of infinite wisdom who understood exactly what life was about in a way that nobody else ever has. His method of dealing with the sick and infirm was a completely comprehensible one. He understood that what is the matter with men, whether mentally, physically, or spiritually, is their fear and guilt, and that if you deliver them from fear and guilt they become well. Now you may say that this couldn't apply to every sick person, and it's quite possible it couldn't; but it certainly applied to the people Christ cured and made whole. For instance, a lot of the sick that he dealt with were off their heads, mad, and he described them as being possessed by evil spirits. And many today, in the light of their own experience of dealing with the mentally afflicted, know that madness *is* possession by an evil spirit. If you can exorcise that evil spirit, and drive it away by introducing the opposite principle—which is the principle of love and harmony rather than of violence and disharmony—a cure automatically follows.

R.T. Is evil personal, as good is personal in God?

M.M. Oh, I think so. There is a Devil—a spirit of evil in us tugging at us to make us animals rather than angels.

R.T. Couldn't this just be the fact that evolutionarily we are still very much nearer the jungle?

M.M. It could be, yes. But even if that was so it wouldn't alter the situation. That situation may have arisen as a result of an evolutionary process, but it's still the same situation.

R.T. But it would cancel out the need to have a personal Devil.

M.M. I am not particular about a personal Devil. I shan't be distressed if there isn't one, but I am absolutely sure that there is a great spirit or force of evil to which men can succumb, individually and collectively, and that this force makes them animals rather than spiritual beings, makes them kill and destroy rather than love and create.

R.T. Do you think that Jesus was a product of evolution, or do you think that this was a miraculous intervention?

M.M. I am always allergic to miraculous interventions, because I don't observe them in life, and I don't think that it makes Jesus any more remarkable if he represents a miraculous intervention than if a process which began when we were created found its culmination in him. It's again a matter of no great moment as far as I am concerned. The thing that matters to me is that he lived and lives.

R.T. So the Virgin Birth doesn't really figure?

M.M. Not in the least. It's understandable, of course, that people were awed, and rightly awed, by this man; by the influence he exerted, and by the stupendous effect of his words and thoughts, transforming the world's darkness into light. So, naturally, they thought he couldn't have come into the world as we did. I can't see that it's of any importance really; it's a natural thought, but how Christ came into the world doesn't matter.

R.T. It matters to me, Malcolm, in this sense, that if Jesus is, shall we say, the apex of an evolutionary process, why has there only ever been one of him, or one of his quality? I know myself well enough to realize that even if I live to be a hundred, I shall still want to get down on my knees and say "Lord" to him, and yet two thousand years have passed, and we haven't had another Jesus Christ.

M.M. Rather than seeing him as the apex of an evolutionary process, I prefer to regard him as a consequence of the creation of life. We don't know how life began, or when it began. But creation presupposes a creator, whom we call God. As a part of some divine purpose Jesus was born, Jesus lived, Jesus taught, Jesus died. If you call that the apex of an evolutionary process, you demean it in actual fact. Nor would it follow at all. Evolution has at best proved to be a very rough-and-ready, sketchy kind of a half guess at something. I don't think it amounts to more than that, though, as usual, much too much importance has been attributed to it. For instance, man has deduced from the theory of evolution such absurdities as the survival of the fittest, which is patently ridiculous. Likewise, the whole system of evolutionary economics, which is now a completely exploded myth.

R.T. Evolution in morals?

M.M. Certainly, in morals—probably the most ludicrous deduction of all.

R.T. But hasn't the same thing been done with Christianity?

M.M. Curiously enough, no, doubtless because the essential truth of Christianity is so strong. There are a certain number of legends associated with Christianity certainly, of a fairly harmless nature, but in modern times no one has been forced to believe in them, or been thought any the worse of for not believing in them. In my opinion these legends are much less harmful than scientific fallacies, because they have no implications. If you say to me that St. Bernadette saw a vision of the Virgin Mary in the Grotto at Lourdes, I might agree or not agree, but it's a perfectly harmless thing, anyway. If you say to me that men are so made that the strongest kicks the weakest in the teeth and then the strongest survive, and go on to argue that if you apply this to economics you will get a happy society, you have done an irreparable wrong, as we know, as we have seen. I think the legend is far less harmful than the fallacy; by comparison it's relatively charming.

R.T. You said that your religious position arose out of asking the question: "What is it all about?" When I asked Marghanita Laski about this she said: "There is no possible answer to that, so I do not tease my brain asking the question." Do you feel that it is possible for us ever to come to any kind of answer that can be satisfactory?

M.M. Yes. I think Christ provides an answer, which I find completely satisfying.

R.T. What is that?

M.M. That we live to the extent that we die. That the purpose of life is to love God and love our neighbor. That insofar as we achieve this we establish a relationship with our creator, with the essential purpose of being here, and with the extraordinary individual, Jesus Christ, who came into the world and explained this.

R.T. What is the guarantee that what you think you are finding is valid, is right?

M.M. In a word—faith, in which I profoundly believe. In this I have with me all the wise men of our civilisation who ever lived. I do not think that the intellect, reason, can produce an answer to life, and I don't know of any person for whom I have any respect, including many scientists, among them the greatest, who have not seen that reason is an inadequate instrument, and that one can only appreciate what life is about through this other dimension which we call faith.

R.T. How is this corroborated? Or does it need to be corroborated?

M.M. It is self-corroborating, because we know it, and if we don't know it we haven't got faith.

R.T. You mean this is an absolute knowledge?

M.M. To me, yes. It is, of course, supported by the fact that there are all these others who had this faith, and that it would be rather extraordinary if each one of them was simply a self-deluded fool, considering that such people are by universal consent the most creative minds and spirits of our civilisation. That in itself is not a proof. There is also the fact that people one has known who strike one as good and true are people who in some degree or another have this faith. The inadequacy of the mind alone is something that is absolutely and dramatically illustrated at every point; everything is built on faith, and faith is the essence of everything.

R.T. But Malcolm, it was asking a tremendous lot when Jesus said to the young rich ruler, Sell all you have and follow me. The demand was total. Aren't people entitled to some kind of assurance that what they are doing is either sane or sensible or reasonable or right?

M.M. Yes, they are entitled to that assurance. The assurance is provided, because to the degree that they have this faith they know it's true. In other words, as Pascal says: "Whoever looks for God has found him." Faith contains its own justification. There is also a mountain of confirmatory evidence in the innumerable cases of all sorts and conditions of people, from the most simple and unsophisticated to the most complicated intelligences that have ever been, who have all reached the same conclusion and found the same certainty. No man that I know of has been able to live a whole life without faith, on a basis of the intellect solely. I doubt there has ever been a single case of it.

R.T. When you say this *faith, what is this faith, what is it faith in?*

M.M. In my particular case, it is in and about the Christian religion.

R.T. Let us talk about what it is for you.

M.M. For me it is the Christian religion, as contained in the Gospels.

R.T. What is contained?

M.M. The message that Christ came to tell us—that we are children of God, and as children of God we are brothers and sisters in one human family, that this human family has a destiny which is beyond the world of time and space and mortality, but which is yet realisable through the experience of living in the world, and that, if we live according to the terms that Christ proposed, we may know and participate in this destiny. Such was Christ's message, enunciated after him so clearly by the apostles, and subsequently elaborated and fulfiled through the tradition of the Christian religion at its best—a tradition which, with innumerable lapses into wickedness and abysmal horror, has somehow been carried on. In other words, through the illumination that Christ provided in his life, we can become new men and find a new happiness and a new zest and a new understanding. That's the Christian religion in brief to me. I read about it and continue to think about it, and note its presentation from generation to generation. In our own time, for me it has been presented by people like Simone Weil and Bonhoeffer and Kierkegaard—new presentations of the same everlasting gospel.

It's quite conceivable, in my opinion, that within the next decades what is called Western civilisation may finally expire, as other civilisations have before it, and that institutional Christianity will be extinguished with it. If this were so, and it may well be so, it wouldn't alter my feeling in the slightest degree. I know that Christianity is true; I believe it. I would venture to put my own interpretation on some of its aspects, but essentially it's true. I propose through my remaining years to attempt to live by and for it. Insofar as I am able to communicate with my fellows, it is what I will communicate to them; this little light, if I am spared the strength to keep it going, will continue to shine.

R.T. *I want to talk now about death. I imagine, Malcolm, that you have had to face this in your personal experience. What do you think about dying? What do you think happens to people when they die? There are all kinds of theories in Christian theology—you go to sleep and you wake up at the Last Judgement, or the Nonconformist view, sudden death, sudden glory. Here we are with somebody that we love and they die. Now the human mind wants to make sense of this. I have been in the position many, many times as a clergyman of ministering to people who want to know if the dead person whom they have loved is alive. Is he all right, will they see him, will they be together again? These are very simple questions, but very, very important, human questions, and I think the Church, or maybe the Christian faith itself, has been so nebulous here that the hungry sheep have looked up and haven't been fed.*

M.M. Of course, this is one of the fundamental things. Death is essentially the reason for religion. We could probably rub along if it wasn't for death, but we can't, because of the fact of death. First of all, my own feeling about it is this—that it is impossible to know. There are certain things we can never know, and the exact circumstances of dying, and what happens afterwards, are among them. Secondly, I have an absolute conviction, without any qualification whatsoever, that this life that we live in time and space for three-score years and ten is not the whole story, that it is only part of a larger story. Therefore, death cannot be for others, or for oneself, an end, any more than birth is a beginning. Death is part of a larger pattern; it fits into a larger, eternal scale, not simply a time scale. This is something

I know. Whether the ego, or what we call the personality, remains intact, or remains at all, whether the separate individuality as we know it remains, are questions to which I don't know the answers. No one knows, and no one ever will know. I think of my own death as something which will transform my way of living into another mode of living rather than as an end; and one thinks of others whom one has loved and who have died as equally participating in that other existence, in that larger dimension. To me this is completely satisfying. I don't want to know any more than this. I'm perfectly content with it. I can honestly say that I have never been afraid of death, and I am less afraid of it now than ever. I just look forward to it as something that will happen. I should like to be spared, obviously, from mental collapse, because I should hate to be that kind of burden on people, but even so I am perfectly certain that if one were so afflicted, it would somehow be part of this larger plan, and as such must be acceptable. I think the most important sentence in the whole Christian religion, devotionally speaking, is *Thy will be done*. This is the essential sentence to be able to say, especially in relation to death.

R.T. Have you any kind of a glimpse, though, into a kind of life that doesn't include self-consciousness or awareness? When I hear people say, as you have said, that after death we get caught up in some new dimension, to me the whole glory of human beings is that we are each a different being, and I am only just beginning to explore the wonder and the mystery of human relationship, of me being related to you, another human being, and it seems to me a little glib when people say, Well, I could well do without this, or, I wouldn't mind if this was all lost. It seems to me that we are cutting something out here that is very important.

M.M. What I said was that to me it's obvious that this existence in a body, in time, on the earth, in this tiny corner of the universe, is part of a larger existence, and that one's relationship to that larger existence will be manifest when one dies here. I think that you are making the mistake of applying a false yardstick. You say that we can only comprehend life in terms of our own egos, and of course that is so, because you are so living at this moment, but if you imagine yourself not living in that way, then some other mode of existence becomes equally comprehensible.

R.T. But I can't imagine myself living in any other way than being myself, or being me.

M.M. Clearly, but that doesn't mean that you won't live in another way: it only means that you can't imagine it.

R.T. But in the New Testament it states that Jesus rose from the dead, and he was the same Jesus that the disciples had known before he died, and he said, God is not the God of the dead but of the living, he is the God of Abraham and Isaac. There seems to be implied in the New Testament some kind of self-continuity. Life after death will obviously be more self-less, it obviously will not be egocentric, but it seems to me that there is a question here that has to be faced.

M.M. I don't see it that way. Obviously, the disciples, when they saw Christ, could only see him as they knew him, because they had no other shape in which they could possibly see him, but that doesn't mean that after his death and his resurrection he was the same person. It only means that they saw him in that way. If Shakespeare kills off one of his characters, and then brings him in as a ghost, it is just as he was in life. This is the only way he can connect the ghost on the stage with the man who was killed.

I think that if you can accept the incredible notion of being here for so short a while, and not knowing how you got here, you ought to be able to accept the mystery of life after death. We are like one of these insects that fly round a lamp, and inside twenty-four hours they have come and gone—this is our earthly life. We haven't the faintest notion what we are at, where we come from, where we are going, if anywhere. We live on a tiny corner of a vast universe which—I am no use at these things—stretches for thousands and thousands of light-years, etc. If we can accept that, we can accept anything, and we have to accept that, because that is in fact our situation.

What it all boils down to is: Do we believe that the significance of our being is exhausted by *this* experience of living? I say it cannot be. I am convinced that the evidence against this is overwhelming. Plenty of people have said that I say this because I have a big ego. I don't think it is only that, but even if it were, all right, then, we have been born into this world as little, tiny creatures with big egos, and the fact that we have big egos must in itself have some significance. But, if these people we love were gone forever, we wouldn't wish to love them any less, we wouldn't part from them in any different way, we wouldn't think of them any differently. I believe that we must trust in God, which I do. I believe that in being here, we are fulfiling some purpose of his; whatever that purpose is, it is the best purpose that we can have. If that purpose involves meeting again after death as we have known one another here, then we *shall* meet again; if it is not God's purpose, then we shan't. In eternity we shall have no worries about it. I think that is all there is really to say about it. I have seen people dead in war. I think it's a dreadful thing that we in our wickedness should kill those who are young, those whose lives are not fulfiled, but the actual fact of death is not a terrifying thing at all.

R.T. What experiences give you now the deepest joy—I'm not talking about happiness, but joy?

M.M. I can answer that very easily. For me now the only great joy is understanding. This means being attuned to God, to the moral purpose of the universe, to the destiny of the human race that I belong to, to the things that are good—this is joy, and it is of course an experience. I find it sometimes in, for instance, music; now that I am older I find that music is the most appealing of the arts. I used not to, but now I do.

R.T. I'm so pleased to hear that, because music hasn't happened to me yet.

M.M. Well, it will. You will find that, because music is so detached from everything else, through it you touch God. That's joy. Misery is to be shut off and in darkness, and of course, alas, there is still no way of avoiding that. Suddenly it's gone; the light of awareness, gone; as you might suddenly lose your love for a person. It's gone, blotted out, and you are in darkness, confined in that terrible little dungeon of the ego, that little dark dungeon down there, tortured by fears, appetites, frustrations, ambitions, greed—all these things crowd in on you like invisible devils, and there you are—lost. That's hell. People ask what hell is. I say that is hell, and that's what it's going to be like. Then suddenly, equally unaccountably, through maybe a sight of nature or of a loved face, or maybe a snatch of music, or just through thinking, being perceptive, it comes back—snap! almost like that—you are in tune, you are in communion; you are back in relationship with God and the moral nature of the universe, and everything is clear; there is nothing to be afraid of, and there is only joy, and only love; it's quite extraordinary.

R.T. *So we reach a stage where God is personal, where Jesus is personal, where Jesus is alive and you are in relationship with God and with Jesus Christ. Now, what form does your communion with God and Jesus Christ take? In other words how do you understand praying?*

M.M. I should have had great difficulty in answering that at one time. I take the view that everybody prays. There is nobody who doesn't pray, and there is nobody who doesn't spare some little moment in his life to look outside his ego. But of late I have learnt more about this. Let's be perfectly factual. I wake up in the morning, and I like to begin the day by thinking what life is about, rather than plunging into the sort of things one is going to have to do. So I like to read the Gospels, the Epistles, St. Augustine, the metaphysical poets like George Herbert, whom I consider to be the most exquisite religious poet in the English language. I read a bit, and then my mind dwells on what I've read, and this I consider to be prayer. Yes, that is prayer. It doesn't for some reason appeal to me to make any specific requests about my own personal affairs, because I do not consider they are likely to be of any great interest, but I don't criticize those who do.

R.T. *But what about this struggle with sin, with worldliness? You said earlier that we need the help that God can give us. Are you never conscious that you need to turn to God and say, "Look, I am in a hopeless condition, incapable and powerless"?*

M.M. My impulse, when the darkness sweeps me up, is not to say, "Please let me out of the darkness," but to seek the light which I know is there. I am frightened, like a child in a dark room; I look for the window, and Christ is the window. That's the thing; he is a window, and when you look out there is a wide, wonderful vista. What's the darkness now?

R.T. *Malcolm, do you ever address God?*

M.M. Yes I do sometimes, but not in the sense of requests. I wrote a little prayer recently, and I'll read it to you:

> O God, stay with me; let no word cross my lips that is not your word, no thoughts enter my mind that are not your thoughts, no deed ever be done or entertained by me that is not your deed. Amen.

That was my own prayer, and its form is an exception. That is why I wrote it down, because I don't very often feel induced to address my creator in that sort of way. To me prayer is a sort of understanding . . .

R.T. What I am after here, Malcolm, is that St. Paul said: In him I live and move and have my being; *other people say, I enjoy God. What I want to know from you is this: Do you believe that God is addressable?*

M.M. Oh, certainly.

R.T. Can you address God in a way that is different from addressing nature?

M.M. My little prayer is addressed to God, but it so happens that it's not my own practice to make this kind of personal address, but of course I believe in God as personal. Otherwise prayer wouldn't work; it wouldn't have any meaning.

R.T. God has a sufficiently objective reality, that although you don't know his form, his nature, and so on, God is such that you can say, O God?

M.M. Most certainly. God is the father, we are a family.

R.T. Malcolm, you know something of the mystics, and one of the things they talk about which fascinates me, fascinates me with horror almost, is what they describe as "the dark night of the soul." Not that I have suffered in this way, but I know what it is like to be in the darkness which you described earlier. I have known what it is like to go for months with no sense of God. God has gone; religion is an illusion; I have been a fool for believing it; this life is all there is; it's all crazy and mad. This is terribly deep, and fills me with despair. Then the light breaks through again, but the mystics seem to be saying, yes, these are simple forms of this kind of spiritual suffering, but the time will come when, in order to be fashioned as God wants you to be fashioned, you must go through "the dark night of the soul," and I must say that, if it's infinitely worse than what I have already experienced, this frightens me.

M.M. First of all, I'm sure it's not, because I am sure that what you have described, and what we all recognize, *is* "the dark night of the soul." As I understand it from St. John of the Cross, and he went most deeply into this, it is something that comes always shortly before a moment of illumination, so that I don't think you have any occasion to fear. Of course it's the only thing *to* fear; there is nothing else to fear at all, nothing at all. Nobody can hurt us, nobody can rob us, not in any real way; but we can be shut off, alas, from the love of God, and if we are, better not to have been born.

R.T. I'm going to be a little bit complicated now: When I go through a time now when God seems to have gone, because I have a lot of experience from the past when it has been like that, but he has come back again, so I can face, shall I say, these wilderness experiences now, and hold on to my faith, and say that all I have to do is to hold on because the darkness will pass—now I sometimes wonder if the "dark night of the soul" is the time when that consolation is taken from you, so that you are left without hope altogether?

M.M. But surely that is where Christ comes in. He's always standing by; his help is always available.

R.T. You don't think there is a specific dark night of the soul? You think there are many dark nights?

M.M. Yes, and if there was a specific one it would only be an intensification of what has already been experienced. Because of Christ there can never be a dark night that doesn't end. The darkness always comes to an end because Christ is here with us now. If he weren't, then when this darkness came down we might never emerge from it.

R.T. You have said that you use the Bible in your prayer times. Why is it that the Bible for most people—again a wild generalisation—is a boring book that is just never read?

M.M. Partly because many people unfortunately are illiterate. Our educational system is making everyone more and more illiterate. Once, people knew the Bible and loved the Bible as children; not just as Christians, but because it is one of the greatest works of literature which exist. If the Christian religion and everything connected with it disappeared, the Authorized Version of the Bible would still be among the three or four supremely great books in the English language. That is absolutely certain. Unfortunately, I suppose it's the way it's presented to people, the way it's read to them, particularly in these new translations. Nowadays when I go to church I have to take an Authorized Version with me in order not to listen to the dreadful gibberish that's liable to be read out to me. It may seem like a paradox, but, in my opinion, looking for the Bible's meaning has destroyed the Bible. The Bible is more than meaning, and, if you take a passage and look only for its meaning, you lose so much. If poetry were to be approached in a similar way, everybody would say it was a very philistine thing to do.

R.T. *But meaning is important.*

M.M. Yes, meaning is important; and the meaning is there, capable of being grasped. But the moment you make the meaning identical with the words, and get some tenth-rate writer to extract the meaning and put it down, you are making, I think, a great mistake, and taking away from people the joy of the Bible. You know, here we needn't be talking about religion at all. With people of little or no education beautiful cadences came into their speech because they knew this one great book, the Authorized Version of the Bible. Think of Bunyan, a writer of supreme and unique genius who knew no other book. The Bible is considered to be something which is out-of-date. It is a most extraordinary idea. I heard a man on the radio complaining that the God of Westminster Abbey is a medieval God. But God can't be medieval or modern, or ancient; he's eternal or nothing. It's as though people of the Middle Ages had complained that the God of the New Testament is a Judaic God, and therefore they were not interested in him. They wanted a medieval God. This notion of the out-of-dateness of the Bible is utterly absurd, but it is implanted in people's minds, I regret to say, to a great extent by the clergy. People say that the Bible is a boring book, that it belongs to the past, but they don't say that about Shakespeare, because the people who teach Shakespeare are zealous for Shakespeare.

R.T. *It doesn't worry you when people say that our selves, our self-consciousness, who we are, everything we are, is all a manifestation of that piece of matter which exists in our head that we call a brain, and, when the brain disintegrates, that is the total disintegration of us?*

M.M. It doesn't worry me at all, because if that turns out to be true I shall not be in a position to realize that I had been wrong, but I think that every single thing I know or have observed suggests the contrary—that I am more than my nervous system, and on that supposition I live. If it could be shown that I have been making a mistake, even then, if it were possible to form a judgement on it, I should prefer to have lived on a basis of this mistake. I shall never be in a position to reach a conclusion about this, but even if you could prove to me to your satisfaction, that what you say might be true, is true, I would still think it better to live on the assumption that it wasn't, with a strong feeling that I should be correct in doing that.

R.T. You are not at all bothered by these people who say that we are just animated lumps of matter?

M.M. I'm not, because I am quite sure that animated lumps of matter don't write the plays of Shakespeare; they don't discover the theory of relativity, and, since man has done this, it is evidently untrue that we are only animated lumps of matter.

R.T. How do you reconcile your belief in the loving purposes of God with the birth of Mongol children and mentally defective children? We have just heard that Helen Keller has died. Do you think that these tragedies are due to the stupidity of man at some point?

M.M. Not at all. I think it is part of the pattern of life. What's more, I think it's an essential part. Imagine human life being drained of suffering! If you could find some means of doing that, you would not ennoble it; you would demean it. Everything I have learnt, whatever it might be—very little I fear—has been learnt through suffering.

R.T. Would you be willing to tell me in what way or is that too personal?

M.M. Not at all. I learnt not to lose my temper through the grief and contrition which afflicted me when I became violently angry with someone infinitely dear to me who had gone temporarily mad. I lost my temper, which is a very easy thing to do, and I marvel, incidentally, that people who look after the mentally sick are able to restrain themselves as they do.

R.T. You mean the fact that this person was mentally ill made you angry with the person?

M.M. Yes, because I hate the unreason, the animality, the almost bestiality of people when they are mad. I lost my temper, and then I realised that this was an utterly evil thing to do, that it was a thing which damaged me, that it could only add to the pain and anguish of someone I loved sorely pressed by a terrible misfortune. I decided that it must never occur again.

R.T. Did it damage the other person?

M.M. Certainly. It always does damage the other person, but of course the thing that one is conscious of is the damage it does to one's self. This was a situation in which someone was sick. If the person had been sick with a broken leg or lung trouble, one would have been ashamed to be other than solicitous, but because it was this scourge of our society, mental disturbance, it produced in me violent anger. I realised in a moment of absolute illumination, which could never have come in any other way, that I had done an utterly despicable thing, and, furthermore, that all anger in all circumstances is equally wicked. Of course I have been angry again, but I have never been *as* angry. You know, there are few things one can point to in one's nature which really change, but thenceforth I was completely changed in that respect, and I could never have learnt it in any other way than through this utterly desolating experience.

Another example occurs to me. There was one point in my life when I decided to kill myself, and I swam out to sea, resolved for a variety of reasons that I didn't want to live any more. Partly it was a mood of deep depression, and partly actual difficulties. I swam out to sea until I felt myself sinking; you get a strange kind of sleepiness that afflicts you, as if you were just about to fall into a deep sleep. I thought that I would take one last look at the coast, and that would be the end. I saw the lights along the coast; and I suddenly realised that that was my home, the earth—the earth, my home, and that I must stay on the earth because I belonged there until my life had run its course. Then somehow, I don't know how, I swam back.

Now that was a time of great trouble for me, and it was very sad that I was forced to contemplate so contemptible an act. At the same time, it was a terrific turning point. I have never doubted since then that in all circumstances, whatever one's condition may be, or the condition of the society one lives in, or the condition of the world, life is good, and that to gain from this experience of living what has to be gained, and to learn what has to be learned, it is necessary to live out one's life to the end until the moment comes for one's release. Then, and only then, can one truly rejoice in that moment. There is no catastrophe, as it seems to me, that can befall human beings which is not an illumination, and no illumination which is not in some sense a catastrophe. It's in an age like ours, an age of great superficiality of thought, that people ask how, if God makes a Mongol, can he be a loving God. It's a very superficial thought, because a Mongol child is part of the process whereby man exists, and we can't judge how that comes about, or what are its full consequences. All we can say is that it's part of the experience of living, and, like all other parts, it can shed light or it can shed darkness. Suffering is an essential element in the Christian religion, as it is in life. After all, the Cross itself is the supreme example. If Christ hadn't suffered, do you imagine that anyone would have paid the slightest attention to the religion he founded? Not at all.

R.T. But it is a mystery that the only way in which God can make us grow up, or help us to grow up, is through suffering.

M.M. It's a mystery in a sense, but just imagine the opposite. Supposing you eliminated suffering—what a dreadful place the world would be! I would almost rather eliminate happiness. The world would be the most ghastly place because everything that corrects the tendency of this unspeakable little creature, man, to feel overimportant and overpleased with himself would disappear. He's bad enough now, but he would be absolutely intolerable if he never suffered. However, we needn't fear that.

R.T. What have you been like as a parent? I have found that being a parent is far from easy.

M.M. Far from easy, but at the same time one of the absolutely major things in life. I find it difficult to think of any human circumstances which would make life intolerable, but I think to be childless would be a truly dreadful catastrophe. Now I've got grandchildren, and I find it all very delightful; but bringing my children up was by no means easy, partly because of deficiencies in myself, partly because of the war.

R.T. *Give me some instances of deficiency.*

M.M. Oh, well, being too egotistic.

R.T. *What does that mean?*

M.M. Being too concerned with my own interests. Quarreling, losing my temper—all the things I despise and hate which I have done. Not sympathising with them when they failed or when they were inadequate. Of course, I married when I was quite young, when I was twenty-four. We were terrific wanderers, which I think was a bad thing really in bringing up children. My wife says she has set up house twenty-two times in the course of our marriage, in all sorts of countries.

R.T. *What were your aims as a parent? Did you have any idea how you should behave in relation to the children?*

M.M. I didn't have any conscious aims. I don't have any now. I think the only thing you can do with children is to love them, and, when they are grown up, provide them with a rest camp, somewhere they can withdraw to from the battle and rest if they happen to be wounded or exhausted.

R.T. *What about discipline?*

M.M. We were poor, and poor people have to have discipline. We had four youngish children rather near in age, and unless you can afford to employ people to keep them in order—which we couldn't—you can't cope unless you have discipline. But it was only discipline imposed for practical reasons; it wasn't a theory. I have no theory for bringing up children at all.

R.T. *You didn't want to make them into anything?*

M.M. No, I didn't at all, except I wanted them to be good men and women, and I am happy to say they are.

R.T. How have you found this whole business of being married? The mystery of another human being, living with another human being—I have found this one of the most demanding experiences of my life, one of the most valuable and profitable experiences, but at the same time a very demanding experience, and I would say that marriage is not a thing to be treated lightly or easily.

M.M. Oh, certainly not. That is why I am against making divorce any easier; very much against it, because I think that in every marriage there are plenty of occasions when you could easily bust it up. If it had been easy to bust it up, I probably should have done so, and then how I should have regretted it! I have been married for over forty years, and I am more contented with my marriage now than when it started. Marriage is very difficult; it has many troubles. Sex, I think, is a frightful trouble, and I consider, myself, that marriage only becomes bearable when that element is largely eliminated. I think sex for procreation is a marvelous thing, and, when one is young, passion is a marvelous thing, but not to build on. I don't think any marriage built on sex can possibly last, because sex doesn't last and can't last, and it would be obscene if it did. If there is one thing I completely loathe in the contemporary world, it is this unashamed effort to devise means to protract physical desire when in the normal way it has disappeared. Marriage, in any case, is an enormously difficult relationship, particularly if, as in our case, the individuals concerned aren't Christians. If the Christian scale of values isn't accepted, then all the questions of jealousy, infidelity, and so on arise and have to be fought through, and sometimes with great pain and strife.

R.T. When you said you weren't Christian, you mean at that stage you weren't consciously a Christian?

M.M. Or even unconsciously. I didn't accept the Christian view of marriage at all, when I married. Marriage, in our eyes, was a purely legal arrangement.

R.T. Why did you bother to struggle through?

M.M. Well, because I loved my wife—for no other reason; and, if there is one single thing I feel grateful for at this moment, it would be that more than anything else at all, far transcending anything in the way of success (utterly bogus anyway) that I might be considered to have had.

R.T. *But there were times when you hated her.*

M.M. I don't know that I hated, but there were times of strife, and this is a terrible thing. Marriage without the comfort of Christian morality is a stormy affair. But it can be survived.

R.T. *I believe, when the storms come in my own marriage, because I believe in an eternal reference to this relationship, that it is worth working through, struggling with or being patient with the present situation, because I believe there is an end to work towards, and this is part of my being a Christian.*

M.M. I entirely agree with that.

R.T. *What was your motivation to make your marriage work, when you didn't have this eternal reference?*

M.M. Without being a Christian? First of all the simple fact again of poverty, and I would here mention that I belong to a minority who think that the poor really are blessed, as the New Testament tells us. There is a great blessing in poverty, which is very little realised today. If you are poor, and you have children, and you accept at any rate the idea that you owe a duty to those children to bring them up, that you can't just jettison them, then to a great extent you are *committed* to a matrimonial relationship. Now, I don't think this is bad; I think it is good. I approve of it, and I pity the rich, who are always in the position that they have no material obstacles to shedding relationships, whether with a wife, children, or anyone else. There is, of course, also the fact of love, which is a very real thing, and which endures, contrary to the modern view. I do not at all identify love and sexual desire. I think the two things coincide for a glorious period of youth, but otherwise they are separate.

R.T. *What do you say to people who would like easy divorce because of people who are married before they grow up—almost, before they understand? They go through the ceremony that locks them together, and yet they are completely unsuitable, and all that can accrue from such marriages will be frustration, hatred, aggressiveness. Don't you think that people ought to be allowed to break these marriages up?*

M.M. Yes, I think that in the last resort they should, but if my advice was sought, my advice would always be in the direction of going on trying, of saying that the difficulty is not incompatibility really, but vanity, egotism, and the answer to this, as to so many things, is to escape from this prison of the ego. I would also accept the idea that in the last resort there are cases, many fewer than are commonly supposed, in which two people have definitely made a mistake; they bring out the worst in each other, and in those circumstances, with the utmost reluctance and caution, I would say it's right to break it. But they are few.

R.T. I would say, as a Christian, if only people were *Christian, very few marriages need to break.*

M.M. I agree with that. Very, very few, surprisingly few, but I think there still would be a few. There would be people who would find it impossible to live together because of a sort of chemistry, but they are few.

R.T. What we are doing with divorce is making it possible to go from one failure to another failure.

M.M. We are establishing a system of promiscuity, a deliberate system of promiscuity, which I think will not make for happiness at all. In fact, it will make for great misery, and I try to tell that to young people, but of course they don't usually listen.

R.T. It can be said of you that it is because physical passion no longer interests you that you are condemning it. People could say, it's all very well for him; he used to enjoy these things, but now he is telling us that we mustn't. People could feel that this is a very odd position to take.

M.M. This is frequently said, and I sympathise with the thought. Some people would put it more bluntly than you politely put it. They say: Here is an old debauchee who has got sick of the senses, particularly of sex, and who therefore turns round and says it's no good. Now, I see the point, but it's not true. Nor is it true that I no longer appreciate the senses. When you are old you still appreciate the senses, as much as ever really, but in a rather different way. But I have never thought, even in the most ardent moments, that the senses could give one any ultimate satisfaction. I have always thought they were delusive, and I think so now more than ever. The reason that one tends to stress this point more now is not merely because one's old, but because society itself is so stridently insisting on the opposite proposition—including a lot of Christians and churchmen. They are all insisting that physical sex is in fact a wholly satisfactory way of achieving satisfaction. I contend, with St. Paul and all the Christian mystics, that it's not, but that doesn't mean that in itself sex is bad, or in itself undesirable. It is undesirable as an end, not as a means. Everything that we perceive or appreciate involves the senses; this natural scene outside my window that I love so much is connected with the senses. If I couldn't smell and touch and feel, I shouldn't be able to appreciate it. But if you say to me that the significance of it is its sensual appeal, and if you go on insisting that is so, as is done with this particular aspect of sensuality which is sex, so that it becomes obsessive, then it is necessary, as it seems to me, to protest, and one protests by saying this is a delusion, a fantasy, which will not even bring the passing satisfaction promised.

R.T. *You have said things earlier that have led me to believe that finally for you sex should only be used for procreation. You seem to eliminate the idea of sex as enjoyment.*

M.M. Yes, I do. I think that the idea of sex as enjoyment is a very dangerous one. The purpose of it is procreation, the justification of it is love; if you separate sex from procreation and love, very rapidly you turn it into a horror.

R.T. *But supposing you separated it from procreation but kept enjoyment within love?*

M.M. Well, yes, I think that is possible, but of course the fact that you are forced, in order to do that, to cut off its procreative function, in other words to sterilize it, will tend, in my opinion, in most cases to produce quite quickly a sense of nausea. Then, of course, one's attitude to this depends upon one's attitude to marriage, the family, and the home. I consider that some form of marriage—and I think that monogamous marriage is probably the highest form—but some form of marriage is essential to civilisation and for bringing up children. I think the family is, and ever must be, the basic and true unit of society. If you base a relationship between two people on their achieving mutual pleasure out of it, it will very soon happen that they don't achieve mutual pleasure out of it at all. This is a fact of life which we all know, and then if they persist, using these various, to me highly disgusting, erotica of various kinds, they will very soon loathe each other, and this is what is going on in our society.

R.T. *What about overpopulation, though?*

M.M. To me, this is a fantasy. You see, when I was young, people used to say the poor had too many children. Or, at the time of the famine in Ireland, they would say that the Irish had too many children. We were taking the food from Ireland, and the Irish were starving, and we said they were starving because they had too many children. Now, we who are sated, who have to adopt the most extravagant and ridiculous devices to consume what we produce, while watching whole, vast populations getting hungrier and hungrier, overcome our feelings of guilt by persuading ourselves that these others are too numerous, have too many children. They ask for bread and we give them contraceptives! In future history books it will be said, and it will be a very ignoble entry, that just at the moment in our history when we, through our scientific and technical ingenuity, could produce virtually as much food as we wanted to, just when we were opening up and exploring the universe, we set up a great whimpering and wailing, and said there were too many people in the world. It's pitiful.

R.T. *Now, Malcolm, I want to ask you about the church. It is my strong feeling that the church is no longer doing the job it was set up to do. The world is passing it by. People are passing it by. The life seems to have gone out of it; the relevance seems to have gone from it.*

M.M. I think this is an irrefutable fact, of course. It so happens that I never really belonged to any church, so that institutional Christianity hasn't meant very much to me. But, of course, I absolutely agree with you. If you take the Anglican Church, I think it's really about as moribund as it could be. If it wasn't an established church, many of its parish churches would just cease to exist. Similarly, nonconformity is steadily declining, and now I think the Roman Church is beginning to run down in the same sort of way. This may be an inevitable development. It wouldn't really affect anything as far as I personally am concerned, although one must remember that whatever deficiencies the various churches have had, it is owing to them that the gospel remains before us; they have kept it alive. The question is: Will Christianity survive if the churches cease to exist?

I am personally convinced that our Western European civilisation is approaching its end. This is an absolutely basic part of my thinking, which governs all my feelings about the world that I live in. There is to me every symptom of our civilisation petering out. This was bound to happen sometime; it just seems to me to be happening now, when I am alive. I think there are advantages in living at a time when a civilisation is coming to an end; in such a situation, one can much better understand the nature of power, just as one can better understand the nature of the body when one is sick. In a dying civilisation one is at least not taken in by power and authority, as one easily might be when conditions are flourishing.

The Christian Church is inevitably involved in this death of our civilisation. I can see that very clearly. If you consider the death symptoms, the foremost is an increasing preoccupation with the material things of life. Here the churches go with the popular trend, and endorse, and even enhance, our affluent society's materialist standards. I thought at one time that the Roman Church would be a final bastion of the Christian religion. I imagined it as a sort of last citadel into which, for no other reason than that it was the last citadel, I should probably climb myself. But I don't think so now. It seems to be clear that the Roman Church is going the same way as the Anglican Church, and will expire with our expiring civilisation.[1]

R.T. What are the marks of weakness of the institutional church that you discern?

[1] Muggeridge became a Catholic in 1982, and he often expressed his grateful respect for the Church that had not forsaken her intractable position on abortion and euthanasia.

M.M. In the first place, the great majority of its ministers and clergy don't believe what they purport to believe. This is a source of terrific weakness. Whether they are right or wrong not to believe is neither here nor there, but the fact is, it puts them in a completely false position.

R.T. I am going to challenge you. You say the vast majority, this is wild isn't it—the vast majority?

M.M. Yes, it is wild, but I would suggest that *a* majority at any rate don't really believe the propositions that, as beneficed clergy, they purport to believe. In their private conversations they don't even pretend to, in my experience. If you employed a solicitor to transfer house property, and then, when he was having a drink with you after the deal, he said: "Of course I don't really believe that those clauses mean anything," it would seem quite disgraceful. It's the same with a clergyman who talks lightheartedly about all the things he's supposed to believe in and doesn't. There is a terrific gap—a credibility gap, to use the popular expression—between what they stand up and say they believe—the creeds they recite—and what they really believe. I can't recite these creeds, and I never do recite them, because I don't believe them in the sense that they're set forth; but a great many clergymen don't believe them either, yet they have to say they do. Then, I think the church, like most institutions of our society, is scared, and is anxious to ingratiate itself with people rather than to tell them the truth. Therefore it takes an extremely equivocal attitude towards many of the moral issues which arise.

R.T. Could it not be that one of the reasons why the clergy appear so unenthusiastic for the things they believe is that it is a pretty soul-destroying job trying to convince people these days that there are any ultimate values?

M.M. It's a very difficult job, and I shouldn't blame them at all if they threw in their hand and said: "I have had a go at this, and it just can't be done, and I am looking for another job." I feel the utmost sympathy for them; but if you ask me why the church is so weak—obviously an institution is weak if its ostensible aims bear little or no relation to the aims and teachings of its ministers.

R.T. What do you think the aims should be?

M.M. The gospel, the Christian gospel; to teach people what Christ taught; to show them how he wanted them to live, how to love God and love their fellows.

R.T. Supposing nobody came to the church where that was done?

M.M. In a way, it wouldn't be surprising if nobody came, because people live in a society in which they are being induced by the most powerful method of persuasion that has ever existed on earth—I mean the mass-communication media, especially television—to believe in the exact opposite. It's perfectly understandable if a clergyman says: "Nobody comes, and I can't go on," but what I think is absolutely fatal is not to say that, and instead to say: "Let's make an adjustment, and see if we can't conform what we are preaching to what these mass-communication media are recommending." There can be no adjustment; they are opposite things. Therein lies the dilemma and fate of the church, I am afraid.

R.T. You have said previously that you believe this civilisation is coming to an end, and you are quite sure that institutional Christianity will come to an end with it, and I agree with you; but this is contrary to what the church has believed for two thousand years. Jesus said to Peter: "You are the rock, and upon this rock I will build my church, and the gates of hell will not prevail against it." Now the implication seems to be that empires can fall, kingdoms can come to an end, but the church will always continue.

M.M. It may, of course; I'm not saying it won't, because it has survived a great many things.

R.T. But my strong feeling—and I thought you echoed this—is that, for the first time, the church is not going to prevail.

M.M. I think it's very doubtful whether institutional Christianity will be able to separate itself from the general process of decomposition. But one always comes back to thinking that with God all things are possible, and it is conceivable, of course, that this whole situation might change. We can only be grateful and delighted if it does, but, as of now, looking at the situation objectively, I see institutional Christianity as irretrievably a part of a world order, a civilisation, which is rushing to destruction. I don't feel particularly perturbed about it, and it doesn't alter in any way, of course, my feelings about the Christian religion. The survival of the church to date is an extraordinary fact, and no doubt churchmen would argue that its survival indicates clearly that God had a hand in it, and wants it to survive today. It might be so. But I find institutional Christianity, with certain exceptions, highly unsympathetic.

R.T. When you say that you feel civilisation is collapsing, do you think this is because the church has failed, or do you think it is man, who has refused the claims of the church and has become world-centered—this *world-centered—and therefore corrupt, and that this is why civilisation is collapsing?*

M.M. I think both processes are taking place. It's very like the Old Testament, and I want to pay my tribute to the Old Testament. You know, people are always telling us not to bother with it, but I think it's the most extraordinary book. The whole of human history is contained in the adventures of this obscure, and in many ways maddening, people. They knew all about the decline of faith and the fall of kingdoms.

R.T. A lot of the people whom you admire and respect were men who were nurtured by the church, and lived inside the church. Isn't it very presumptuous of us to sit here and calmly decide that of course the church is now coming to an end, when we owe it so much? Going back to the Old Testament—the Jews had to leave Jerusalem, the Temple was destroyed, they went into captivity in Babylon, but God kept a remnant, and in that sense the church can never die.

M.M. I think this is absolutely true. Every Christian owes an immeasurable debt to the church because it has kept Christ's message alive. Through its worship, through its music, through marvelous things like the Book of Common Prayer, it has enshrined the Christian religion in an artistic excellence which has enormously enhanced it. Think just of the cathedrals—the Christian cathedrals of Europe; what a contribution they have made! No one is going to pretend to himself that at the same time that this was happening there were not very corrupt men in the church, false doctrines being preached, and very wicked things being done; clearly there were. I have a pessimistic view of the future of the church because it seems to me that many of its leaders have, of their own accord, allied themselves with the forces of this world, and that is the one disastrous thing they can do.

R.T. Shouldn't you be inside the church, being part of the pull away from the worldliness? After all, the direction of the church has been wrong many times in the past, but, thank God, there have been people within it who have corrected it, and when I talk about the church I mean the whole church.

M.M. I feel deeply hostile to the general direction of the Christian churches today, one and all, including the Roman Catholic Church; deeply suspicious and hostile. I couldn't produce an apologia for them if I was associated with them, and I find it easier to pronounce my views, such as they are, on the Christian position, from without, rather than from within. There might be a case for being inside, but, if so, which particular denomination should be preferred? That question arises then, doesn't it? One might say the Roman Catholic Church, because Roman Catholics are more numerous, international, and altogether, in certain respects, very appealing to me, but on the other hand there are other aspects which are very unappealing. The Quakers, likewise, are very appealing, but they have certain things which are unappealing. I don't know, I have a sort of feeling at this moment that institutional Christianity is careering away in a direction that I don't approve of—you may say I should be there trying to pull them back, but I don't think that I could take that on. My own picture of the future is that our society is going in the next decades to be totally non-Christian; I mean its institutions, everything about it, will lose whatever relationship they now have with Christian religion. Then, I think, there will be people, in the very stressful circumstances that are likely to arise, who will still want to live as Christians, and I think they are much more likely to find themselves in the position of a Christian underground, a sort of *maquis*. I imagine the forces of paganism occupying our world, and the Christians drawn together in those conditions, rather as I remember surviving Christians in the USSR. who appealed to me very much. They seemed to me to be enormously pure—simply a collection of people who, in extremely hostile circumstances, clung to their faith, and tried to cling to their Christian way of life. This might easily happen, and I hope that if I were still alive, I should be among those people.

R.T. So much for the church and clergymen—but what about your claim that civilisation itself is coming to an end? On what grounds do you come to this judgement?

M.M. The basic condition for a civilisation is that there should be law and order. Obviously, this is coming to an end, the world is falling into chaos, even—perhaps especially—our Western world. Furthermore, I firmly believe that our civilisation began with the Christian religion, and has been sustained and fortified by the values of the Christian religion, by which admittedly most men have not lived, but to which they have assented, and by which the greatest of them have tried to live. The Christian religion and these values no longer prevail; they no longer mean anything at all to ordinary people. Some suppose that you can have a Christian civilisation without Christian values. I disbelieve this. I think that the basis of order is a moral order; if there is no moral order there will be no political or social order, and we see this happening. This is how civilisations end.

R.T. So we are either moving into a new kind of civilisation with a new moral order, or we are moving into a new Dark Age.

M.M. Yes, and the Dark Age is likely to intervene anyway. It is very unusual for one moral order to slide into another with no intervening chaos. There are many other symptoms. The excessive interest in eroticism is characteristic of the end of a civilisation, because it really means a growing impotence, and a fear of impotence. Then the obsessive need for excitement, vicarious excitement, which of course the games provided for the Romans, and which television provides for our population. Even the enormously complicated structure of taxation and administration is, funnily enough, a symptom of the end of a civilisation; these things become so elaborate that in the end they become insupportable because of their very elaboration. Above all, there is this truly terrible thing which afflicts materialist societies—boredom; an obsessive boredom, which I note on every hand. Mine is, admittedly, a minority view; a lot of people think that we are just on the verge of a new marvelous way of life. I see no signs of it at all myself. I notice that where our way of life is most successful materially it is most disastrous morally and spiritually; that the psychiatric wards are the largest and most crowded, and the suicides most numerous, precisely where material prosperity is greatest, where most money is spent on education.

I don't regard this at all as a gloomy point of view. If one considers the nature and present objectives of our society, I think it's much more optimistic to suppose it's going to collapse than that it's going to succeed. Its success would be a nightmare beyond all thought or belief. If a place like, for instance, California really were viable, this would be the end of everything. Consider our actual circumstances at this moment: We have made ourselves so strong that we can destroy ourselves. We spend a great part of our wealth and our research resources and so on, elaborating the means to destroy ourselves and the earth. Our corner of the world is getting richer, to the point that its main preoccupation is to stimulate consumption by all sorts of asinine means, while the rest of the world is getting poorer and hungrier. And the only answer we can produce is that there are too many of the others. Our ultimate offering to our less fortunate brethren is what? A contraceptive! I don't think any civilisation has ever produced such a contemptible product as its major offering to the world.

R.T. *Do you think that there is any chance of our civilisation being redeemed?*

M.M. It seems to me very unlikely, but everything is possible. All historical prognostications are false. Nobody can know; I can only say, that is what it looks like to me. I sometimes think to myself: Supposing I had been the sort of person that I am, as a Roman in the time of Nero, shall we say. I should, I am sure, have said exactly what I am saying now. I should have said: The barbarians are coming in, Rome will be destroyed; our whole structure of paganism and so on is all over, nobody believes in it; the administration won't work, the expenses of administration exceed all bounds; the Roman Empire is top-heavy and it's going to collapse. And I should have been absolutely right. The only thing I shouldn't have known was that these very obscure Christian events in a distant outpost of the empire—events involving almost totally illiterate people, subject people, people of absolutely no interest or importance to a sophisticated, educated Roman—were going to lay the foundation of a new and infinitely greater civilisation that in terms of art and science and understanding was going to reach unimaginable heights.

R.T. *Can you see that happening now?*

M.M. I wouldn't know, and you wouldn't know. We are precisely the sort of people who above all don't and can't know.

R.T. *But can you see signs of it?*

M.M. I find an increasing scepticism about the utopian hopes which, in the first flush of scientific achievement, made people more or less drunk with expectation. I find that hope disappearing. I find a new mood of humility. Even these half-baked students, for whom I have considerable contempt, in a blind sort of way feel dissatisfied. It's good that they should feel dissatisfied; there's nothing to be satisfied with.

R.T. If you are right and this civilisation is coming to an end, the death pangs will probably take quite a long time. In the meantime somebody has to govern, somebody has to accept responsibility, the world has to go on. Some people have to be, for instance, the managers of the Central Electricity Board or the managers of the coal mines, the fruit of whose work we enjoy. Now isn't it a little bit off to criticise people who have positions of power, depending, as we do, on somebody having it?

M.M. Of course. I entirely agree that power is necessary in a society, and it would be absurd to say that all men who exercise power are bad men, but I think you could say that all men who seek power are dangerous men and require very careful watching. Power as a passion is a bad passion. My favorite example is in the New Testament. We read that the kingdoms of the earth are in the gift of the Devil. This is a very interesting fact which isn't sufficiently regarded. Why are they in the gift of the Devil? How can it be that the Devil has the gift of the kingdoms of the earth, and not God? The reason is that the kingdoms of the earth signify power, which is a devilish pursuit.

The other day I was turning up some old notes I had made, and I found a copy of an inscription that had been set up in the Libyan desert by a Roman centurion: "I, serving as a captain of a legion of Rome in the Libyan desert, have learnt and pondered this thought—in life there are two pursuits, love and power, and no man can have both." That is very much what I have in mind. The same notion arises in the Book of Genesis. Through eating the fruit of knowledge—like power, a necessary pursuit—the happiness of the Garden of Eden was destroyed.

R.T. The Book of Genesis is a myth, but do you think the myth of the fall of man represents something true which you can observe in life now?

M.M. I would go further and say this—that I think legends and myths are probably truer than history. As Kierkegaard says, in the case of the greatest happenings, such as Christ's life and death, historicity is completely without importance. It is very important to know the history of Socrates because Socrates is dead, but the history of Christ doesn't matter, because he is alive. If and when we know the final truth about human life, we shall find that the legends, or what pass for legends, are far nearer the truth than what passes for fact or science or history.

R.T. Going back to the fall of man, one has to wrestle with this: Why is man fallen? If God is the creator and he made man good, why were the seeds of corruption in him?

M.M. This, of course, is the most fundamental and difficult question of all. I find I can grasp it better if I think of the creation of man and the universe by God as being of the same nature as creation by man, only of course multiplied by billions and billions. On however a lowly scale, insofar as I have tried to create something in words, written or spoken, as an expression of truth, that process is painful. It's not easy or pleasurable, but it can give ecstasy. Also it contains within itself the same essential principle that, in order to reach after perfection, it has to be itself intrinsically imperfect. So I see that if God had created man perfect, man without pain, man without sin, there would have been, in this sense, no creation, any more than if King Lear had not suffered, there would have been a play for Shakespeare to write about him. The life we know, with all its pains and ecstasies, wouldn't have existed. If you imagine your life made by a different god, made perfect, it wouldn't be life. The process of creation contains in itself its own imperfection; the pursuit of perfection is via imperfection, as the pursuit of spiritual love is via the physical body. This is how it is, and this is the majesty of it, and why it is interesting. This is why there is literature, why there is art, why there is thought, and how we may know there is a God—a loving God—whose children we all are.

EPILOGUE

BY SALLY MUGGERIDGE

Cecil Kuhne has managed to assemble within this anthology a quite remarkable collection of writing, talks, sermons, and interviews by my late uncle Malcolm Muggeridge on the subject of faith. Whilst much of the content has been previously published, the sources are mostly long out of print and increasingly difficult to find. Muggeridge's thought-provoking expressions of faith have always found resonance and thoroughly deserve a fresh airing to what I also hope will be a new generation of readers.

Malcolm Muggeridge had a poet's love of life. Well into his eighties he still particularly loved his long country walks. He revelled in the beauty of nature with all its shapes, smells and colours, and the company of his friends and family. But with an ever-growing faith and conviction, I recall him in declining health looking forward quite impatiently, and almost enthusiastically, to death, or as he called it "that other life". For him, it represented the natural end of a lifelong, twentieth-century pilgrimage of exploring and finding faith. In *The Pilgrim's Progress*, Bunyan used metaphor and allegory to chronicle a journey through life "wherein is discovered, the manner of his setting out, his dangerous journey, and safe arrival at the desired country". The headstone over Muggeridge's grave in Whatlington churchyard, Sussex, England, bears the epitaph "Valiant for Truth". Valiant-for-Truth is a character appearing near the end of the book, a fellow traveller going to the Celestial City whose greatest virtue is a single-minded pursuit of truth. Over the past few years, I have been discovering just how much Malcolm's life represented a pilgrimage, always with a constant need to hurry on, always seeking answers to fundamental questions of man's existence, and hoping perhaps finally to see the Holy City set on a hill. He sought from an early age to chronicle his thoughts through writing and so make some sense of his own varied and turbulent life. From boyhood in Croydon to his college days at Cambridge. From teaching stints in India and Cairo to his career as a writer and journalist experiencing Britain, Russia, and India in the 1930s. From life as a soldier-spy in the Second World War to becoming an esteemed radio and television celebrity, rubbing shoulders with presidents, popes, and future saints. He had a face and voice that became instantly recognised around the world.

Muggeridge has often been described as one of the foremost writers of the twentieth century. Despite the fact that some of his most enduring work was writing and broadcasting about Christianity and faith, Muggeridge never regarded himself as a theologian. Whilst he had been strongly encouraged to enter the priesthood whilst at Cambridge in the early 1920s, he had doubts about the nature of the institutional church and thereby his vocation. He resisted it in favour of becoming a teacher and a writer. He was to become, however, a man with an unshakable conviction in a living Jesus, a consciousness of a spirit that somehow animated and guided mankind's whole existence. Life, he claimed, was a gift of God. He wrote, lectured, and broadcast about Christianity using words that were wholly understandable and to which very many people found they could relate.

For those new to the work of Malcolm Muggeridge, and also for the many who have long appreciated his unique literary style and challenging approach to spiritual matters, this book is a veritable feast. But, fortunately, you need not gorge yourself in one sitting, working steadily through all the courses. Like an anthology of poems, it should be dipped into at random as the mood may take you, to be slowly savoured and reflected over. All Muggeridge's writing emanates from a fine, thinking mind, but unusually, it is combined with a unique journalistic style. In places, it is also very entertaining.

An intellectual of immense depth of thought, his philosophy on life and afterlife were shaped by saints, particularly Saint Francis, Saint Augustine, and Saint Paul. He was truly fascinated by them, and together with Blake, they crop up repeatedly in his writings. With this interest, it is not so surprising that he discovered a modern-day "saint" of his own, an Albanian nun called Mother Teresa, working for God in the squalor and deprivation of Calcutta. In his career, Muggeridge had experienced affliction and poverty in abundance. Perhaps that was why he immediately recognised in Mother Teresa a divine purpose, what he immediately felt to be saintliness. He found that in her presence, all the foolish material aspirations and distractions were as nothing, as he witnessed love being freely and unconditionally offered to the dying and destitute. Indeed, so inspired was he by this example of selfless work carried out by the Sisters of Charity that he felt he wanted to participate in the Church of which they were members. He came to see the Catholic Church, alone of contemporary institutions, as offering serious and stubborn resistance to a drift into moral chaos. Mother Teresa had the most powerful and profound influence on him, leading him through constant encouragement eventually to find Christ. Mother Teresa was not the only influence on him. He also greatly admired the work of Father Bidone, working tirelessly in Sussex, England, looking after severely mentally handicapped children. He was also staunch friends with the Earl of Longford, a near neighbour and a leading Catholic.

Like Valiant-for-Truth, Malcolm's life reads as a series of adventures, fights, and struggles. It was punctuated with occasional mishaps and misjudgements, but always with that restless, self-destructive urge. However, events on the way often served as important moments of revelation, and he recorded his growing disillusionment with the twentieth century's utopian dreams. As he gained maturity and experience, there was a corresponding confirmation of his own unique views about Christianity. It appears to many that Muggeridge made a journey of faith through life from complete agnostic to ardent believer and evangelist. Closer study shows that the path was not as straightforward. From an early age, he was certainly aware that another dimension existed—that there was somehow and somewhere a destiny beyond the devices and desires of the ego. But even with a profound realisation that earthly life could not be the end, for many years he struggled in admitting to himself and to others his possessing a Christian faith. There was never to be a total certainty. In fact, he later claimed that the only people who never doubted or wavered in their deeply held beliefs were materialists or atheists. Doubt, he came to recognise, was an integral part of coming to have faith, and conversely, an integral part of belief was to have doubt. It is perhaps for this reason that his writings find such an appeal. He comes to the subject of faith from the standpoint of an agnostic believer, a position with which many can readily identify.

To Muggeridge, embracing Christianity was necessarily always going to be a question of faith, not one of rational proof. Whilst he came to believe firmly in the Incarnation, he often chose to describe the event as a drama—in other words an artistic truth rather than an historical truth.

His faith had been greatly confirmed and consolidated by his experiences working for the BBC on religious programmes in the Middle East, particularly in the Holy Land. Far from being the cynical hack, the journalist observing at a distance with a job to do and a schedule to keep, he admitted to being incredibly moved by many of the experiences encountered whilst the cameras were filming. For instance, he later recounted his personal feelings speaking to pilgrims at Lourdes, or of visiting the birthplace of Christ in Bethlehem. He found he could not be dispassionate and uninfluenced by the faith of those he met and closely observed, and this helped strengthen him in finding his own faith.

In turn, it should be said, Malcolm Muggeridge appears to have had a profound effect on others—through his writing and broadcasts, he has helped turned millions to faith, and more than once from despair and suicide. He both absorbed and reflected the human condition. Able to use the new twentieth-century media to great effect and with a brilliant mind, he was a skilled documentary maker with a great gift for imparting obviously heartfelt truth. I have had the pleasure to meet a remarkably large number of journalists, eminent churchmen, media celebrities, and ordinary men and women, on both sides of the Atlantic and as far afield as Australia, whose lives have at some time been variously touched by Malcolm Muggeridge. I have met with actors, writers, painters, cartoonists, and sculptors. Fifteen years after his death, there remains a huge following worldwide.

In interviews in later life, Malcolm was frequently asked what he most wanted in the short time that remained to him. He would answer, "I should like my light to shine even if only very fitfully, like a match struck in a dark cavernous night and then flickering out."

I have found myself somewhat left by default to hold the flame in my uncle's memory, encouraging it to burn ever more brightly, keeping the literary and broadcast legacy alive. With so much darkness in the world, it struck me that we all need every bit of extra illumination. A very active secondary market in his out-of-print books takes place on the Internet, and a vast amount of information can be found, including biographies, articles, lectures, sermons, quotations, and even jokes. He was a great writer and frequently regarded himself, like Saint Augustine, as a vendor of words. He once said that he would like as an epitaph, "He used words well." Many have now come to feel as I do that the legacy of his writing and broadcasts have provided not just that momentary flicker he hoped for but a bright and shining light, albeit with perhaps only a small part of the certainty and luminosity of Saint Paul in whose footsteps he once so memorably trod in 1970 for British television.

Considered now in retrospect, Muggeridge's legacy is one of accurate prophesy on many of the major issues of our time. Today we bear the fruit of many of his dire predictions about sexual permissiveness, immigration, advances in medical science, the spread of Islam, the lowering of standards on the media, etc. He was memorably described "as the prophetic scourge of the follies and fantasies of our time, a political radical and a cultural iconoclast". It is always in the nature of things that a true prophet may not be recognised by his own people in his own time. His exposition of conservative Christian values certainly resonates more readily today in America than at home in more liberal Britain, but this may simply be due to the number of charitable and educational foundations in the U.S. motivated by Catholic and conservative agendas.

In recent years, we have seen the beatification of Mother Teresa, and there is a movement toward achieving her eventual canonisation. However, Malcolm Muggeridge was long before canonised by the media. He became, and indeed remains today, affectionately known universally as "Saint Mugg", latter-day people's saint and twentieth-century prophet. No doubt intended at first as a term of mild derision, with cartoons depicting him with a halo, it has since become a term of genuine respect. Perhaps of all the honours, sainthood on earth is as much as anyone could ask. The "shrine" for Saint Mugg, patron saint of religious broadcasting, such that it is, can be found in the Buswell Library in Wheaton College, Illinois. Letters, journals, sermons, book reviews, videotapes, and radio and television scripts, his solid silver ink stand bearing the caricature of Mr. Punch—a gift from his Daily Telegraph colleagues, his bronze bust, even his Olympia typewriter form the relics. Visitors are welcomed by appointment. Wheaton, as a Christian College, is an appropriate venue, and they have been generous in their support.

Sally Muggeridge, President

The Malcolm Muggeridge Society
Pilgrim's Cottage, Tilmanstone
Kent, England
CT15 4DJ

www.malcolmmuggeridge.org